Caesar Country

Cocktails, Clams & Canada

Aaron Harowitz &
Zack Silverman

Cocktail & Food Photography
Tanya Pilgrim

appetite

Appetite by Random House® and colophon are registered trademarks of
Penguin Random House LLC.

Walter® is a registered trademark of Brutus Beverages Inc.

Library and Archives Canada Cataloguing in Publication is available upon request.

ISBN: 9780525611370
eBook ISBN: 9780525611387

Design: Aaron Harowitz
Cocktail and food photography: Tanya Pilgrim

Supplemental photography: Nataliia Kvitovska (back cover), RADD Collective (page iv),
Yann Allegre (page 3), Erik Mclean (pages 14–15, 228, 229), Laurent Beique (pages 72–73),
Glen Jackson (page 76), Jean da Silva (page 92), Zosia & Ruben Bialons (pages 93), Kyle
Thacker (page 108), Ksenia Makagonova (page 109), Priscilla du Preez (pages 116–117,
133), Bryton Udy (page 132), Tandem X Visuals (page 144), Subtle Cinematics (page 145),
Ferdinand Stohr (pages 154–155), Matthias Mullie (page 157), Albert Laurence (page 158),
JD Gipson (page 174), Alice Triquet (page 175), Yalin Kaya (page 190), Steven Wright
(page 191), Tobias Negele (pages 212–213), Mark Timberlake (page 215), Michael & Diane
Weidner (page 216), Kalen Emsley (pages 246–247), Kwan Fung (page 249), Ian Keefe
(page 250), Chris Boyer (page 260), JP Valery (page 261), Leonard Laub (page 269)

Printed in China

Published in Canada by Appetite by Random House®,
a division of Penguin Random House Canada Limited.

www.penguinrandomhouse.ca

10 9 8 7 6 5 4 3 2 1

Helen, you make it all possible.
Quinn & Avery, go to bed.
And I love you all.

—Aaron

For Amanda, you may not be a Caesar lover but I love you anyways. For Sienna, Stella, and Nolan, I'm sure you'll all grow up to be Caesar lovers but if you don't, I'll still love you.

—Zack

Contents

Recipes

Introduction

September 3, 2013. 3:22 a.m.
Aaron and Zack stand in a cold bottling plant in Toronto looking at a stack of skids containing about 8,000 bottles of Caesar mix that have just come off the bottling line. Aaron starts to feel pretty dizzy and breaks out in a sweat. He feels like he's on the verge of a heart attack. He turns to Zack and asks, "What have we done?"

What we had done was pour our life savings into producing our first-ever batch of Walter Caesar mix with the idea of trying to reinvent Canada's national cocktail. We knew Canadians love Caesars, and that Caesar culture in Canada runs deep. We also recognized that Canadians, for years, had only one option for Caesar mix on the market, and that we had an opportunity to do something totally different—offer Canadians a premium, all-natural mix made here in Canada. We spent a year developing the recipe and then figuring out how to make it. We named it in honour of Walter Chell, who invented the Caesar in Calgary in 1969. We thought we had a great idea. But nobody had tried it before.

On that early September morning, facing the cold reality of 8,000 bottles of juice—that we'd not yet figured out how or even where to sell—we were starting to wonder if we'd missed seeing the reason no one before us had put this "great idea" into action.

2021
Our company now sells enough Walter Craft Caesar mix in a year to make more than 6 million craft Caesars. In that time we've had the chance to travel across the country talking Caesars, learning about Caesars, meeting people who've been serving Caesars for generations, seeing people push the boundaries of what a Caesar is and can be, and of course, making and consuming many thousands of Caesars (some better than others) along the way.

Also along the way, a friend introduced us to Robert McCullough, who had published some of our favourite cookbooks and cocktail books. Our friend said something like "You guys should talk. Maybe you could write a Caesar book." Not really knowing what we were getting ourselves into, we said "Cool. That would be fun." Robert agreed, and all of a sudden we were writing a cocktail book.

We've spent two years developing and collecting recipes for this book, and we're eager to share them with you. Hopefully by the time you read this COVID-19 will be starting to fade from memory, but as we write these words, we're still deep in a global pandemic that has thrown everyone's lives out of whack and made this project—in which we've worked with more than 40 contributors from places as varied as Victoria, British Columbia;

Iqaluit, Nunavut; and Fogo Island, Newfoundland—even more of an undertaking than we'd anticipated.

The recipes in this book are arranged geographically, tracing a journey from west to east and then north. We asked bartenders, chefs, purveyors, and other people with a variety of backgrounds, food philosophies, natural environments, local ingredients, and techniques to share their recipes, showing us how the Caesar can be pushed and stretched and reinvented. We offer some of our own recipes, too, inspired by our many travels across Canada and some of the people and places we've encountered along the way.

Caesar Country is an exploration of a nation that happens to be in the form of a book about a cocktail made with clam juice and tomatoes. We hope that, by seeing all these ideas that have sprung out of a single concoction made in a Calgary bar in 1969, you'll also get some sense of Canada in its vastness and complexity: how we grow things, how we fish and hunt, how we transport and preserve; how amid our abundance we've also had to learn to make magic out of scarcity, not in defiance of nature but in harmony with it; how we share, how we celebrate, how we play host, welcoming people different from ourselves, how we gather in restaurants and bars, and above all, how we connect.

By guiding you step by step through the creation of a huge variety of Caesar cocktails (as well as showing you a few ways to cook with Caesar flavours), we hope this book will inspire you to approach your own Caesar making—and indeed all cocktail making—in new ways. And if you've never made a Caesar before, welcome to the team. We hope you'll enjoy the journey as much as we have.

Cheers,

Aaron Harowitz
& Zack Silverman

A National Cocktail

When we started Walter Caesar we recognized that we were walking on hallowed ground. We were trying to reimagine a drink that is so much more than a drink: it's part of our national heritage. But the Caesar's more than just the most popular cocktail in Canada—roughly 400 million are consumed each year—it also ranks among the country's most iconic and recognizable symbols, period. In a 2007 CBC series on great Canadian inventions, the Caesar placed 13th; not as high as insulin, the telephone, or the Robertson screw, but higher than the Canadarm, basketball, and the snowmobile.

And yet, while the Caesar has become a ubiquitous part of the Canadian landscape, it remains almost totally obscure everywhere else. We think it's worth exploring what our decades-long fascination with this (admittedly strange) clam-and-tomato cocktail might say about us as a nation.

A Brief History of the Caesar

1969. It's a year for wild innovations, unexpected upheavals, and bold leaps forward. Hair is getting longer, music louder, cars faster. Led Zeppelin release their first album. *Easy Rider* roars into the theatres. *Monty Python's Flying Circus* debuts on TV. Four computers from different universities "talk" to one another for the first time, through the ARPANET. People take to the streets to protest the war in Vietnam. The Zodiac Killer stalks northern California, while Charles Manson and his "family" gather in the south. Roughly 400,000 people travel to a dairy farm near Woodstock, NY, for a music festival.

Here in Canada, Trudeaumania (father, not son) is in full swing. The Front de libération du Québec bomb the Montréal Stock Exchange. The Montréal Expos play their inaugural home game at Jarry Park, securing a rare victory on their way to tying for the worst record in the league. A few blocks away from the stadium, John Lennon and Yoko Ono spend a week in bed in Room 1742 of the Queen Elizabeth Hotel, where they record "Give Peace a Chance."

And everyone everywhere watches Neil Armstrong take a walk on the moon.

In the middle of all this change, Walter Chell stands behind the counter of the Owl's Nest, the fine-dining lounge of the Calgary Inn, a downtown hotel a short walk from the recently completed Husky Tower.[1] Tonight, as always, Walter's wearing his steel-rimmed glasses,

---

1. The Calgary Inn is now the Westin and the Husky Tower is now the Calgary Tower.

an expertly tailored blazer, a white Oxford shirt, an understated black tie, and a fine Swiss watch. With his dark pomaded hair and carefully groomed moustache, he's more Jazz Age than Summer of Love. And unbeknownst to him, he's about to secure a spot in the history books for himself.

The owners of the Calgary Inn had asked Walter, their food and beverage manager, to create a signature drink to celebrate the opening of Marco's, the hotel's new Italian restaurant.[2] The request got him thinking about his favourite meal from his years living in Italy, spaghetti alle vongole, and wondering if he could recreate its flavours in a cocktail.[3] He cooked clams and strained tomatoes, adding and subtracting ingredients until he found the perfect combination.

Behind the bar in the dimly lit Owl's Nest, Walter gets ready to serve his new cocktail. We can't know for sure what's playing on the lounge stereo, but it being 1969 in Canada, there's a good chance it's Winnipeg's own The Guess Who, whose "These Eyes" has recently become their first top-ten hit. The regulars could be making their cases for best player in the then 12-team NHL: Esposito or Gordie? Which Bobby: Hull or Orr? Serge Savard, whose Habs have just won their second Stanley Cup in a row? Or, like many others across the country, maybe they're complaining about the CBC cancelling the folk musical variety show *Don Messer's Jubilee*, which often rivalled *Hockey Night in Canada* as the most popular show in the nation during its 12-year run. Walter, however, prefers listening to talking, even though, hailing from Montenegro by way of Italy and Switzerland, he speaks seven languages.

Quietly, then, he pours some celery salt on a plate, rubs the rim of a highball glass with some lime, and rolls the rim into the salt before placing a couple of ice cubes in the glass. In a cocktail shaker he combines his house-made mix of clam juice and tomato juice with a shot of vodka, four dashes of Worcestershire sauce, pepper, and what he later says was his "secret ingredient": a dash of oregano.[4] He fills the shaker with ice, stirs the mix gently with a bar spoon, and strains the drink into the glass. He garnishes the cocktail with a wedge of fresh lime and a celery stick, and serves it for the first time. Price: $1.80.

---

2. Though part of the Calgary Inn property, Marco's is located across the way from the main building on the other side of bustling 4th Street. In crossing 4th to run food and drink between the main hotel and the restaurant, the staff made use of the first instalment of Calgary's now ubiquitous +15 Skyway, an elevated pedestrian walkway.

3. Walter, who was born in Montenegro, was reportedly an excellent cook, and no stranger to Italian cuisine. His mother was a countess, and he spent his early years in Italy, schooled by Jesuits in Trieste, before running away to Switzerland at age 16.

4. Caesar aficionados will note the absence of hot sauce in Walter's original recipe.

Walter himself is not actually a fan of his cocktail. It's just "not his cup tea," as he'll later tell reporters. He prefers scotch on the rocks, with a splash of water. But he knows a hit when he tastes it. And he knows that a great drink needs a great name. With a nod to the homeland of spaghetti alle vongole, he calls it the Caesar.[5]

So begins a local craze. You can imagine it travelling, almost block by block, as the bartenders of Calgary start adding it to their arsenal, and then to Edmonton, Banff, and across the country. Home bartenders start serving it at parties, helped by the arrival in Canada that same year of Mott's Clamato Cocktail, a canned blend of clam and tomato juices made by Duffy-Mott, an American company specializing in juices and sauces.

At least, this is the version of the Caesar's origin story that we find most convincing, based on our research. Cocktail origin stories are, by their nature, often a bit murky. As bartender and historian Jim Meehan points out, "Given the sensitive and private nature of the guest/bartender relationship, the history of what happens in bars is largely an oral tradition, transmitted through the hazy fog of a night of drinking . . . Depending on whom you ask, even recent innovations are shrouded in mystery."[6]

Certainly, there were earlier iterations of clam-based cocktails, and there are records of cocktails featuring some combination of clams, tomatoes, spices, and vodka being served at various moments in the first half of the 20th century in bars in Paris and New York. We don't know if Walter Chell ever sampled such a drink on his travels or if he was aware that such a combination had been tried before. He would have been familiar with the Bloody Mary, to be sure.

What we do know beyond doubt is that Walter Chell popularized the clam, tomato, and vodka cocktail, coming up with its ideal portions, spicing, flavour additions, and garnish. And that he gave it the name that helped it to become iconic, while doing more than any other person to popularize it. Walter Chell and the origin of the Caesar are inextricably linked.[7]

---

5. There's some contention as to whether Walter Chell first called his drink Caesar or Bloody Caesar, the name by which it was popularly known for many years, and which you still hear used sometimes in Québec. Walter maintains that he called it only Caesar, and there's a well-worn story that the Bloody was informally added after a British regular commented, "That's a bloody good Caesar you make!" But the earliest press reports about the drink refer to it as Bloody Caesar, and it would make sense that it would be referred to that way, as a riff on the Bloody Mary—transforming Queen Mary I of England, supposed namesake of the Bloody Mary, into Julius Caesar, bloodied after being stabbed by several Roman senators.

6. Jim Meehan, *Meehan's Bartender Manual*. Ten Speed Press, 2017, 4.

7. See page 303 for information on sources for this section.

A Brief History of the Bloody Mary

One simple way to define a Caesar is that it's not a Bloody Mary. It would be nice to think of the Bloody Mary as the American Caesar—as though someone found our drink and decided to make it less interesting. But unfortunately, that's not historically accurate. Since the Bloody Mary pre-dates the Caesar, any history of the Caesar should include a history of the Bloody Mary. From our own research we can confirm that Walter Chell was undoubtedly familiar with the drink by the time he came up with the Caesar. Thanks to the research in Brian Bartels' book *The Bloody Mary* (Ten Speed Press, 2017), we can briefly recount that history here.

Legend holds that a French bartender named Fernand "Pete" Petiot served an early iteration of the Bloody Mary in the 1920s at Harry's New York Bar in Paris, a favourite among American expats such as Ernest Hemingway and George Gershwin. Petiot offered a simple combination of tomato juice and vodka. But, as Bartels argues, if the drink did originate at Harry's Bar, it doesn't make sense that when Harry McElhone of Harry's Bar published a book of recipes in 1927, he didn't mention Petiot's Bloody Mary.

An American comedian named George Jessel also claimed to have come up with a cocktail that he called the Bloody Mary, which combined tomato juice, Worcestershire sauce, and potato vodka, and that it originated during a late-night drinking session in 1927. Bartels is also skeptical about this claim, because commercial mass-produced tomato juice wasn't on the market in 1927.

In the 1930s, Petiot moved to the United States and started running the King Cole bar at the St. Regis in New York, where he served a drink called the Red Snapper, made with citrus, spices, tomato, and vodka—a drink very much like a Bloody Mary but with a different name, supposedly because the owner of the St. Regis thought that the name was offensive.

Cut to a 1964 *New Yorker* article on Petiot, where he lays out what Bartels deems the most plausible theory: the comedian George Jessel may indeed have come up with the name Bloody Mary, but his version was simply tomato juice and vodka. Petiot refined the drink, and over the years he created what is now the classic Bloody Mary recipe: tomato juice, vodka, hot sauce, Worcestershire sauce, lemon juice, salt, pepper, and ice. Petiot claimed to be serving about 150 Bloody Marys a day at the King Cole bar in the 1960s.

So What Does Our Love of Caesars Say About Canada?

So: In 1969 Walter Chell served a drink called the Caesar in Calgary. And in the roughly 50 years since, the Caesar, relatively unchanged, has become our national cocktail and ranks among the country's most iconic food-and-beverage items. Through the years of Banana Daiquiris, Harvey Wallbangers, iceberg lettuce with seven seas dressing, and lobster thermidor, the Caesar endured. Through the years of chicken tetrazzini, Salisbury steak, tuna casserole, Appletinis, Long Island Ice Teas, and sundried-tomatoes-everything, through just over a half-century of ever more quickly changing food trends, the Caesar is still here and as popular as ever. That is a rare thing. By any measure, the Caesar can be called a classic.

But how did it happen? Admittedly, it's an unusual combination. Tomato juice, clam juice, and vodka. It's not an obvious hit.

And yet, it is.

There's no one simple way to explain why the Caesar caught on like it did. In part, it was the right thing at the right time in the right place. In 1969 Calgary was still a small western town (population: 369,025) but beginning to buzz. Cowboy culture was huge. That year's number one movie at the box office was *Butch Cassidy and the Sundance Kid*, and another classic, *True Grit*, came out the same year. Hippie culture, with its back-to-the-land ethos and celebration of rugged individualism, included a fascination with the west, and people were coming to Alberta to check out the Stampede and scenes beyond.

The Owl's Nest, with its heady mix of Rat Pack glamour, cowboy cool, and European sensibility, was the place to be in Calgary. Frank Sinatra passed through, as did the notorious Chicago mobster Sam Giancana, rubbing shoulders with real cowboys and with people who just played them on TV in shows such as *Bonanza* and *The Big Valley* that had been sent by the networks to promote their shows at the Stampede. Visitors to Calgary would have wanted to make their memories of the place last long after they'd returned home, and they could do so by trying to replicate the unique drink they'd sampled: the Caesar, star of the Owl's Nest's menu.

But knowing that an unexpected clam-and-tomato cocktail was introduced at a hotspot in a growing city at an exciting time still doesn't answer the question of why the Caesar became a national icon, or why it remains one half a century later.

Our theory: As the Caesar started to gain recognition, with help from Walter Chell's skills as a promoter and some marketing muscle from Mott's, people started to sense that the drink was something that bound us—and only us—together. We started to see the Caesar as one more peculiarly Canadian phenomenon, something that we cared about in the same way we might care about things like world junior hockey or curling far more deeply than people anywhere else do. We started to enjoy our Caesars just a little more in the knowledge that drinking one in our hometown bar or at a party somehow connected us to all sorts of strangers across Canada.

And if drinking a Caesar became about more than just what was in the glass, the ritual of making one was also fun and delicious. Cocktails that become classics do so like any other examples of enduring popular culture: at some point a lot of people have to choose to like the thing itself enough to want to consume it regularly. No matter how appealing or bizarre something might seem at the outset, no matter how much or how little money gets spent on promoting it, getting a lot of people to choose this thing and keep choosing it can only happen organically. People choose their icons, not the other way round.

But even if Caesars have become canonical, that doesn't mean people shouldn't mess with them. The drink can be poked and prodded and tweaked in ways no one would dream of doing with a Gin and Tonic or a Negroni. Like Canada, the Caesar is confident in its lack of rigidity. Just as there's no one "right" way to be Canadian, so are there infinite ways to make a Caesar. All you need to do is draw inspiration from some underlying principles, introduce your own variations, and find the version that works best for you. It's fitting, then, that this drink that has become so symbolic of our country was originally crafted by someone born far beyond its borders.

Canada is huge. And varied. And always changing. So it's all the more amazing that we should have this one drink that unites us. And if the Caesar is our beloved national secret, we're happy for it to stay that way. We like to think of it as the Tragically Hip of drinks. If you don't get it, that's fine. We do. It's ours.

We Started a Caesar Company

To talk about how we came to start a Caesar company, we first need to talk about slushies. We'll explain.

In 2009, Zack was working as an attorney at a large firm in midtown Manhattan. While he loved New York, he didn't love being a lawyer. He dreamed of ways to escape. He wasn't alone. While he and his officemate Alex Rein were reminiscing about their love of Slurpees and lamenting the dearth of 7-Elevens in the city, they wondered if there was a way to make a premium version of the slushie, using top-quality natural ingredients to create sophisticated flavours. Thinking it was a wacky but actually pretty good idea, Zack and Alex bought a slush machine and started experimenting.

In 2009, Aaron was running his own design studio in Vancouver. Aaron loved Vancouver and loved running a design studio. Escape was the last thing on his mind. That year a client project took him to New York, so he popped in to see his childhood friend Zack at his Chelsea apartment. And that slush machine would actually end up changing his life.

Aaron and Zack grew up as family friends in Richmond, BC, and hung out a lot while they both attended the University of British Columbia. They'd seen far less of one another after graduating. Zack had stayed at UBC for law school and business school before moving to New York. Aaron had gone on to design school at Emily Carr University of Art + Design and worked at agencies in Vancouver before starting his own studio. They'd never considered that they might one day work together; their lives seemed headed in such different directions. And while they'd both worked in restaurants and bars to help pay the bills during school, neither one had ever envisioned a career in the food and drink industry.

But then Aaron saw that slushie machine in the corner of Zack's kitchen and naturally asked, "What's up with that?" Zack pitched him the idea. Aaron thought Zack was nuts. But he said, "If you ever decide to actually do this, I'll help." Six months later, Zack emailed him with the subject line: **Slushie Time!** Aaron, true to his word replied: **I'm in.**

And so it began. Kelvin Slush Co. (nerdily named after the Kelvin temperature scale) launched in 2010. Zack and Alex left their jobs as lawyers, bought an old mail truck, put in some slush machines, and gave cash in a brown paper bag to a sketchy dude for a "vending permit" (actually). Aaron flew back to New York for "opening" weekend, which is a fancy way of saying parking the truck in Union Square and opening the service window. We had no idea what we were doing. But sometimes things just work out. There were big lines. Awards. Features on CNN and in the *New York Times*. Food trucks were new and cool and having a moment, and we were part of it. It was a laugh, and a huge learning experience. People started bringing booze to the truck to spike their slush. This led to another light bulb going on: It's cool to drive around selling what one reporter called "slush for hipsters," but the real business opportunity was to sell the organic mix we'd created for the truck to restaurants and bars looking to reimagine their frozen cocktail programs. Better frozen cocktails made with real ingredients instead of the usual super-sweet chemical-laden concoctions. Zack became the salesperson and started selling Kelvin Slush mix to restaurants and bars, and even a few grocery stores, like Whole Foods.

And then another light bulb went on.

Caesars. We love them. Canadians love them. And we realized two key things: One, the Caesar is by far the most popular cocktail in Canada. Two, there were sure to be many Canadians like us who would welcome a Caesar mix crafted with great ingredients and made here in Canada. In an era of premium everything, there was no premium Caesar mix.

Why hadn't anyone made one? The idea seemed so . . . obvious.

We started to talk about the idea. First by email. And then, more frequently, on marathon phone calls well into the night and early morning. We discussed how Kelvin had gone from food truck to wholesale, and all the things we'd learned as a result. We'd shown that people would embrace a better version of a popular but pedestrian product. We knew how to make a premium product on a commercial scale and how to sell it. We also knew that we liked working together, Zack with his business skill set (in other words, spreadsheets) and Aaron with his background in branding and marketing (not spreadsheets). As the weeks went by, we started to get nervous that somebody would have the same idea, scoop us, and be first to market. We knew we had to do it. And fast.

We each cleared some space in our calendars and started testing recipes in our kitchens at night. We spent countless hours sourcing ingredients and packaging. We tasted more than 50 kinds of hot sauce, drank clam juice straight (don't: it's not good this way), and got super deep into tomatoes. We called every beverage manufacturer in Canada we could find, trying to convince someone to help us make our product. Nobody called us back. Finally, though, we found someone willing to take us on.

After getting the encouragement he needed from his wife, Helen, Aaron closed his design studio to work on Walter full-time. He really didn't want to. But he realized he had to. With our savings and some seed money from friends and family we produced an initial run, setting out to prove that Canadians, if given the option, would actually want a premium Caesar mix. We made 8,000 bottles. We had zero customers. But life's funny. Just as we were getting ready to launch, Joshua Linde, another childhood friend and a restaurant industry veteran, reached out to Zack with some questions about possibly doing an MBA. They got to talking about Walter. Josh thought it was cool and started working with us right away, armed with no salary, no contract, and a stack of Walter to sell. He is now a partner in the business and head of sales. It ended up being his ongoing MBA program.

We launched Walter Craft Caesar in October 2013 and quickly settled into panic mode. But the first run quickly sold out. The response from both retailers and customers was overwhelmingly positive. We'd passed our test: clearly there was a market for a better Caesar. People loved the product, and Walter started to grow. We got some press. Awards. A five-star review in the *National Post*. For the first few years our biggest problem was trying to keep up with growth.

We didn't have a playbook for how to turn a cool idea with a small cult following into a national brand. Building a distribution network, getting on shelves, securing production and working capital—we figured it out on the fly. We asked *a lot* of questions. Still do. We lived our version of the entrepreneurial cliché: Sleepless nights. Maxed-out credit cards. Partner-to-partner pep talks. Some tears. Some big wins. A few hard losses. Lots of mistakes. Lots of learning.

Nearly a decade after its launch, Walter is now a national brand and available in thousands of grocery stores, restaurants, and bars across Canada. We sell enough mix to make more than 6 million Caesars annually. That feels like a lot when we think back to how freaked out we were by the challenge of selling 8,000 bottles. But since Canadians drink 400 million Caesars a year, we've still got some room to grow.

Nerding Out

This section offers a deep dive into the theory and practice of crafting quality cocktails, and a step-by-step guide to building quality Caesars. By exploring all the different components, equipment, and techniques that go into making the Caesar so delicious and unique, we want to give you the tools you'll need to best execute the recipes in this book and the confidence to develop your own custom recipes. The Caesar is an especially useful case study in the art and science of drink making, since it's a relative unicorn in the cocktail world in that it can be customized in so many different ways.

We promise that if you spend some time nerding out with us over the minutiae of the Caesar, a world of possibilities will open up to you the next time you reach for the cocktail shaker, whether you're making a Caesar, another classic cocktail, or something new of your own invention.

A note before we start: *Be not afraid.* We're just making cocktails. It's not life or death. We've poured many a botched drink down the drain. Life's too short to suffer through failed Caesar experiments. Mix, build, test, taste, adjust, taste some more, try again.

What Is a Caesar, Anyway?

If we answered that question based only on Walter Chell's original recipe for the Caesar back in 1969, we'd define a Caesar as a cocktail consisting of tomato juice, vodka, spices, Worcestershire sauce, and clam juice.

But people have taken the Caesar in many different directions in the 50-plus years since Mr. Chell welcomed it to the world, and the definition of a Caesar should be broadened to reflect the drink's continuing evolution. We suggest that few of the ingredients from Mr. Chell's recipe are now *absolutely necessary* to make a Caesar. We've

enjoyed Caesars built around every spirit under the sun, without a drop of vodka in sight; Caesars with no alcohol at all; Caesars where the tomato juice has been replaced by other vegetable juices; Caesars without Worcestershire sauce; Caesars spiced in countless ways. We'll even go so far as to say that clam juice, the drink's most distinguishing element, isn't vital to what makes a Caesar a Caesar.

At Walter we've used dulse, a red seaweed, to create our Vegan Caesar mix, and lobster stock features in our seasonal Holiday mix. You'll notice that in each of these two non-clam-based mixes we're still drawing on an *element of the sea*. This, to us, is the key to the whole thing, the major insight that Mr. Chell hit on way back when in Calgary: that the briny, mineral-rich umami hit (which in his case was achieved through clam juice) is what gives the Caesar its particular *je ne sais quoi*. It's this connection to the sea that makes the Caesar so much better than a Bloody Mary (with all due respect to our southern neighbours) and what sets it apart from every other drink out there.

And so, we define the Caesar as: *a cocktail (alcoholic or non-alcoholic) made with a base of vegetable juice and an element of the sea.*

Take away the vegetable juice and you're drinking something other than a Caesar. Take away the element of the sea and you're enjoying a Bloody Mary. Everything else is optional. (And, yes, we know the tomato is botanically defined as a fruit but culinarily we're going to call it a vegetable.)

With the Caesar now defined, we should, before further discussion, categorize it properly within the cocktail kingdom. Technically, the Caesar qualifies as a *highball,* the rubric for any tall drink in which the volume of a mixer, usually soda or juice, is greater than that of its anchoring spirit or spirits (your Gin and Tonics, Rum and Cokes, Screwdrivers, etc.). However, we feel it's more precise to classify the Caesar as a *culinary highball* (alongside its cousin the Bloody Mary), given the savoury ingredients involved. The culinary nature of the Caesar presents all sorts of challenges and opportunities for creativity not offered by typical highballs, and it's also why we think the mixing of a Caesar should be done a little differently than the mixing of a typical highball (as we'll explain later).

Making Great Cocktails:
The Search for *Balance* & *Tension*

There's one word you'll see time and again in cocktail books: *balance*. Everyone wants you to carefully measure and combine ingredients until you reach some ideal equilibrium where all flavours, textures, and visual elements come together in harmony in a single perfect glass. But the term "balance" shows up so often in cocktail books (cookbooks, too) that it's at risk of losing its meaning altogether. And balance can be boring. On its own, the idea of balance fails to capture the excitement and wizardry that go into a well-made cocktail. While measuring accurately and mixing ingredients judiciously are vital to the process, making a drink should ideally feel a little dangerous, or at least more exciting than playing with a paint-by-numbers set. The best drinks, like the best foods, always have some ineffable, almost mysterious quality to them, something that goes beyond ticking off boxes.

That is why we approach cocktail making as a search for both *balance* and *tension*. Of course, we want the various elements of a drink to cohere into some kind of order that pleases the senses. But the hint of danger is what takes a cocktail from drinkable to delicious.

A tightrope walker crossing perfectly and mechanically between two points is impressive but instantly forgotten, which is why the best tightrope walker will lift a leg and point it outward to raise the stakes and then, just before the end of the line, suddenly teeter as if about to fall, jolting the audience, making them instinctively lean forward in their seats. The tightrope walker knows they won't fall. But they want you to think they might. While no one's at risk of getting injured while making a cocktail, we should still aspire to the same level of artistry and drama as the tightrope walker.

Don't get us wrong: there are rules and we want you to follow them. But over time you'll amass enough experience to learn where the edge is, the confidence to know you won't fall, and the audacity to push as close to it as you can get, while pulling your various elements together less

---

Caesar vs. Bloody Mary:
The Key Differences

The Bloody Mary is as malleable as the Caesar, and you'll find innumerable twists and expansions on its basic formula, especially across the United States (see *The Bloody Mary* by Brian Bartels), but the "classic" or "typical" Caesar tends to differentiate from the "classic" or "typical" Bloody Mary in the following ways: 1) It contains clam juice or another element of the sea; 2) It's thinner in consistency and a little sweeter; 3) It's garnished with a lime wedge rather than a lemon wedge; 4) It has a celery salt rim rather than a rock salt rim.

Another way to tell them apart:
Caesar: excellent.
Bloody Mary: fine (if a Caesar isn't available).

A Note from Ocean Wise
By Claire Dawson, Senior Science Lead
Ocean Wise Seafood

Ocean Wise Seafood is a not-for-profit ocean conservation program that researches and recommends sustainable seafood options that support healthy oceans, lakes, and rivers. Ocean Wise Seafood's sustainability recommendations are based on the most up-to-date science regarding fishery and aquaculture practices to inform responsible purchasing decisions by businesses and consumers.

Walter Craft Caesar joined Ocean Wise Seafood in 2015 as the program's first beverage partner. The clam juice used in Walter Caesar products has been verified as sustainable by the Ocean Wise Seafood team, and they have been an active collaborator and supporter of ocean conservation throughout their partnership.

The Walter team's commitment to Ocean Wise Seafood recommended sourcing ensures their Caesars will not harm wild ocean habitats. In many cases, clams improve the quality of the ecosystems in which they are grown. As filter feeders, clams clean waterways while they grow, which increases water quality and clarity and reduces nutrient overloading. They also create structural habitats, which can support local biodiversity. This behaviour is rare in food production.

By making informed decisions, we can all have a positive impact on the health of our oceans, lakes, and rivers. Look for the Ocean Wise symbol for an assurance of a sustainable choice.

How Do You Juice a Clam?

The term "clam juice" is confusing. It's a misnomer, really. You can't *juice* a hard-shelled bivalve. It would be more accurate to say clam broth or clam stock, but clam juice is the name that has stuck and it's what we use in this book. Clam juice refers to the briny, mineral-rich liquid that comes from clams when they're cooked, and to the reserved liquid in which the clams cook and is then used for canning or jarring clam meat. In other words, *broth* or *stock,* right? How exactly the standard industry term came to be "clam juice" (sometimes you'll see "clam nectar") we couldn't say. By the way, you'll find a recipe to make your own clam juice on page 71.

with an eye to perfectly matched proportions and more to recognizing that only in tandem can these particular ingredients serve some broader purpose.

If cocktail making was *only* about balance, we'd put up one recipe for a nice steady Caesar on our website and be done with it. The different ways that people search for tension are what keep things interesting in cocktail land and why there are more than 50 recipes for a Caesar in this book, with no two alike. What constitutes an ideal sense of balance and tension will vary according to who's in charge of making the drink, and a big part of the fun of the whole process is discovering what works for you.

We think the most appealing cocktails are the ones that risk a bit of criticism—where, for instance, a touch of acid might on first sip seem out of place until your palate and brain come to agree that this very acidity is what makes the drink sing. Which is to say that creating drinks with the idea of tension in mind isn't about showing off but about seeking out those beautiful and unforeseen moments that can only come through exploration.

Henri Matisse said it was better to risk ruining a painting by pushing it to its limits than to be satisfied with the results reached by taking the easiest route, no matter how pleasing or harmonious they might be. We feel the same way about cocktails.

Why the Caesar Is the Unicorn of the Cocktail World

Two words: *complexity* and *flexibility*.

Complexity
When we talk about the Caesar's complexity, we don't mean that it's complicated to make. We mean that it stands apart from so many other cocktails because it encompasses such a wide range of flavours—a wider range, in fact, than found in almost any other cocktail.

Most cocktails feature some combination of the four flavours in drink making: sweet, sour, bitter, and strong (alcohol). In a Gin and Tonic, for instance, the *strength* comes from the gin, the tonic water lends *bitterness* through its quinine, the *sweetness* comes from the sugar in the tonic water, and the *sourness* comes from the lime. The pattern repeats in cocktail after cocktail, although some contain only three flavours, such as a Daiquiri, which lacks a *bitter* component. And while the cocktail world focuses on four flavours, the culinary world focuses on five: sweet, sour, bitter, salty, umami.

What makes culinary highballs like the Caesar unique is that they typically contain all five basic culinary flavours *plus* the *strong* flavour from alcohol. Knowing where each of those flavours tend to come from in a typical Caesar will help you know where to push and pull as you look for balance and tension in bringing these flavours together.

1. **Sweet**
   Tomatoes, being naturally sweet, are usually among the largest providers of sweetness in a Caesar. Worcestershire sauce also adds some sweetness, as does citrus juice. And any Caesar mix will likely have some amount of sweetener added. At Walter, we add a touch of organic cane sugar.

2. **Sour**
   Most Caesar recipes call for some kind of acid, such as citrus juice (and/or garnish), brine, vinegar, and sometimes hot sauce, which is typically made with vinegar. And while tomatoes are sweet, they're also acidic, adding an element of sourness.

3. **Bitter**
   Horseradish and celery salt (as a rim and/or in a mix) will very often be the source of a Caesar's bitter elements. Some recipes might call for cocktail bitters, or beer that can bring some bitterness. Some folks want to avoid bitterness altogether. And remember Exodus (12:8): With bitter herbs they shall eat it.

Why the Caesar Is a Culinary Highball

Cocktails: 4 Basic Flavours

Sweet	Sour	Bitter	Strong

Culinary: 5 Basic Flavours

Sweet	Sour	Bitter	Salty	Umami

Caesars: 6 Basic Flavours + Heat

Sweet	Sour	Bitter	Strong	Salty	Umami	Heat
Tomatoes	Citrus	Horseradish	Alcohol	Salt	Tomatoes	Hot Sauce
Sugar	Tomatoes	Celery Salt		Clam Juice	Clam Juice	Pepper
Citrus Juice	Brine/Vinegar			Hot Sauce	Worcestershire	Horseradish
Worcestershire				Rim		Chili

4. Salty

A Caesar will almost always have at least some salt added, which heightens other flavours—especially tomatoes. Salt will also enhance sweetness (think salted caramel) while balancing out bitterness. Typically, Caesar rims will have some kind of saltiness. Plus, hot sauce and clam juice are usually quite salty.

5. Umami

A classic Caesar is in many ways an umami bomb. Umami flavour can be found in tomatoes, Worcestershire sauce, and clam juice. (And if you read the sidebar on umami, you'll discover that the most common mass market brands of Caesar mix use monosodium glutamate—better known as MSG—for a reason: it's an umami enhancer).

6. Strong

Last but not least, the Caesar typically contains vodka or some other spirit. Hooray for that!

Honourable Mention: Heat

While not technically a flavour, the Caesar almost always contains *heat,* usually delivered through some kind of spicy ingredient, typically a chili-based hot sauce.

And so, to create a well-made Caesar, you need to harness all of the five flavours a chef would be dealing with when cooking a dish, while also integrating the strong alcohol flavours and deciding on how (or if) to deploy your heat. Like we said: complexity!

Flexibility

Another way the Caesar stands apart from so many other cocktails is through its *flexibility.* Making an excellent Caesar requires following very few rules, even when it comes to the drink's most basic elements.

Traditionally, Caesars are anchored by vodka, but a simple way to add more depth to the drink is to switch the vodka for gin, tequila, mezcal, aquavit, or any number of other spirits or beer. And as we've argued above, a Caesar can be a Caesar even without the classic red tomato juice or clam juice in its base. When you factor in the number of sauces, brines, garnishes, and rim options at your disposal, the possibilities for variation are endless.

Umami & MSG

One of the five basic tastes, umami refers to the pleasant sense of savouriness we get from certain foods. When we say something has umami, we're technically describing the taste and mouthfeel of glutamates and nucleotides. Foods such as soy sauce, mushrooms, cheese, tomatoes, shellfish, Worcestershire sauce, seaweed, and meat broths are naturally high in glutamates, which gives them their rich flavour. Walter Caesar mix is naturally high in glutamates—and therefore umami flavour— as we use lots of tomatoes, clam juice, and Worcestershire sauce in our recipe, so we don't have to add any glutamates to provide a strong umami flavour. Monosodium glutamate (MSG), first extracted in 1908, gives food scientists an easy way to pack mass-produced products with something resembling the flavour of naturally occurring glutamates. MSG can be found in many products, including soups, bouillon, gravy—and the most common mass market Caesar mixes.

The Components

Breaking down the six components that typically go into preparing a Caesar will help us to better understand how best to bring them all together when it comes time to make one. They are:

1. **Base Mix**
2. **Base Spirits & Modifiers**
3. **Flavour Additions**
4. **Rim**
5. **Garnish**
6. **Ice**

1. Base Mix

By "base mix" we mean some kind of vegetable juice combined with an element of the sea. The easiest (and most common) way to get those elements into your glass is to start with a pre-made Caesar mix. Of course, we recommend Walter, but there are others available. Find your favourite.

As an alternative to a pre-made mix, you can start with commercial tomato juice, or, if you want to forego tomatoes altogether, any vegetable juice: carrot, beet, multi-veggie "garden cocktail," the sky (or soil) is the limit. To add that vital sea element to a vegetable juice base you can add store-bought clam juice or, better yet, make your own clam juice using the recipe on page 71. It stores well in the freezer and you can whip up some bar clams for snacking while you're at it (page 272). If clams aren't your thing, seaweed, fish sauce, lobster stock, and squid ink can all serve as substitutes.

And of course, you can make your own base Caesar mix from scratch. This is how we first started developing our recipes for Walter in our kitchens, and it's actually really fun and satisfying. Find our base recipes on pages 68 to 71.

Or for a different spin, you can try making a fresh tomato water base, using raw tomatoes rather than the usual cooked version (page 299).

Tomatoes: The Raw & the Cooked

We're often asked if Caesars can be made with fresh tomato juice rather than cooked. The answer is yes, as we show in Tomato Water Last Word (page 164), but rarely. There are several reasons Caesars, Bloody Marys, tomato juice, pasta sauce, pizza sauce, ketchup, etc., all use cooked tomatoes. First, the caramelization that results from cooking creates a sweeter and more complex profile that you can't find in raw tomatoes. Second, heating tomatoes breaks down their cell walls, which gives the tomatoes a smoother consistency and improves their digestibility. Third, cooking removes water from the tomatoes, concentrating and intensifying their flavour. And as a bonus, food scientists suggest that tomatoes, unlike many other fruits and vegetables, actually gain nutritional value when cooked, as more of the antioxidant lycopene is released. Gazpacho made with raw tomatoes is delicious, bright, and fresh, but it tastes totally different from the sweet, rich, caramelized flavours of a warm bowl of cooked tomato soup. Those deeper cooked tomato flavours stand up far better than the flavours of raw tomatoes to the generous seasoning and strong alcohol flavours in a Caesar.

2. Base Spirits & Modifiers

A base spirit is the alcohol that anchors a cocktail, and a modifier is anything else alcoholic that complements the base without overshadowing it. If a drink were a movie, the base would be the star and the modifier the quirky sidekick. (Some drinks will call for a "split base," meaning two base spirits in roughly equal proportions, or to extend the movie metaphor, two co-stars sharing top billing.)

Walter Chell's original Caesar recipe had a vodka base, and it remains the most commonly used Caesar spirit base in bars and restaurants across the country. There's a good reason for its popularity: vodka's relative neutrality, taste-wise, makes it an ideal starting point through which to showcase the classic Caesar's defining characteristics of clams and tomatoes. This book contains plenty of recipes that follow in the tradition of the vodka-based Caesar, while also reimagining what can be done while maintaining this classic anchor.

But, as we said earlier, the beauty of the Caesar is that it offers so many chances for personalization because of all of its moving and interlocking parts. And one of the key ways to customize your Caesar is through the spirit (or non-alcoholic alternative) you choose for your base. By looking beyond vodka to options spanning from gin to mezcal to vermouth to so many other spirits or beer, Canada's bartending community has dramatically expanded the possibilities for what can make a great Caesar, and we encourage you to have some fun and get creative with your bases.

Just as great dishes start with great ingredients, high-quality liquor is vital to a successful cocktail. You don't have to use the most expensive super-premium spirits you can find, but the quickest route to a disappointing drink is to use the cheapest stuff. When choosing your spirits, take note of the many world-class spirits being produced in Canada. We've seen a coast-to-coast-to-coast boom in craft distilleries over the past few years, and we encourage you to seek them out and support them.

One last thing. Since spirits belonging to the same category can vary significantly in their flavours and alcohol levels, you'll want to consider how those potential differences can affect your cocktail. Let's take gin, for example: some are dry, some feature strong botanicals, others favour bold citrus notes—there's even gin made with kelp (the award-winning Seaside Gin from Vancouver Island's Sheringham Distillery). You can imagine how each of those styles of gin could take your Caesar in a different direction.

Base Spirits

A quick walk through the major spirits will give you some ideas about why you might choose one over the other for your cocktail.

Vodka

The original. A neutral but flexible spirit that takes you everywhere from clean and bright (wheat), to earthy (potato), to super-refined and sweet (corn). This is the safe bet. If you're ever in doubt about which spirit to use, start with vodka. You can't go too far wrong.

Gin

A real team player and likely the second most common Caesar base. Because of its flavourful mix of botanicals (including juniper, citrus peel, and/or coriander), gin is especially good at complementing Caesars with sophisticated and more subtle seasoning where its herbaceous qualities won't get lost in the shuffle. People sometimes call a gin-based Bloody Mary a Red Snapper, and we've sometimes seen the term applied to gin-based Caesars.

Tequila

A unique (and sometimes polarizing) choice, tequila's assertive flavour works well as the base for confidently spiced and citrus-forward Caesars. Also check out our recipe for a Sangrita (page 98), the traditional non-alcoholic accompaniment to tequila blanco.

Mezcal

Tequila's smoky brother mezcal has been having its moment in the sun here in Canada. While most often drunk straight in Mexico, people around the world have discovered all sorts of ways of using it in cocktails. Mezcal is a bold choice, capable of giving Caesars smoky and earthy undertones that can't be fully replicated with any other spirit. We typically use mezcal as a modifier or in a split base. As with tequila, Mezcal is best with sweeter and more acidic Caesars, and it can handle some pretty serious seasoning and spicing.

Whisky

Whisky can sometimes work well in a Caesar, but it's an assertive flavour that you need to use wisely. This is another spirit we often use as a split base with equal parts vodka so that the whisky doesn't overpower the whole cocktail. A nice peaty (read: smoky) scotch, used sparingly, can be a particularly effective modifier. Pro tip to help you remember the spelling: It's *whisky* if it comes from a place with no "e" in the name (Scotland, Japan, Canada) and *whiskey* if it comes from a place with an "e" in the name (Ireland, the United States of America).

Aquavit

Our fellow Northerners in Scandinavia make this fine wheat (sometimes potato) spirit with all sorts of herbs, spices, and fruit oils (typically caraway, anise, fennel, citrus), which is why bartenders love to use aquavit for all kinds of unconventional cocktails. We feel the same way about using it in Caesars. Aquavit pairs especially well with recipes featuring horseradish, black pepper, and lemon.

Rum

Made from cane sugar or molasses, rum isn't a typical Caesar addition, but it can work if you're feeling adventurous, especially if you're seeking a tropical and/or tiki-inspired flavour profile. Note that rum, more so than many other spirits, will vary widely in flavour and colour according to where and how it was distilled.

Other Spirits

Anything you can find at the liquor store could potentially find a place in your Caesar. You just need to take the risk and keep experimenting. We've had a lot of fun tasting innovative Caesars made with all sorts of unconventional alcohol choices from around the world, from baijiu, cachaça, and pisco to sake, shochu, soju, and beyond.

Beer

Beer and Caesar mix is really a beautiful thing. Some people find the combination surprising. We think it's fantastic. You can use beer in Caesars in many different ways.

1. **Use beer instead of a spirit as your base.** This lets you offer a lower-alcohol cocktail option while also bringing some carbonation to the party. Beer-based Caesars are sometimes called Beesars but we usually just say "Beer Caesar" or "Session Caesar" because the low ABV (that would be its alcohol by volume) makes it very sessionable (meaning light enough to allow for drinking a few in one session). For an example of a Session Caesar see The Merman (page 90). Beer Caesars seem to be an especially popular option in Québec and Alberta. Latinx communities have long favoured the Michelada, a *cerveza preparada,* with a tomato and beer base, spiced somewhat similarly to a traditional Caesar.

2. **Add a splash of beer as a modifier to your spirit-based Caesar.** This is a simple way to bring a new flavour (and light carbonation) to your Caesar. See the Bug Repellent (page 258), which uses just a couple of ounces of a hoppy IPA to add a hint of bitterness. Another beer-modifier option is to make a beer reduction. In It's a Thing, Man (page 128) we use a stout or porter reduction for a concentrated dose of malty aromas paired with molasses-like sweetness.

3. **Pair your usual Caesar with a small glass or shot of beer.** This is a perfect palate cleanser (for an example, see Ponyboy on page 138). As you go back and

forth between the two drinks, you'll find a surprising interplay of flavours, which can break up the richness of the Caesar, making it easier to drink. And the tiny glass will make you feel like a giant.

4. **Instead of adding beer to a Caesar, do the opposite.** Many Canadians, particularly Albertans, have been known to splash just a little Caesar mix into a beer to spruce up a not-so-great lager (see Calgary Redeye on page 140).

If you're using beer in a Caesar, we generally recommend ones with low IBU (international bitterness units) and low to moderate malt. We tend to focus on more neutral beers. A few good options are:

Lagers/Pilsners: Fairly neutral, lagers and pilsners are likely the most common choice for Beer Caesars. Mexican-style lager is, unsurprisingly, the go-to for Micheladas. Along with the many Mexican beers available in Canada there are several Canadian brewers making Mexican-style cerveza.

Wheat Beers: A light option that will lend some refreshing herbal notes to your Caesar. Wheat beers tend to be sweeter, so this is a great option when looking to add some sweetness.

Sour: Sour beers make an excellent choice for your Beer Caesar, as they come close to replicating the flavour of citrus juice that would be used in a traditional Caesar.

Stout/Porter: With their heavier flavour, we find that 1 or 2 ounces (30 or 60 ml) of stout or porter is plenty for a Caesar, and they work best alongside one of the clear spirits: vodka, gin, aquavit.

Modifiers

Since the term "modifier" refers to anything alcoholic that changes the flavour of your drink without serving as its anchoring liquor, you could use any of the base spirits or beers listed above as a modifier just by using it in a smaller quantity than your base. But there are also many items that typically serve exclusively as modifiers when they're used in cocktails, including liqueurs, aperitif wines, and bitters, which we cover below. Choosing different modifiers is a great way to start experimenting.

Cocktail Bitters

Bartenders will sometimes speak of their assortment of bitters as their "spice rack." Since we draw on the real spice rack (often liberally) when making Caesars, we use bitters more modestly than you might in other cocktails. Think of bitters as supercharged bursts of flavour that also emphasize the qualities of other ingredients you're already using. Anything more than a few drops and you risk pushing your drink past the point of no return. Some bitters flavours ideally suited for Caesars are black pepper, celery, chili, citrus, rosemary, and salt.

Liqueurs

Some examples of liqueurs with different flavour profiles that can be incorporated into Caesars include:

Bitter Liqueurs: Most often associated with Italy and typically infused with herbs, citrus peels, spices, and roots, these *apertivo* or *digestivo* drinks have become increasingly popular in North America and appear frequently as cocktail modifiers. They get their respective names by being traditionally served as appetite-stimulating drinks before a meal or digestive aids afterward. The best-known brands are Campari (the Negroni's key ingredient) and Aperol (anchor for the eponymous Spritz). We generally find Campari and Aperol flavours too distinct to be incorporated into a Caesar. When it comes to Caesars, our preference is for Amaro, and you'll find an example of that in Untitled (The Amaro One) on page 186.

Orange Liqueur: Orange liqueurs (or curaçao) such as triple sec, Cointreau, and Grand Marnier are most commonly associated with Margaritas, Cosmopolitans, and Long Island Iced Tea. The latter serves as the tongue-in-cheek inspiration for our Vancouver Island Iced Tea, which also uses triple sec (page 94).

Chartreuse: Green and Yellow Chartreuse are French liqueurs crafted with a proprietary combination of botanicals that give them their unique flavours. Green is more herbaceous, while yellow's on the sweeter side.

Pernod: Pernod is the classic French anise-flavoured liqueur best known for its delicate licorice flavours. It's often used in cooking seafood including, classically, bouillabaisse. We use it in Cabane à Sucre on page 160.

Wines, Fruit Spirits & More

Red, white, and rosé wines can all be used as modifiers in a Caesar, as can fortified wines such as sherry and aromatized wines like vermouth. Fruit brandies, such as cognac, and pomace brandies, such as grappa, have roles to play as well.

Red and white wine tend to be the most common choices under this rubric, with red being a strong choice for when you're looking for some earthiness and tannins, and white a simple option for adding acidity and sweetness. We've seen bartenders add a dash of anything from brandy to madeira to give their Caesars a dose of sweetness. Vermouths, and other aromatized wines (meaning fortified wines that are further flavoured by botanicals and/or fruits), can take things a step further, adding not only dryness or sweetness but also new flavour notes.

You'll find an example of dry vermouth as a modifier in Hot & Sour on page 84. While we rarely see it used as a base, Matthew Boyle and Jeffrey Van Horne have brilliantly shown how it can be done, creating a low-ABV Caesar with a dry vermouth base in Dear Friend on page 232.

Infusions

Alcoholic infusions are produced by adding a non-liquid ingredient or ingredients to a spirit, letting them sit, and then removing the non-alcoholic ingredient, leaving you with a spirit that has been infused with the flavours of the other ingredients. Making your own alcoholic infusions opens up a host of possibilities for your Caesars because it allows you to incorporate other flavours into your base spirit. Infusions are typically made with a neutrally flavoured spirit, usually vodka, but you should feel free to explore using any others you fancy. There's no law against a whisky or tequila infusion, for instance.

In the Appendix, starting on page 270, you'll find a number of infusion recipes, but don't feel limited by them. You can infuse almost any ingredients using the same basic technique that we discuss below, so feel free to get creative.

Infusion Tips & Tricks

Always ensure that infusions are made in a clean glass container with airtight lids and mouths wide enough to allow you to get your infusion ingredients in and then out again. In most cases you're going to need to strain out some of your ingredients. Do so with a fine-mesh sieve or cheesecloth, or both.

The longer you leave the infusion before straining out the solid bits, the more intense the flavour. While some infusions could be ready to go after just a few hours (or minutes for a really spicy pepper!), a good rule of thumb is to let your infusion sit for between 5 and 7 days before consuming it—if you can stand the wait. There's little benefit to waiting any longer than a week, though. Shaking the infusion a few times a day speeds up the process somewhat. The higher the alcohol content of your spirit, the faster the infusion process tends to go. Some people prefer over-proof spirits to make infusions for the sake of speed. Don't worry about leaving your infusion out at room temperature, because the alcohol will serve as the

stabilizer, although there's nothing wrong with putting it in the refrigerator if you prefer. Finished infusions can be stored on a cool and dark shelf or in the refrigerator.

Remember to taste along the way, especially if it's your first time trying a particular infusion. This is important with spicy infusions where things can get out of hand quickly. When testing new infusions, we start small and infuse only a cup or two of alcohol before committing to a larger amount.

Fat Washes

If infusing lets you get the flavour of herbs, spices, and other dry ingredients into a spirit, fat washing is the equivalent but for fat. By combining fat with alcohol and then freezing it, you can easily separate the fat. You're left with the flavour of the fat in the alcohol. This is especially useful for a Caesar because the savoury flavours that come from fat (bacon fat, butter, olive oil, sesame oil, etc.) pair extremely well with the rich tomato and clam base. And the beauty of fat washing is that it allows you to incorporate those satisfying fatty flavours without actually adding fat. And, to state the obvious, you typically wouldn't want to add actual fat to a cocktail because it would have an oily, greasy mouthfeel, not to mention potentially solidifying at cold temperatures.

A few of the leading figures credited with pioneering this revolutionary but surprisingly simple technique are Eben Freeman, Sam Mason, Don Lee, and Tona Palomino. In this book you'll find three different fat washes, each one highlighting the use of a different kind of fat:

1. Fat that is liquid at room temperature, such as olive oil or sesame oil, which can be used without modifying it. See Sesame Fat Washed Vodka (page 302).

2. Fat that remains solid at room temperature, such as butter, which needs to be melted before use. See Citrus Brown Butter Washed Vodka (page 301).

3. Animal fat, such as bacon fat, which can't be added raw (in solid form). The fat must first be rendered from the protein, by cooking. See Duck Fat Washed Gin (page 301).

You can use these three techniques to create almost any flavour fat wash you can imagine. Olive oil and bacon are especially popular fat wash options for bartenders, and both can work well in Caesars. And as with infusions, you aren't limited to any particular type of spirit.

As a rule of thumb, we use the following ratios of fat-to-spirit when creating fat washes. If the fat has a stronger flavour (like sesame oil), we'll use less of it, and if it has a more delicate flavour (like butter), we'll use more.

A Note on Non-Alcoholic Drinks

Restaurants and bars across Canada are making increasing efforts to offer low-proof and non-alcoholic cocktails (a.k.a. mocktails). We've included a few non-alcoholic cocktails (see Double Double, page 102, and Garden, page 176) made with Seedlip, a non-alcoholic distilled spirit. Given how much flavour and textural interest already comes from its non-alcoholic ingredients, the Caesar translates especially well into its alcohol-free versions, arguably more so than any other cocktail.

Fat-to-Spirit Ratios

	Fat	Spirit
Liquid Fat	1 oz (30 ml)	6¾ oz (200 ml)
Solid Fat (melted)	2 oz (60 ml)	6¾ oz (200 ml)
Rendered Fat	2 oz (60 ml)	8 oz (240 ml)

The safest bet is to test and taste a small batch before making a big batch. Fat washed spirits should be stored in the refrigerator.

3. Flavour Additions

This section covers some of the main ingredients that you can add to bases and modifiers to form the foundation of a Caesar cocktail. These flavour additions play a key role in giving the Caesar its unique personality.

Worcestershire Sauce

This fermented fish sauce was included in Mr. Chell's original Caesar recipe for a reason: it provides a background flavour enhancement, adding a significant amount of umami (or savouriness) to the overall drink, as well as a touch of sweetness. People don't generally think of Worcestershire sauce as sweet, but try tasting it on its own and you'll find it actually is. When someone says they want a "muddy" Caesar, they want extra Worcestershire sauce. And while Worcestershire sauce is used in the vast majority of Caesars, it isn't mandatory.

Hot Sauce

Walter Chell didn't use hot sauce in his original Caesar recipe, explaining that "it kills the taste of the clam." It would seem a half-century's worth of home and professional bartenders have respectfully disagreed, since today hot sauce is a standard Caesar ingredient. Whether it's Louisiana-style, Mexican-style, green (jalapeño-based), Buffalo-style, sriracha, or whatever your favourite might be, most any hot sauce will work. There are shelves of hot sauces at the local grocer and more online; there are

What's-This-Here Sauce?

Wonderful sauce, hard to spell, daunting to pronounce. Saying the name of this fermented condiment strikes terror into the hearts of many people. Blame the Brits. The sauce gets its name from the town of Worcester, England, where it was first made by a couple of chemists with the last names of Lea and Perrins. (Worcester-*shire* because adding "shire" is like adding "county" to the end of a place name.)

In Britain, the *proper* way to pronounce it is simply *Wooster* (rhymes with *rooster*). Why? Because, in the Queen's English, the letters *Worcester* are pronounced *Wooster* (obviously) and, of course, in Britain everyone knows you just drop the *shire* (again, obviously).

Or you can use the more common North American pronunciation. Try *woo-stuh-sure* in three even syllables, dropping that last R sound so it ends the same way you would say New Hampshire (*New Hamp-sure*). Or you could just say *Worch*, as many pressed-for-time bartenders do.

whole cookbooks dedicated to the stuff. So, rather than trying to cover the enormous variety of options here, we'll just advise you to pay attention to the differences in taste, quality, and pungency in any given sauce and to remember that choosing one isn't about adding just *heat* but also *flavour*. Since each one is made from its own particular blends of chili peppers, salts, sugars, vinegars, fruits and vegetables, spices, and other ingredients, a hot sauce can take you anywhere from smoky to fruity to nutty.

You might also want to try your hand at making your own funky fermented hot sauce, using Josh's Fermented Hot Sauce recipe on page 295. Or, try making the super-secret Rodney's Back from Hell Hot Sauce on page 297.

Note: Recipes in the book that recommend a certain style or brand of hot sauce do so because the sauce in question provides a specific flavour profile. But, as with spirit brand recommendations, our suggestions are exactly that: suggestions. We understand that people have very particular preferences when it comes to spice levels. Feel free to adjust the amount of hot sauce in any recipe, or to omit it completely.

Other Sauces

You'll find there are many other sauces that can do wonders for your Caesar, either alongside or in lieu of Worcestershire and hot sauces. We encourage you to explore them. Some of the common commercially available sauces we've seen used effectively are soy sauce, tamari, Maggi, HP Sauce, BBQ sauce, fish sauce, chili bean sauce, oyster sauce, tandoori paste, teriyaki sauce, sweet chili sauce, adobo sauce, and gochujang paste.

You can also custom-make your own sauces, syrups, or reductions to suit your particular needs. Some of the recipes in this book will show you how. For example, Cloudberry Syrup (page 294), Pomegranate Syrup (page 296), Tare (page 298), and Concord Grape Vincotto (page 294).

Sweeteners

Sometimes a Caesar just needs a little boost of sweetness to get it to where it needs to be. Sugar, honey, maple syrup, and agave can all fulfill that need. When we're using sweeteners whose consistencies make them harder to dissolve in a cocktail (sugar, honey, agave), we first convert them to syrup through some version of adding water and heating. (Maple syrup is liquid enough in its natural state that we use it as is.) You'll find a variety of syrup recipes in the Appendix (pages 270 to 302).

Juices

Juices offer another way to add sweetness, as well as new flavours and usually some acid too. To keep things fresh, try whenever possible to squeeze your own juices as close as possible to when you're ready to make your drink. The taste of juice will change for the worse as time marches forward. Use high-quality ripe fruits. Whenever possible we try to use organic.

Lemon & Lime: These are the two citrus juices most often associated with the Caesar. With their natural tartness, they're perfect for adding brightness, freshness, and a punch of acidity. Walter Chell's original Caesar used lime, which remains the more commonly used of the two. Lime leans more bitter than lemon, which helps to offset the sweetness from the tomatoes and other elements. So you should be looking to lemon whenever you have a Caesar whose ingredients lean more to the sour or bitter side and could use some rounding out by the lemon's sweetness.

Truth be told, more often than not, we reach for lemons rather than limes when making Caesars. We find that lemon's more neutral flavour, relative to lime, gives the other ingredients in the cocktail the chance to shine. But each one has its place and they both make many appearances in the recipes that follow.

A rule of thumb for shopping and planning: limes tend to give you 1 oz (30 ml) of juice each, while lemons will usually give 1 to 1½ oz (30 to 45 ml).

Grapefruit, Orange, Pineapple, Mango, & Other Fruit Juices: Other fruit juices, while a less obvious choice, can also offer effective ways to add sweetness and flavour. They should be considered as background characters, however, meant to support or emphasize the allures of other ingredients—so take a light hand with these. Typically, ½ oz (15 ml) per drink is plenty. If you're squeezing these juices yourself, think about straining them to remove pulp as you see fit. For a particularly unexpected combination, try watermelon juice, as used in our Waltermelon on page 226.

Seasonings & Spices

Salt & Pepper: As the Caesar is a culinary highball, we need to think about seasoning more carefully than we would with regular cocktails. We always have a salt and pepper grinder ready when making Caesars, and we approach the drink's seasoning in the same way we would a sauce or soup, adding salt and pepper to taste as we go.

Horseradish: This bitter root vegetable has long been a fixture in Caesars. We use a healthy dose of it in our Classic Walter mix. Horseradish offers a great combination of bitter and pungent, which cuts through all the other ingredients without overwhelming them, so long as it's used in the right proportion. The heat from horseradish is enough to get you crying but lingers on the tongue for a much shorter time than does heat from chili peppers, so it's ideal for giving you a quick zing without commanding all of your attention. Store-bought jarred horseradish will be floating in vinegar or brine, so account for those added tastes when choosing this option over grating the fresh stuff.

Spices: Caesar makers have been known to reach for the spice rack, most often in the base mix stage. Garlic powder, onion powder, cayenne, chili pepper, cumin, celery seed, paprika, and sumac are all at home in a Caesar— we'd go so far as to say that almost anything in your spice jar could be used.

Fresh Herbs (& Muddling)
Dried herbs have their place in a Caesar, but when we're looking to bring herbaceous flavours we far prefer using fresh herbs, which we muddle just as you would muddle fresh mint in a Mojito. Muddling fresh herbs lets you extract fresh and vibrant flavours that you just can't get from the dried variety. While you can get herb flavours into a cocktail by making infusions, we find muddling is faster, requires less planning, and yields a brighter, more robust herbal flavour in the finished cocktail. While anything you have on hand will work, some of our favourites are basil, rosemary, thyme, dill, celery leaves, lemongrass, sage, tarragon, and oregano (though use this last one sparingly, given its strong flavour).

Brines, Vinegars, & Shrubs
Think of brines, vinegars, and shrubs (drinking vinegars) as flavour shortcuts. The acids they provide make them great for adding a touch of sourness to Caesars as needed. Among our favourites are pickling brine, olive brine, apple cider vinegar, red wine vinegar, white wine vinegar, champagne vinegar, and rice vinegar. Bold, sometimes even brash, they require a careful hand. They can quickly take over your whole drink if you let them. You'll find a number of recipes for shrubs and infused vinegars in the Appendix, pages 270 to 302.

Smoke
Smoke pairs really well with the Caesar's flavours, which is why we make a Smoky Maple Walter mix. You can add smoke to a Caesar in many ways, several of which you'll see in this book: from charring rosemary and thyme to liquid smoke and smoky mezcal. You can also add other smoked ingredients, such as smoked paprika or smoked sea salt. If you're really serious about smoke, know that we've seen people put finished cocktails into smokers to infuse them.

4. Rim

Rarely would you be served a Caesar in a bar or restaurant without some kind of rim. After all, a nice dose of salt in your drink makes you yearn for more. Choosing the right rim is a key step when conceiving of a Caesar recipe, because the rim offers the chance to add an entirely new flavour element to the drink, emphasize flavours that are already present, or both. Rims give you simple ways to add saltiness, sweetness, more spice, or something more herbaceous.

Since the rim is the first thing to hit your guests' lips when they take a sip, you want to make a strong impression. It can be tempting to overdo it and overpower the drink rather than complementing it. The most important thing a rim can do is pair well with the liquid in the glass. That's why a Caesar is sometimes better with no rim at all, either because the cocktail has a subtle profile that would be overwhelmed by a rim's flavour, or because it's an assertively seasoned drink that has no need for added saltiness or spice.

The Caesar rim is made up of two parts. First, the liquid to which the dry ingredients will stick (which we call the base coat) and second, the rim spice. We'll cover rim technique below. But for now, let's walk through some potential ingredient ideas for base coats and rim spices.

Base Coat
Every rim starts with a sticky liquid base to which the spice will cling. The base coat plays a double role: along with its stickiness, this foundation allows you to add a new flavour element. The key here is to choose something with some sugar content so that the stuff actually sticks. (Water won't work. The rim spice will drip down the side of your glass.) Some base coat ideas to get you started:

Lime Juice: The classic Caesar basecoat, offering a sharp citrus note.

Lemon Juice: Lemon tends to be a touch sweeter and rounder in flavour than lime. It's a more neutral option and the one we use most often.

Pineapple Juice: A great blend of acid and sweetness, this may seem like an odd choice, but it works really well. We've converted many a skeptic into pineapple-Caesar fans.

Maple Syrup: It doesn't get more Canadian than this. Just make sure you get the good stuff from Québec or Ontario. A Caesar with Vermont maple syrup could be delicious— but we wouldn't know.

Honey Syrup: We generally use Honey Syrup (page 295) rather than honey out of the jar for applying a rim because it's thinner and easier to apply, but you can also use straight honey. Either way, honey's super sticky so it'll do the job. As with all ingredients, the better the honey, the better your rim. We generally choose a neutral variety, such as clover honey.

Agave Syrup: As you'd expect, this is a great choice for tequila- or mezcal-based Caesars. We typically use Agave Syrup (page 292), but you can also use straight agave nectar.

Rim Spice
There are no real rules or limits to what you might add as a rim spice. Options range from the classic celery salt to the totally absurd (and awesome) crushed ketchup chips, as made famous by our pal Chef Stephen La Salle (see The Diplomat on page 180). In the recipes that follow you'll find different rim spices used on almost every cocktail. If you're looking for inspiration, several rim spice recipes are listed in the Appendix, starting on page 270.

Just as you can reach into your spice drawer to make up your own grilling rub, so can you scour your pantry for the makings of your own signature rim. Be creative. And there's always the Walter Rim Spice, made with a blend of flaked sea salt, paprika, organic cane sugar, and some secret spices. Bonus: it's delicious on buttered popcorn.

5. Garnish

It's easy to get lost when it comes to garnishing a Caesar. There's a temptation to treat the garnish as an excessive final flourish. While we encourage you to think well beyond celery stalks and lime wedges, we want to stress that garnishing should be considered as one of the elemental steps in building a Caesar rather than as ornamentation. With a thoughtfully assembled garnish you can reflect and enhance the ingredients in the glass, or take the drink into a whole new realm through unexpected flavour combinations. Meanwhile, your garnish heightens the Caesar's visual appeal. And also: snacks!

For our own Caesars we generally subscribe to the less-is-more school of garnish thinking. Get wild and fancy, by all means, but try to stick to one or two things that complement what's in the glass, and focus on executing them well. In other words, don't make it all about the garnish. When thinking about garnishes, we organize them into two broad categories, produce and protein, with each of these having its own subcategories.

Produce

We sub-categorize produce according to preparation technique: fresh, pickled and fermented, and cooked. Fresh produce offers brightness (and yes, freshness). From the stalwarts of lime, lemon, and celery to less common choices like tomato, cucumber, radish, and grated horseradish (a personal favourite), fresh items are an easy choice, straightforward and simple. Pickled and fermented garnishes can serve as a kind of foil, cutting through a Caesar's rich and savoury character with a sharp, acidic bite. There are all sorts of ways to cook produce to create dazzling garnishes; some of our favourites are grilling pineapple, dehydrating lemon, roasting carrots, and simmering beets.

Protein

Garnishes made from land proteins can offer your cocktail a fatty, umami component. Options abound, including all kinds of jerky, charcuterie, seared meats, smoked bacon and sausage, pickled eggs, cheese, and tofu. Given that one of the Caesar's defining characteristics is an "element of the sea," sea proteins are Caesar garnishes that are as logical as they are luxurious. An underwater world of options awaits, including poached crab, steamed lobster, grilled shrimp or octopus, smoked, candied, or jerkied fish, and raw shucked oysters or clams.

Skewers

Skewering garnishes allows you to expand your garnish options to include smaller items that wouldn't stand up in, or rest on top of, a glass by themselves. Skewering also lets you collect a variety of garnish elements into one single, tidy presentation. When we're thinking about building skewers, we take a mix-and-match approach, often combining items from both the produce and protein categories. The following pages show some of our favourite produce, protein, and skewer garnishes as a means for general garnish inspiration. You'll find dozens of garnish recipes in the pages of this book, and you can browse more garnish ideas in the Appendix, starting on page 270.

Quick Pickles

When it comes to garnishing a Caesar, pickles are always a good bet. We're big fans of quick pickles (a.k.a. refrigerator pickles), and we usually have a jar or two going at any time. To make quick pickles, we generally use a standard ratio of one part water to one part vinegar, a little sugar, a little salt, and a sprinkling of whatever herbs and spices catch our fancy. (Or you can always use a pre-mixed pickling spice.) See the Appendix (page 270) for our Quick-Pickle Basic Recipe and a few of our favourite variations.

6. Ice

Don't overlook the importance of ice. A few bad cubes are enough to ruin a drink. We think of ice as another vital cocktail ingredient alongside the liquid, rim, and garnish.

As Jeffrey Morgenthaler writes in *The Bar Book* (Chronicle Books, 2014), "In the same way a skilled chef uses heat to prepare food, the professional bartender uses ice to prepare cocktails." Old-Fashioneds, Gin and Tonics, Margaritas: they can all fall flat if the ice isn't right. Same for Caesars. Ice is about more than making things cold. It's there to provide some necessary dilution to your cocktail ingredients, which is why it's fundamental to a good Caesar. The drink tastes better with some dilution to open up the flavours, and the cold helps too. (We'll talk more about dilution later.)

Classic cubes are the default ice choice for Caesars but it's worth exploring your options. Just don't use any of that half-melted stuff at the bottom of the ice bucket. You've come this far in choosing quality ingredients. Don't let bad ice destroy your drink and your mood. You want something solid, dry, and flavourless. We say flavourless because ice absorbs odours if it's left sitting open in the freezer. We suggest refreshing your trays often and storing ice in airtight containers whenever possible. Or do what we do and empty your freezer of everything except ice for Caesars.

Pro Tip: If you make your ice with hot water it will freeze significantly faster (because of the Mpemba effect). And hot water has fewer air bubbles than cold, so you'll get clearer ice.

Cubes

The classic preparation, which should be used for the vast majority of Caesar cocktails. We find that silicone moulds are the best for prepping cubes. Dilution: *medium.* Used: *often.*

Crushed

Oyster-bar style. Crushed ice is the best option when your mix is pre-chilled and you're dealing with lots of strong flavours (hot sauce, Worcestershire, horseradish) that could benefit from serious dilution. Dilution: *high.* Used: *occasionally.*

Sphere & Block

Certain cocktails, such as the Old-Fashioned, tend to be served over one big block of ice, the reasons being a lower and slower dilution (and because it looks cool). The big block of ice is not a typical Caesar preparation but can work well for small-portioned Caesars with subtle flavours where you want to minimize dilution. Dilution: *low.* Used: *moderately.*

No Ice

Otherwise known as being served "up" or "straight up", on rare occasions your Caesar may just be better without the ice, as in the Tomato Water Last Word (page 164) or in Ryan Reynolds' The Crescent Caesar (page 106). In this case, it's critical to mix the cocktail over ice in a separate glass or shaker to chill and dilute it a bit before straining it into your chilled glass. Ice-free is also a good option for people who simply want a thicker, richer cocktail. Dilution: *none.* Used: *rarely.*

Caesar as a Hangover Cure

The Caesar is famously known as a hangover cure, which explains much about its association with brunch. Speaking from our own experiences, we can say that having a Caesar "the morning after the night before" does seem to ease the effects of a hangover. But we never knew why. Until, that is, we read Canadian journalist Shaughnessy Bishop-Stall's informative *Hungover: The Morning After and One Man's Quest for the Cure* (Harper, 2018). Turns out there's scientific research that may support our hunch. Bishop-Stall points to how providing the body with B12 and B6, depleted by alcohol consumption, can effectively thwart the complex chain-reaction that creates a hangover—but only so long as the body also fights against cell inflammation. One way to get a concentrated dose of B12? Clam juice. B6? Tomato juice. And it so happens that garlic and pepper, two of the main ingredients in Worcestershire sauce (and Walter), are also two hard-working anti-inflammatories. Worcestershire also contains piperine, the alkaloid that lends black pepper its kick, and which, in 1979, was the first ever discovered bioavailability enhancer, meaning that it gives the body a better chance of absorbing and making use of all the other helpful hangover-fighters listed above. And it turns out that there is some scientific truth to the old "hair of the dog" cure, which is to say that drinking some more alcohol can actually help to decrease the harshness of a hangover by curbing the brutal downswing of withdrawal. The trick, of course, is finding the balance between a morning-after drink and starting the process of a whole new hangover. So, while we're not suggesting the Caesar as the be-all, end-all of hangover cures, we do think it might hold some promise. Clearly more research is needed.

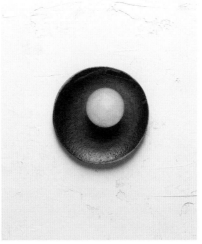

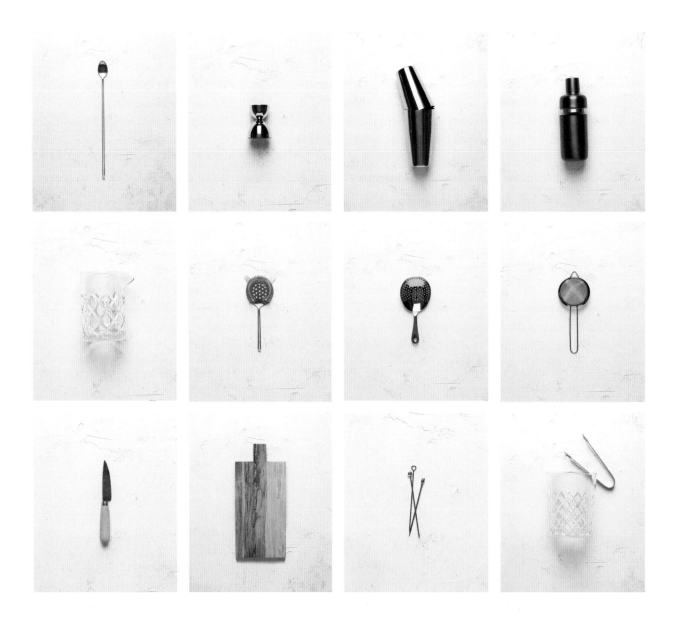

Left to Right

Bar Spoon, Jigger, The Boston Shaker, Cobbler Shaker

Mixing Glass, Hawthorne Strainer, Julep Strainer, Fine-Mesh Sieve

Bar Knife, Cutting Board, Garnish Skewers, Ice Bucket and Tongs

Tools & Equipment

Great chefs all have their go-to tools: the perfectly-seasoned cast iron skillets and hard-to-find Japanese boning knives. Great bartenders approach their own tools with the same level of care and appreciation. With the right tools at your fingertips, not only will you find it easier to craft great cocktails but the process will become more enjoyable as well, especially as you get more comfortable with your arsenal and start to expand and personalize your assortment of gear. We advise you to start with a few high-quality items and then build your barware collection as you go, adding specialty pieces as the mood strikes.

What follows is by no means a definitive guide to kitting out a complete and professional level bar but instead comprises those items we think are especially useful for making Caesars, and which, of course, will serve their purposes on those rare occasions you might crave something else.

The Essentials

Bar Spoon

Pull that random fork (or finger) out of your drink and get yourself a nice bar spoon, essential for all mixing, stirring, and measuring. Any kind will do, but we're partial to the long-handled swizzle-necked variety for usefulness and aesthetics. With a long and lean bar spoon you can quickly stir your drink to spread around the coldness of the ice and dilute the contents evenly.

Note: Bar spoons vary in the relative sizes of their bowls, typically from ½ tsp (2.5 ml) to 2 tsp (10 ml). To keep things simple when following recipes, we favour spoons with bowls equivalent to 1 tsp (5 ml).

Jigger

People sometimes say "jigger" when they mean a shot of liquor. But in bartending parlance, and for the purposes of this book, a jigger refers to the tool designed for measuring spirits. Typically, jiggers look like two concave cups glued end to end, creating an hourglass shape, with each cup offering a different volume of measurement. They come in a variety of size combinations but we suggest starting with a jigger that offers 1 oz (30 ml) on one side and 2 oz (60 ml) on the other. Try to find jiggers that have marks inside the bowls for smaller measurements (e.g., ½ oz/15 ml, ¾ oz/22.5 ml). We prefer the Japanese-style jiggers, because their tall and slender shape makes them more accurate than the typical hourglass jiggers.

Mixing Vessels

If you're going to stir or roll your Caesars (as we recommend and discuss in detail below) you're going to need some kind of mixing vessel. There are a few different choices:

The Boston Shaker: Preferred by most professional bartenders, this combo consists of two parts: a bottom and a top. The bottom is a large metal shaking tin, typically with a capacity of 28 oz (840 ml), or thereabouts. The top is a smaller metal shaking tin, typically around 16 oz (480 ml), which fits snugly upside down within the rim of the bottom tin. Because we recommend stirring or rolling a Caesar, our preferred mixing vessel is the basic metal shaker (a.k.a. tin). For stirring, all you need is the larger tin; for rolling, you use both tins. Metal shaker tins have lots of advantages. They're inexpensive and practically indestructible. And they cool very quickly, so that a higher ratio of the ice's cooling effect goes toward chilling your cocktail than to the vessel it's in.[8] There are also "footed" versions of Boston Shakers, with a wider

---

8. For more technical details on the impact of different materials and mixing vessels on cooling we recommend Dave Arnold's *Liquid Intelligence* (Norton, 2014).

lip around the bottom for added stability, which comes in handy when stirring two drinks at once.

Cobbler Shaker: This is the iconic cocktail shaker with a three-part assembly that does it all. There's a main tin, a cap, and a built-in strainer. All the parts are made of metal and fit together snugly. It's easier for novice mixers to get the hang of the Cobbler than it is to hold two cups together, as with a Boston shaker. But Cobbler shakers are more expensive than Bostons and since we never recommend shaking a Caesar, the cap and strainer aren't needed. Also, the built-in strainer tends to clog if you have lots of solids, as is often the case in a Caesar, which is why we prefer to use a separate strainer.

Mixing Glass: This can be as simple as an empty pint glass. These are inexpensive and very utilitarian but they're also breakable and they have a narrow base, so they sometimes tip. If you want to get a little fancier, you can use a cut-crystal Japanese mixing glass or a large-stemmed mixing glass. Technically, glass mixing cups cool more slowly than thin metal tins, which diverts energy from cooling your drink. So, if you're using a glass mixing cup, be sure to chill it beforehand. We rarely use glass mixing vessels for making Caesars but the fancy ones do look cool.

Strainer

One of the key items for any self-respecting bartender, this keeps out ice, citrus, and other solids while stirred or shaken liquids seep into the glass. A few of the main types:

Hawthorne: The most commonly used cocktail strainer, this workhorse sports a flat, perforated disc of metal lined with a flexible and movable spring coil, often accompanied by a tab that lets you adjust the levels of flow as needed. Simple to use, this fits easily into most shakers or mixing glasses, is relatively inexpensive, and is our preferred strainer for making Caesars.

Julep: Dating back to the early 19th century, the julep strainer gets its name because it was first designed to sit inside a julep cup, staying there to strain with every sip of that sweet mint julep. It's really just a large spoon with a bunch of perforations that fits over a mixing tin or glass. The julep strainer is durable and easy to clean but somewhat trickier to use in certain mixing vessels, as opposed to the versatile Hawthorne.

Fine-Mesh Sieve (a.k.a. Cone Strainer): Used to double-strain cocktails when you want to catch finer particles (e.g., citrus pulp, herbs) that won't get caught by a Hawthorne strainer. To use it, hold your shaker and Hawthorne strainer in one hand and the fine-mesh sieve in the other and pour the liquid from the shaker-with-strainer through the sieve into your vessel. This is a useful option for when you have a lot of ingredients you want in your shaker but not your finished cocktail, and for when you want a super-smooth Caesar.

Bar Knife (Paring Knife)

You can't have a great bar kit without a great knife. How else are you going to cut your fruits and garnishes? While choosing a knife can be a deeply personal experience (hello, fellow knife nerds), we think that basically a bar knife should: 1) measure somewhere between 3½ and 5 inches (8.75 and 12.5 cm); 2) be sharp as hell.

Cutting Board

For cutting citrus and garnishes. We like a heavy wooden board—the bigger the better so it can do double duty as the base of a Caesar bar set-up. It's the perfect platform for setting up your rim tools, prepping your garnishes, and building your cocktails.

Garnish Skewers

For skewering garnishes. There are lots of cool ones out there. Just take your pick. (Pun!) At home we prefer the reusable ones. If we are using disposable (like at an event), we try to use wooden ones.

Ice Bucket & Scoop or Tongs

An insulated ice bucket is handy for keeping ice frozen longer. A perforated scoop (to allow any melted water to drain off) or tongs is better for scooping than a spoon.

Rimming Plate or Tray

You could use any old plate or tray you have on hand, but it's helpful to have something with a decent-size lip to keep mess to a minimum when you're applying a rim. A shallow disk of stainless steel or plastic works just fine.

Muddler

A nice wooden muddler is affordable and durable, and the go-to tool for the recipes in this book that call for muddling, the ideal technique for making certain kinds of herbaceous Caesars. Bonus: Mojitos!

Bar Rag

You'll want some close at hand, especially if you're making Caesars for a crowd. We never said this wouldn't get messy.

The Nice-to-Haves

Citrus Juicer or Reamer

Any juicer will do as long it makes it easy to extract juice from citrus fruit. Aaron's partial to the simple handheld citrus reamer, equally effective whether made from wood, plastic, stainless steel, or porcelain. Zack prefers the double-handle hinged juicer where you stick one citrus half in and squeeze. Also easy and very handy.

Speed Pourer

The speed pourer streamlines the flow of liquid coming out of a bottle, helping to avoid spills and splashes while giving you greater control over the amount of alcohol that gets poured. The funny thing is, it's actually speedier to pour liquid straight from a bottle, so don't be misled by the name.

Wine/Beer Opener

We're assuming you have one. So much better than using your teeth. If you don't have one, send us an email and we'll send you one.

Zester, Grater, or Microplane

For grating almost anything (horseradish, citrus, ginger, garlic), these do the trick. Get something half-decent and it'll last you for years.

Pitcher

Great for pre-batching for parties. No need to overthink this. Ideally, something glass that's easy to pour. About 34 oz (1 L) tends to be a good size.

Sealable Glass Vessels

You'll need these if you want to make any infusions and pickle any kind of garnish. The classic Mason jars work great, or try to find something more interesting. We like to reuse jars and bottles from other products as our sealable vessel option whenever possible.

Funnel

If you're going to be pre-batching cocktails for a party or making infusions in various glass bottles, the funnel is your friend.

Measuring Cup or Glass

These are essential for batching cocktails but we find them useful for making single cocktails too, as we typically use 4 to 6 oz (120 to 180 ml) of mix in a recipe and it's faster to measure something once in a measuring glass than to fill a jigger repeatedly. We prefer the tall thin measuring glasses without handles because they take up less space and look a bit more sophisticated.

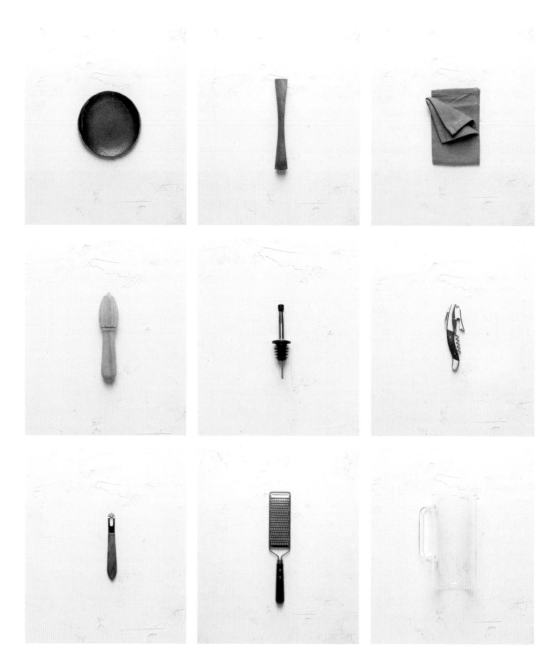

Left to Right

Rimming Plate, Muddler, Bar Rag

Citrus Juicer, Speed Pourer, Wine/Beer Opener

Zester, Grater, Pitcher

Glassware

People can be finicky when it comes to glassware. Walter Chell, ever the perfectionist, said a 15 oz (450 ml) glass is the "only glass to use" for a Caesar but we don't think you should get too hung up about size. Any glass between 8 and 18 oz (240 to 540 ml) will do the trick. For Caesars, it's usually something without a stem. But we'll drink a Caesar out of a coffee mug in a pinch. (Or maybe your mischievous friend—hey, Helena—stole you a kick-ass mug from the famed Chicago tiki house Three Dots and a Dash and that became your favourite drinking vessel.) What we're saying is that if it holds liquid, you're set. So, rather than being an exhaustive list of every kind of glassware available, this list focuses on the glasses we think are most appropriate for serving Caesars.

Rocks (& Double Rocks)
An excellent multipurpose glass, good for everything from spirits served neat to more complicated cocktails, it's best for drinks with smaller volumes and simpler pared-down Caesar concoctions.

Highball or Collins
These are usually our go-tos. Classic looks, not too big, but not too small. (Note: the highball is just a bit shorter than the Collins.)

Sleeve (or Pint Glass)
While not the best-looking glassware, the standard sleeve (typically about 16 oz/480 ml of tempered glass) is a solid option and can also double as a mixing glass.

Mason Jar
We tend to avoid Mason jars because they're awkward to drink from due to the threads on the lip, which also makes applying a rim tricky. But people seem to love 'em, so god bless.

Coupe/Martini Glass
Probably not your everyday Caesar glass but once in a while, for the right cocktail, it's an elegant presentation option.

Technique (Bringing It All Together)

Temperature

It isn't just cooks and bakers who need to pay attention to temperature; cocktail makers also strive to hit their desired target on the thermometer. Flavours at colder temperatures tend to be more muted. They get stronger as the heat increases, which is why a glass of red wine served too cold might be hiding some of its nuance, while a glass of white wine that's too warm might come off as overly sweet or acidic.

With Caesars, however, the issue of temperature is as clear as, well, ice. We want things super cold. With all of the Caesar's richness, spiciness, and bold (and potentially overwhelming) flavours, it drinks best when served chilled, with everything dialled back a notch by the cold temperature. Another benefit of serving a Caesar super cold that shouldn't be overlooked is that the colder the mixed cocktail is when it goes into the glass, the slower the ice in that glass will melt, which means less ongoing dilution, so the cocktail will change less as you drink it.

Dilution

Ice not only chills the room-temperature ingredients that go into your cocktail, it also dilutes those ingredients as it melts, weakening the force of their flavours. You can't have a chilled drink without some dilution, and vice versa.[9] In most cases, some dilution is *desirable* in a cocktail, which could otherwise taste too strong—as in, for instance, the stirring or shaking of a Martini, which tamps down the potentially overpowering gin (or vodka) and vermouth. And this is why we make Walter thicker than the most common mass market Caesar mixes. Walter is designed for dilution.

That way, the final cocktail will hit the ideal consistency once it's been chilled and diluted with ice.

Note: Though it might sound counterintuitive, if you prefer your drinks on the more refreshing, thinner side, you should start with your mix at room temperature rather than chilled. Dilution levels vary based on the starting temperature of a base mix: drinks made with room-temperature mix will be a little bit thinner and smoother since the ice will melt slightly more (meaning more dilution) than it would in drinks made with a refrigerated mix.

Mixing Techniques

If we asked for your typical image of a bartender mixing a cocktail, you might picture someone (who may or may not look like Tom Cruise) shaking their mixing vessel so vigorously you'd think they were angry at the thing. This is not the way of the Caesar maker. We want to mix and chill our ingredients more gently. Which is why our two preferred methods for mixing a Caesar are *stirring* and *rolling,* explained below alongside the other main techniques, *building*, *shaking,* and *throwing.* While we don't recommend shaking and throwing for making Caesars, we thought you might want to read why not in order to better understand the benefits of the techniques we do recommend.

Stirring

Our preferred method for making a Caesar is to stir the drink contents with ice and then strain them over fresh ice. Stirring a cocktail sounds easy but it takes practice. To start, you'll need a bar spoon and a mixing vessel.

First, pour your cocktail ingredients into the empty shaker. Then fill the shaker with ice until the ice sits slightly above

---

9. If you want a really deep dive into the thermodynamics of ice, dilution, and chilling, we again point you to Dave Arnold's *Liquid Intelligence.*

the top of the liquid. Any more ice than that will only make it harder to stir without any added benefit of chilling or dilution; any less and your drink won't get properly chilled. Make sure your ice is "dry" (not dripping with melted water), as "wet" ice only adds water without the benefit of chilling.

With ice in the shaker you're ready to stir. With one hand planted firmly on the base of the mixing vessel, hold the bar spoon near its top between your thumb, forefinger, and middle finger of your other hand. Rotate the spoon around the inside wall of the shaker, keeping the flat side of the spoon against the shaker's wall. If your cocktail has a lot of ingredients that might require some extra mixing force, raise and lower the spoon (going from the bottom to the top of the liquid and back down again) while spinning it around in the glass. To avoid adding unnecessary aeration, always rotate in one direction, not back and forth or side to side. Using a finger or two of the hand holding the base of the mixing vessel, feel the outside of the shaker to test the temperature of the drink as you stir. The shaker should feel very cold to the touch. Stir for longer, or more quickly, for more chilling. Once the drink reaches your desired temperature, strain it over fresh ice.

Rolling

Pour all your ingredients, including the ice, back and forth from one mixing vessel to another until the drink is chilled. Then you strain it over fresh ice. That's it. You've just rolled a drink.

Unlike shaking, rolling lets you mix ingredients together and chill them while adding a little bit of aeration into the drink but without so much that things get overly frothy. And no less an authority than Dale DeGroff, in *The Craft of the Cocktail*, recommends rolling for Bloody Marys. We fully endorse rolling your Caesar. We just like stirring a little more.

Building

Building a cocktail in the glass is just what it sounds like: place all your ingredients into a glass and maybe give it a stir. That's it. Simple and easy, building has been the technique used for the vast majority of Caesars from the beginning. Most highballs do get built in the glass (think Rum and Coke or Gin and Tonic), and that's because most highballs are made with carbonated mixers that lose their carbonation if overly stirred or rolled.

But we think that building isn't the best way to make a culinary highball such as the Caesar. We first want to get our drink super cold (by stirring or rolling) before straining it over fresh ice so that the now-chilled drink melts the ice in the glass slowly, meaning less dilution in the glass and a more consistent drinking experience. Building's fine if you're in a pinch. Just make sure to stir.

Shaking (not recommended)

We don't recommend shaking a Caesar, but we thought it useful to explain why not. Shaking is an efficient method for chilling, but with a Caesar, it aerates the cocktail too much. Bartenders seek out aeration—which adds texture to the drink in the form of tiny air bubbles—in traditionally shaken drinks like Daiquiris and Margaritas. With the Caesar's existing pleasant mouthfeel and viscosity from its tomato base, aeration brings no added benefit. And shaking a Caesar can create an unappetizing foamy or frothy consistency.

Throwing (also not recommended)

Throwing (straining from one vessel to another via a long pour, working back and forth) is undeniably cool to look at if done well, but not ideal for making Caesars. Aeration is the culprit again, though not as much as with shaking.

How to Make a Caesar

Okay, you've made it this far and you're finally ready to make (and drink) a Caesar. Here's how we do it, broken down step by step.

Select Glassware

Can't have a cocktail without a glass. Choose one. Make sure it's a suitable size for the amount of liquid you'll be pouring in while leaving room for the garnish if it will be sitting in the drink.

Prepare Ingredients & Tools

Any good chef or bartender knows it's all about the mise en place. Getting everything ready in advance and within reach is incredibly helpful, especially if you're making a bunch of Caesars. (We'll show you how to set up a Caesar bar for guests so you don't have to make all the drinks yourself on page 56.) Squeeze your juices, mix and pour your rim spice on a plate, make any syrups or sauces, and gather your spirits. Make sure you have your ice and a scoop ready for when you need them.

Prepare the Garnish

Same mise en place logic here. Get your garnish ready before you start making your drink. Even if it's a simple celery stalk and a lime wedge, having it ready to go means one less thing to worry about once you get into the thick of things. You definitely don't want to be making your garnish while your mixed cocktail is sitting in a glass of melting ice.

Rim the Glass

Rim your glass before you start making your drink so you're not doing it while the dilution clock is ticking. If you have time to pre-chill your glass, all the better. It will keep your drink colder for longer and avoid further dilution. But consider that step optional. To be honest, we almost never have the time, refrigerator space, or foresight to chill glasses.

Base Coat

The first thing you have to do is put something on the rim of the glass for the rim spice to stick to. There are a few methods you can use to apply the base coat.

The Base Dip: This method works best for liquids such as citrus juice or syrups. Fill a shallow rimming dish or plate with enough liquid to coat the rim of your glass and dunk the overturned glass into the liquid. Be aware that with a **base dip** or the **wedge squeeze** (see below), your base coat has been applied to both the outside and *inside* of your glass, meaning the rim spice can stick there, too, and as that spice falls into the drink, it will change the flavour. Not a huge issue but worth noting.

The Wedge Squeeze: Cut a citrus wedge and slice it vertically down the middle, stopping at the pith. Place the slice that you've cut into the citrus wedge on the rim of your glass. Run the citrus wedge around the circumference of the rim, squeezing gently with your fingers to make sure the citrus touches the glass all the way around. You don't want any gaps in your rim. This method is fast and easy, but be aware you'll get citrus juice (and potentially rim spice) inside the rim of your glass. If you only squeeze the portion of the wedge that is outside the glass, this is reduced.

The Wheel Roll: Cut a wheel of citrus and lay it on a plate or cutting board. Holding the edge of your glass at a 45-degree angle, roll it along the cut citrus wheel. Now you have a wide section of base coat on the outside of your glass with none on the inside. And it looks pretty once the rim's on. You can adjust the width of your base coast by adjusting the angle of the glass, whereas the **base dip** method typically results in a short rim.

Rim Spice

Now that you've got your base coat, time to apply the rim. Here are a few of our favourite methods.

Left to Right

The Base Dip, The Wedge Squeeze, The Wheel Roll

The Rim Spice Dip, The Rim Spice Roll, The Half-Rim

The Rim Spice Dip: Spread your dry rim spice ingredients on a wide but shallow dish or small plate, then dunk in your base-coated glass.

The Rim Spice Roll: Spread your dry rim spice ingredients on a wide but shallow dish or small plate. Gently roll your glass at a 45-degree angle in the rim spice so that it only sticks to the outside of the vessel.

The Half-Rim: Using the Rim Spice Roll technique, as the name suggests, you rim only half of the glass. We're fans of the half-rim. It's all about giving people options. Drink the Caesar through a rim or don't. Plus, it shows that just a little extra thought and artistry went into your drink.

Assemble the Drink in the Mixing Vessel

Measuring

Now that you have your ingredients and tools gathered, your garnish prepped, and your glass rimmed, you're ready to make a drink. Start with an empty mixing vessel. Since we prefer a simple metal shaker, that's what we'll be describing here. Add your ingredients to the shaker one at a time. Don't add any ice to the shaker or your rimmed glass just yet. When adding your ingredients, make friends with your jiggers and be sure to have some measuring spoons handy (or your bar spoon—just note its volume). A good bartender is like a good baker when it comes to valuing accurate measuring.

If we're making a complicated Caesar recipe, we'll line the ingredients up in the order we plan to add them. If our mind wanders or we get interrupted, it's easier to remember where we left off.

Ice the Mixing Vessel & Stir

Once you have all the ingredients in the mixing vessel, add ice and stir (or roll), applying what you've learned from Mixing Techniques above. Remember, you're looking for a nice cold drink, which you should be able to feel on the outside of the mixing vessel, along with the ideal

dilution—the drink shouldn't knock you over with its spirits but neither should it taste limpid and watery.

Taste as You Go

When you think the drink's ready, taste some from the mixing vessel before serving. We do this after stirring with ice in the mixing vessel but before straining so we can get a sense of what the diluted drink will taste like, and its temperature, before we pour it. Are all the ingredients nicely integrated? Do we have the smooth texture we want? Is the temperature as cold as it should be? The official bartender method for tasting is to dip a clean metal straw into the mixing vessel and then create a vacuum by placing a finger over the top of the straw and lifting it out to taste, like a lab technician with a pipette, except way more fun.

Strain Over Fresh Ice

Now that your cocktail is perfectly chilled and diluted, quickly fill your rimmed glass with fresh ice. Fill the glass only about three-quarters of the way up with ice to leave room for the liquid and potentially a garnish. Now strain your cocktail into the glass. Unless you've taken your Caesar into space, straining is the simplest part of the operation. Just secure your (Hawthorne) strainer against the mixing vessel, tilt the vessel, and pour gently, giving the vessel a little bump and shake at the end to make sure you've released any liquid that might still be sticking to the ice inside. Avoid the theatrics of pouring from great heights because this will add unwanted aeration to your drink. And you might spill some, too. If the glass looks a little underfilled after you've poured your drink, you can always add some more ice to top it up.

Garnish

Last but not least, finish the cocktail with your prepared garnish. And serve.

Recipe Creation

Okay. You've read this whole section, you've made some of the recipes in this book, and now you want to start creating your own custom Caesar recipes. Where do you start? Here are some tips that we use when creating our own Caesar recipes.

Find Inspiration

When we're coming up with a new Caesar recipe, whether for an account, an event, or this book, we'll often start by searching for some kernel of an idea around which to build the drink. Maybe it's a place whose essence you somehow want to evoke in liquid form. Sometimes it's as simple as wanting to feature a specific spirit or non-alcoholic ingredient. You got a new bottle of something cool. Great. Build around that. You wonder if a particular fruit juice or sauce could bring something new to Caesar country. Go for it. In this book you'll find examples of drinks that were inspired by dishes (Hot & Sour, page 84), ingredients (Waltermelon, page 226), places (Cabane à Sucre, page 160), and a song (Friend of the Devil, page 234). Whatever the inspiration—and it can come from anywhere—we've found that having even the faintest glimmer of a concept anchoring our imagined drink is exceptionally useful, guiding our thinking as we start developing the recipe. Plus, it gives you a story to tell.

Choose Your Base Mix

Once you've got your idea, start thinking about a base mix. You can use any Walter mix (or another brand) or homemade mix that you want, depending on the flavour profile you're seeking. When we're creating recipes that will have a lot of flavour additions we'll usually start with the Mild version of Walter.

Choose Your Spirit(s) & Modifiers

The Caesar's spirit or spirits will, in many ways, have the biggest impact on the flavour of your cocktail. A unique spirit choice is the simplest way to detour off the road toward making yet another classically flavoured vodka-based Caesar. We have more fun playing around with different spirits, split bases, and modifiers than almost anything else.

Decide on Ratios

We generally keep it simple. We use three standard ratios when making pretty much all of our Caesars. From strongest to weakest, they are:

- 1 part spirit to 4 parts mix
- 1 part spirit to 5 parts mix
- 1 part spirit to 6 parts mix

Play around with these ratios and see which one you prefer—keeping in mind that the drink will taste different after you've stirred in ice and strained it over fresh ice. Different spirits will also likely lead you to different ratio choices. It all depends on the drink. When we're testing a new cocktail, we usually try it with all three ratios to see which works best.

Choose Your Flavour Additions

This is the stage where you can really start personalizing the drink. Pick your hot sauce and other sauces. Decide what citrus (or other) juice(s) you want to add. Muddle some herbs. Maybe smoke or char something. Add some spices. Skim through this book for ideas. Open your cupboard and look for inspiration. Go to your local Asian or European grocery store and walk the aisles. Make some pickles. Do whatever you want. It's your drink. As Doc Brown says, "Roads? Where we're going, we don't need roads."

Think about Balance & Tension

The first time you taste your new creation, it won't be perfect. That means you're doing it right. This is where the work and also the fun begin. Now you have to start adjusting it to try to find the ideal balance and tension. Remember, you're looking to combine your ingredients in proportions where everything balances "just right" but there's still that hanging note of tension that brings an element of excitement.

Drink!

Once you think you have your recipe dialled-in and the flavours just perfect, there's one last critical test. You have to sit down and drink a whole one. Beginning to end. You can't judge a cocktail based on one taste. The drink that tastes amazing on sip one may be completely overpowering once you're halfway through a glass.
So, seriously, before you add this new creation to your repertoire or menu—drink one, top to bottom. It's hard work, but somebody has to do it.

Some Final Tips

- Don't pick some wild ingredient and add 3 oz (90 ml) of it to start. Tread lightly.

- Taste each potential ingredient on its own, particularly spirits or modifiers with which you might be unfamiliar. Try to picture how this particular player will fit in with the rest of the team.

- To start, add ingredients in small quantities—¼ oz/7.5 ml— is usually a good starting point while you try to figure out your best ratios. You can always add more as you go. Taking away is another story.

- If your recipe has 20 ingredients, you should probably ask yourself why and start cutting. There's a reason so many classic cocktails have only three ingredients. Less is usually more.

Measurements & Ingredients

For the purposes of this book:

1 oz = 30 ml (as opposed to the imperial ounce, which is 28 ml)

1 cup = 8 oz = 240 ml

Juice: is freshly squeezed, unless otherwise noted

Hot sauces: in some cases, we've provided a recommendation; if you don't have it, use what you have

Butter: is unsalted

Olive oil: is extra virgin

Caesar mix: refers to various flavours of Walter, but of course you can use any other pre-made Caesar mix or make your own (pages 68 to 71). At Walter we currently make the following flavours:

- **Classic:** crafted with hot sauce, select spices, horseradish, and Worcestershire sauce, it's our take on a "classic" Caesar, pre-seasoned and ready to go.

- **Mild:** more gently seasoned than Classic, it's our most "neutral" mix and is often a good starting point for customizing a Caesar.

- **Extra Spicy:** made with a blend of ancho, habanero, cayenne, Tabasco, and fire-roasted jalapeño chili peppers, it's meaningfully spicy with a touch of extra sweetness.

- **Smoky Maple:** crafted with hickory wood smoke and maple syrup.

- **Holiday:** a seasonal product, this mix is made with sage, tarragon, and lobster stock.

- **Vegan:** a plant-based version of our Classic mix made with dulse (edible seaweed) in place of clam juice.

Rim Spice: every recipe in this book calls for a different rim spice, but if you don't have the ingredients, you can always substitute an alternative rim spice.

A Note on Spirit Brands

Some of the recipes in this book recommend specific brands of spirits, particularly where one of our contributors has specified a preference. You should, of course, feel free to use whatever you have on hand and in no way feel pressured to run out and buy that specific bottle. Just be aware that with a substitute, your drink could taste somewhat different than the recipe intends.

A Note on Spice Levels

The recipes in this book are generally intended to give you a medium spice level: a good amount of heat but not too spicy for the average drinker. (Don't worry, spice seekers, there are a few recipes here that pack some substantial punch.) Whether you love spice or avoid it, feel free to add or subtract hot sauces and other spicy elements as you see fit.

Safety Note

Certain recipes in this book call for raw or very lightly cooked eggs, meat, fish, and fermented products. These foods should be avoided by pregnant women, infants, the elderly, and anyone who is immunocompromised.

Caesar Bar at Home

We once threw a tiki-themed party. Our guests were outraged that we didn't have a tiki-Caesar option. Call it an occupational hazard: whenever we play host, from the smallest get-together to the biggest party, we're *always* expected to have Caesars on offer. We are, of course, happy to do so, but we don't want to miss the party by playing bartender all event long.

The solution, as we've learned, is to set up a Caesar bar in advance. Doing so not only allows us to enjoy spending time with our friends but also lets them have some fun customizing their own drinks. We've tried organizing our Caesar bars a few different ways over the years, and we've found that the following two bar set-up methods work best. Each one is relatively simple and efficient while offering a range of options for drink customization. Regardless of which option you choose, you'll want to include a garnish station—because everyone loves the garnish station—and we'll give you some tips on how to put that together (page 64).

Option 1: The True DIY Caesar Bar

This DIY option is about providing your guests with all the tools and ingredients they'll need to make their own Caesar cocktail from start to finish. This option is fairly easy to execute from a set-up standpoint and lets your guests really get creative and have some fun customizing their drinks to their hearts' content. We tend to find this fully DIY option is best done for a crowd that (a) actually knows how to make a proper Caesar, and (b) is happy to spend time doing so. Otherwise, you'll end up manning the DIY Caesar bar as a sort of Caesar-spirit-guide, shepherding your guests through the "experience."

Here is what we recommend:

Glassware: 2 glasses per guest works well.

Tools: Mixing spoons, garnish skewers, jiggers, cutting board, bar knife.

Ice Station: Make sure ice is plentiful and in a properly insulated ice bucket to avoid mid-party melt. Don't forget the ice tongs or an ice scoop.

Rim Station: A bowl of citrus wedges, Walter Rim Spice or your own custom rim, and a small plate to hold the rim spice for dipping.

Caesar Mix: We tend to put out a few options. We find that a combo of Walter Classic, Walter Mild, and Walter Vegan will accommodate a range of Caesar tastes.

Spirits: Typically, we put out a few options for these as well: usually vodka, gin, and tequila. For extra style points, make some spirit infusions ahead of time (page 300) and have these out as well.

Sauces & Flavour Additions: We like to include a selection of various hot sauces, Worcestershire sauce, cocktail bitters, horseradish (freshly grated or prepared), salt, and pepper.

Beer (optional): A bucket of ice-cold beer to make Beer Caesars (or simply to drink) is a nice addition.

Mimosa Station (optional, but awesome): Depending on the crowd, we sometimes also add a Mimosa station to the bar, putting out a couple bottles of sparkling wine on ice and a pitcher of OJ.

Option 2: The Pre-Batched Caesar Bar

Truth be told, this is the style of Caesar bar that we generally set up. While it does take a bit more work to set up pre-batched pitchers of various Caesars in advance of the party, in the long run it always proves successful and well worth the effort. This style of Caesar bar removes the guesswork and labour in Caesar making for your guests, ensures the Caesars served are actually good, and frees you up as host from tending bar.

Here you'll find our standard base batch recipe that you can serve as is or use as a guide to customize your own. We've also included a few of our favourite batched-up recipes for you to try. It's always a good idea to have a non-alcoholic option available for your guests, so we've also included a handy non-alcoholic batch recipe. (Note: all batch recipes are designed to fit comfortably in a 34 oz/1 L pitcher.)

How Much to Batch: We tend to plan for 1 to 2 drinks per guest, with each batch recipe yielding 4 to 6 drinks. Ask yourself, are my guests the tame type, or do they *party* party? It's just math from then on out. Also, it's kinda like pizza—better to have too much than too little. Order the extra one, just to be sure. It'll keep and so will your batched Caesars—for a few days at the very least.

Rounding: When we're making batch cocktails, we find rounding to the nearest whole or logical number in terms of measurements makes your life easy. You could simply multiply a single cocktail recipe by the number of drinks you want but that will often yield odd measurements, which is just annoying.

Do It in Advance of the Party & Serve Cold: These recipes can be made as much as a full day in advance of the party (you don't want to be batching right before your guests arrive). Store in the refrigerator and serve cold. This will help reduce the amount of ice dilution in the cocktails your guests serve themselves.

Pre-Rim the Glasses: We think putting out a bunch of pre-rimmed glasses is a great way to help your guests quickly and easily get going with their cocktail.

Basic Batch Recipe

Makes 4 to 6 drinks

3 cups (720 ml) Caesar mix, any flavour
¾ cup (180 ml) spirit of choice
2 Tbsp (30 ml) citrus juice (ideally lemon or lime)

Combine all the ingredients in a pitcher and stir to combine. Store in the refrigerator until ready to serve. Do not add ice to the pitcher, as this will cause unwelcome dilution. The better method is to have an ice station where your guests can add fresh ice to their glass immediately prior to serving.

Note: This is the basic recipe we use to start all our batch recipes. If you want to create your own batch cocktails, start with these basic ratios and adjust as needed. But to make things easy, following are a few of our favourite tried-and-true batch recipes.

Batch Recipe: The Vodka One

Makes 4 to 6 drinks

¾ cup (180 ml) vodka
3 cups (720 ml) Caesar mix, Mild
1½ Tbsp (22.5 ml) Worcestershire sauce
1 Tbsp (15 ml) hot sauce
3 Tbsp (45 ml) pickle brine
2 Tbsp (30 ml) freshly grated horseradish
2 Tbsp (30 ml) lime juice

Batch Recipe: The Gin One

Makes 4 to 6 drinks

¾ cup (180 ml) gin
3 cups (720 ml) Caesar mix, Classic
2 Tbsp (30 ml) cucumber purée (see note)
2 Tbsp (30 ml) lemon juice
½ tsp black pepper, freshly cracked

Note: Just blend (or smash up) some peeled and seeded cucumber into a smooth paste, then push it through a fine-mesh sieve.

Batch Recipe: The Tequila (& Mezcal) One

Makes 4 to 6 drinks

½ cup (120 ml) tequila blanco
¼ cup (60 ml) mezcal (optional) (see note)
3 cups (720 ml) Caesar mix, Extra Spicy
⅓ cup (80 ml) pineapple juice (store-bought is fine)
2 Tbsp (30 ml) lime juice

Note: Mezcal in this drink is optional. If you don't want to use it, just increase the tequila to ¾ cup (180 ml).

Batch Recipe: The Non-Alcoholic One

Adapted from Garden (page 176)
Makes 4 to 6 drinks

¾ cup (180 ml) Seedlip Garden 108
3 cups (720 ml) Caesar mix, Vegan
2 Tbsp (30 ml) Herb-Infused White Wine Vinegar (page 295)
6 dashes Cholula green pepper sauce
½ tsp Lemon Pepper Sea Salt (page 290)

Garnish Station

Undoubtedly, part of the appeal of the Caesar is the garnish, so this is an important aspect of setting up a Caesar bar for your guests. Keeping it simple and elegant is great, but depending on how elaborate you go, a garnish station effectively does double duty as an appetizer station. When we set up a Caesar bar we look to have a selection of easy-to-use, delicious, and thoughtful options, including fresh veg cut into bite-size pieces, house-made pickles, seafood (crab legs, shrimp), jerky or cured meats, cubed cheese, citrus wedges. You'll find lots of inspiration for garnish ideas in the recipes that follow and in the Garnish section of the Appendix starting on page 272.

We've also had great success using pre-made skewers. Having skewers ready to go makes it easy for guests to just grab one and be done. Get creative with your skewers. Here are a few of our favourites:

- Cherry tomato, bocconcini, fresh basil, balsamic reduction drizzle
- Grilled shrimp, pickled onion, pepperoncini
- Prosciutto, green olive, marinated artichoke
- Pickled cucumber, cheddar, jerky
- Salmon (candied or smoked), pickled beet, lemon wheel

Remember, whether you're putting out individual garnish items or pre-made skewers, presentation matters—so set out your garnish station with some thought and attention. And while a wide selection is great, aim for quality over quantity on this front.

Base Mix Recipes

Given that we define a Caesar as a cocktail made with a base of vegetable juice and an element of the sea, there are lots of different base mixes you can use—from a pre-made Caesar mix, such as Walter, to almost any other kind of vegetable juice. To add an element of the sea, you could also use store-bought clam juice, seaweed, lobster stock, or squid ink, for example. And of course, you can also make your own Caesar mix or clam juice from scratch. In this section, we'll teach you how to make three different base Caesar mixes, as well as homemade clam juice.

Red Caesar Mix

This is your starting point for a classic homemade Caesar mix. The key is roasting the tomatoes to caramelize them for a sweeter, richer flavour profile. Roasting also helps break down the cell walls for smoothness while intensifying the flavours by cooking down the tomatoes' juices. To this deeply roasted tomato base, we add some acid (lemon juice), some sweetness (simple syrup), and a taste of the sea from the clam juice. Note that the recipe adds back a touch of water to get it to a perfect drinkable consistency, which is key. (You can adjust the amount of water as needed but remember to plan for additional dilution from ice and spirits.) This recipe offers a suggested blend of spices and seasoning that works well for a traditional Caesar. But the spice blend is completely customizable. We encourage you to play around with the spices based on the flavour you're looking for, or—more pragmatically—what you have in your pantry.

Green Caesar Mix

This viridescent mix uses the tomato's tangier cousin, the tomatillo, as its base. Here, we broil the tomatillos—rather than roast—to add some additional smoky charred flavour and then combine it with fresh cucumber and lime juice to balance out those charred acidic flavours inherent in the tomatillos. This recipe includes very little seasoning beyond sea salt and a touch of simple syrup to let the fresh flavours of the vegetables shine through.

Yellow Caesar Mix

Chances are you've never been served a yellow Caesar. This enticing recipe produces a striking, colourful mix and shows how dramatically you can transform a Caesar simply by changing the base vegetable(s). The use of yellow tomatoes, yellow bell peppers, habanero, and turmeric combine to create a vibrant base that tastes as good as it looks. As with the other mixes, you can adjust the seasoning to taste (but try not to add anything that will muddy the bright yellow colour).

Note: There is no hot sauce or Worcestershire sauce in these recipes, as we consider those to be flavour additions and not part of the base mix.

Red Caesar Mix

Used in Original (page 120)

Makes about 42 oz (1.25 L),
enough for 6 to 8 drinks

4½ lb (2 kg) tomatoes, halved
    lengthwise (ideally Roma,
    about 24)
1 to 2 jalapeños, stemmed,
    halved, and seeded
2 to 4 whole cloves garlic,
    skin on (optional)
1 cup (240 ml) water + more as
    needed
½ cup (120 ml) clam juice
    (page 71 or store-bought)
¼ cup (60 ml) lemon juice
¼ cup (60 ml) Simple Syrup
    (page 297)
2 tsp sea salt
¼ tsp cayenne powder
¼ tsp celery seed
¼ tsp cracked black pepper
¼ tsp onion powder
¼ tsp Spanish paprika

1. Preheat your oven to 500°F (260°C) and line a baking sheet with parchment paper.
2. Place the tomatoes cut-side down on the prepared baking sheet. Place the jalapeños skin-side up on the baking sheet along with the garlic cloves.
3. Roast the vegetables until nicely browned, about 30 minutes, then let cool completely.
4. Once completely cooled, remove the skins from the garlic and place the tomatoes, ½ jalapeño (skin on), and garlic in a blender. Blend until very smooth. You can adjust the heat level by adding more jalapeño to taste. We recommend starting with half a jalapeño and tasting the mixture before adding more. (You can always add heat but you can't take it away!) Similarly, you can add more or less garlic to your taste. (We like to use 2 garlic cloves but roasted garlic is delicious, so feel free to add more.)
5. Add the water, clam juice, lemon juice, simple syrup, and salt. Give it a quick blend to homogenize. The water will help you get the right, very drinkable consistency for making a cocktail. If your tomatoes are very thick, or they reduced down significantly during the cooking process, you can add more water to get your desired consistency.
6. Add the cayenne powder, celery seed, pepper, onion powder, and paprika and quickly blend one more time. (If you don't have exactly these spices or want to try something different, you do you. Feel free to mix it up and add whatever spices you have on hand and think would work.)
7. Strain the mixture through a fine-mesh strainer set over a large bowl to remove the larger chunks and seeds. It helps to push everything through with a spatula. Now strain the mixture again through a large piece of cheesecloth and squeeze it hard over a large bowl to get as much liquid as possible out. Discard the seeds and remaining solids. The finished mix should be very smooth with no seeds or large chunks. If the mixture is a little too thick, add a touch more water. Season to taste with additional salt if desired.
8. Store in a glass bottle or jar in the refrigerator for up to 4 days.

Green Caesar Mix

Used in Green (page 88)

Makes about 20 oz (600 ml),
enough for 3 to 4 drinks

2.2 lb (1 kg) tomatillos, husks
    removed and sliced in half
1 to 2 jalapeños, stemmed,
    halved, and seeded
2 to 4 whole cloves garlic, skin on
    (optional)
1 lb (450 g) mini cucumbers,
    roughly chopped (about 6)
¼ cup (60 ml) lime juice
¼ cup (60 ml) clam juice
    (page 71 or store-bought)
1 tsp sea salt
2 Tbsp Simple Syrup (page 297)
Water, as needed

1. Turn your oven broiler to high and line a baking sheet with parchment paper.
2. Place the tomatillos and jalapeños, cut-side down, on the prepared baking sheet, along with the garlic.
3. Roast the vegetables until nicely charred and blistered, about 8 to 12 minutes. Depending on how roasted or smoky you like the flavour, you can leave them in longer or take them out earlier, but watch them carefully to avoid burning.
4. While the roasted vegetables are cooling, place the cucumbers, lime juice, clam juice, and salt in a blender and blend until well combined.
5. Once completely cooled, remove the skins from the garlic and place the tomatillos, ½ jalapeño (skin on), and garlic in a blender. Blend until very smooth. You can adjust the heat level by adding more jalapeño to taste. We recommend starting with half a jalapeño and tasting the mixture before adding more. We like to use 2 garlic cloves but feel free to add more.
6. Add the simple syrup to the mix 1 tsp at a time, tasting as you go. Depending on the sweetness of your tomatillos you might want to add a little more or less simple syrup.
7. Strain the mixture through a fine-mesh strainer set over a large bowl to remove the larger chunks and seeds. It helps to push everything through with a spatula. Now strain the mixture again through a large piece of cheesecloth and squeeze it hard over a large bowl to get as much liquid as possible out. Discard the seeds and remaining solids. The finished mix should be very smooth with no seeds or large chunks. If the mixture is a little too thick, you can add a touch of water. Season to taste with additional salt if desired.
8. Store in a glass bottle or jar in the refrigerator for up to 4 days.

Yellow Caesar Mix

Used in Yellow (page 222)

Makes about 42 oz (1.25 L),
enough for 6 to 8 drinks

4½ lb (2 kg) yellow heirloom
    tomatoes (about 12), halved
1 yellow bell pepper, stemmed,
    halved, and seeded
1 habanero pepper, stemmed,
    halved, and seeded (see note)
2 to 4 whole cloves garlic, skin on
    (optional)
1 cup (240 ml) water + more as
    needed
½ cup (120 ml) clam juice
    (page 71 or store-bought)
¼ cup (60 ml) lemon juice
1 Tbsp honey
2 tsp sea salt
¼ tsp white pepper
¼ tsp ground turmeric

1. Preheat your oven to 500°F (260°C) and line a baking sheet with parchment paper.
2. Place the tomatoes, yellow pepper, and habanero pepper cut-side down on the prepared baking sheet, along with the garlic cloves.
3. Roast the vegetables until nicely browned, about 30 minutes, then let cool completely. Once completely cooled, remove the charred skins from the tomatoes, yellow pepper, and habanero (they should slide off very easily). You want to remove as much char as possible so you don't get black flakes in the final drink. Remove the skins from the roasted garlic cloves.
4. Place the tomatoes, yellow pepper, ½ habanero, and garlic in a blender and blend until very smooth. You can adjust the level of heat by adding more or less habanero. We recommend starting with half a habanero and tasting the mixture before adding more. You can also add more or less garlic to taste.
5. Add the water, clam juice, lemon juice, and honey, and blend again. The water will help you get the right, very drinkable consistency for making a cocktail. If your tomatoes are very thick, or they reduced down significantly during the cooking process, you can add more water to get your desired consistency.
6. Add the salt, pepper, and turmeric, and quickly blend to incorporate.
7. Strain the mixture through a fine-mesh strainer set over a large bowl to remove the larger chunks and seeds. It helps to push everything through with a spatula. Now strain the mixture again through a large piece of cheesecloth and squeeze it hard over a large bowl to get as much liquid as possible out. Discard the seeds and remaining solids. The finished mix should be very smooth with no seeds or large chunks. If the mixture is a little too thick, add a touch more water. Season to taste with additional salt if desired.
8. Store in a glass bottle or jar in the refrigerator for up to 4 days.

Note: Consider wearing gloves when cutting chili peppers. Be careful not to touch your eyes after cutting. Wash your hands well.

Clam Juice

Makes 5 cups (1.2 L) clam juice
and 1 lb (450 g) clam meat

Making your own clam juice is a relatively simple exercise and a rewarding one, too, resulting in a rich, briny, slightly sweet, umami-packed broth. Just a splash of this juice will do wonders for your next Caesar. We also like to set some aside as a substitute for fish stock. It's a quick way to transform risottos, chowders, bouillabaisses, and all sorts of other fish stock–dependent dishes.

In the Appendix (page 270), we've included two ways to make bar clams so you can put the leftover meat to good use. The first method uses chili garlic (bold, savoury, and assertive), and the second, orange fennel (sweeter and more delicate). For those who want to keep things traditional, skip the flavoured options altogether and simply pack the clams back in some of the juice they were cooked in. Regardless of how we prepare them, our favourite way to eat these bar clams is chilled, with a squeeze of fresh lemon and some toasted crusty bread.

5 lb (2.25 kg) fresh BC clams
(ideally Manila or Savoury, as
they have high meat yields)
5 cups (1.2 L) cold water
Sea salt

1. Soak the clams in fresh cold water for 20 minutes. Scrub off any residual dirt or sand. Discard any clams with broken shells or that don't open when tapped.
2. Bring the water to a boil in a large pot over high heat, then drop in them clams. Cover and bring back to a boil, shaking occasionally to evenly cook the clams. After 3 to 4 minutes, all the clams should be opened. Discard any that are still closed. Take the pot off the heat to prevent overcooking.
3. Leave the clams in the pot to cool enough to handle. Without draining the flavourful cooking liquid (the coveted clam juice!), lift out the clams and carefully begin to remove the meat from each shell, ensuring you pour any residual nectar in the shells back into the pot.
4. Reserve the clam meat in an airtight container in the refrigerator for Bar Clams (either Chili Garlic or Orange Fennel, page 272), making sure to keep the individual plump pieces of meat as intact as possible.
5. Double-strain the remaining clam juice through cheesecloth or a very fine-mesh strainer set over a large bowl. Before straining each time, allow the juice to sit for a couple minutes so any residual grit falls to the bottom of the bowl. Carefully pour the juice through the cheesecloth, discarding the last little bit of liquid where all the grit has gathered.
6. Taste, and add salt if desired (you may not need to add any).
7. Store the fresh clam juice in a glass jar in the refrigerator and consume within 2 to 3 days. Excess fresh clam juice (and clam meat) can be frozen for up to 3 months in individual portions and thawed in the refrigerator as needed.

West Coast

We grew up a few minutes from each other in the 1980s in a suburb of Vancouver called Richmond. It was a small town then, built across a few muddy islands at the mouth of the Fraser River. Along with the usual suburban sprawl, Richmond was rich with farmland and had a bustling fishing trade in Steveston Village, where the Fraser River feeds into the Strait of Georgia on its way to the Pacific. Steveston boasted British Columbia's largest cannery (salmon mostly) and served as a major hub for the whole fishing industry along the Pacific coast. Back then, depending on the wind conditions, you knew the cannery was hard at work by the smell that carried several kilometres—right into Aaron's childhood bedroom.

The Steveston Village of our youth was a pretty exciting place, a multi-ethnic and multi-class mix of working fishing village and bedroom community. The Steveston Barbershop never took appointments and educated young minds in curse words and nudie magazines; the smoky pool hall a few doors down was where the tough guys hung out. There were rusty chain-link fences where fishing boats sat in dry dock, and countless net lofts—some boasted shiny new iron, while others were weather-stripped woodsheds that looked like they'd come straight from the set of *The Beachcombers*.

On weekends, we would wander down to the floating docks and watch as our parents paid cash for fresh fish and seafood. Salmon was king, but depending on the season, mussels, clams, crab, and the occasional bag of spot prawns also featured.

As you'd expect, fish and chips was the thing here, freshly fried and served in a rolled-up newspaper cone (with malt vinegar and a lemon wedge, never ketchup). Locals learned the art of shielding their meals from the hordes of battle-hardened seagulls ready to strike at any time. Many a Steveston visitor learned their lesson the hard way, as their lunches were liberated with a quick snatch and sacrificed to the maritime gods.

Perhaps it was Steveston Village that got us wondering about the natural world beyond our sleepy suburb. Watching the hard-working fishers and the trawlers with their nets helped to give us a sense of how many people, faraway places, and collective effort went into getting food on our plates. And like so many locals, as a teenager, Aaron would play his own small part in that effort, getting his first job at a bustling restaurant on the pier serving fish and chips and ice-cold beer.

The Steveston of our youth is not the Steveston of today—its fishing and canning heyday passed years ago. The Gulf of Georgia Cannery is a museum now, and the old smoky pool hall and marine outfitters are now fancy coffee shops and housewares stores. But there's still some fishing. Still lots of fish and chips. Still those battled-hardened seagulls.

You can find versions of Steveston all along Canada's West Coast. Places that have shaped so much of how people eat, drink, and approach life across the region, carrying not just the natural bounty but also the stories of the Pacific Ocean hundreds of miles inland. Which is why, as much as West Coasters feel connected to their fellow Canadians to the east, many also feel a special kinship with seafaring people far beyond our borders.

While Richmond served as our home base when we were growing up, we also thought of much of the rest of BC as our backyard. And while you can get around by car, train, seaplane, and all sorts of things that float, even the most well-travelled local will likely have only seen a tiny fraction of it—BC's coastline alone is over 25,000 kilometres long—and its almost otherworldly palette of cold blues, misty greys, and deep greens. There are fruit-bearing desert regions, countless pristine lakes, mysterious uninhabited islands, deep and dense old-growth rain forests, saltwater waves, and world-renowned mountains all close at hand. And the same variety of environments that makes the West Coast a favourite for film location scouts means that the chefs and bartenders around here suffer from an embarrassment of riches when it comes to locally sourced ingredients.

Living on the edge of a continent breeds a healthy independent streak but also an openness to ideas from far away. Chefs, sommeliers, and bartenders are known to hop down to the Santa Monica farmers' market just to see what's new—not to mention making the occasional pilgrimage south to iconic bars and restaurants in Seattle, Portland (arguably the birthplace of the craft beer movement), and San Francisco, as well as to Mexico's capital and coastal towns and along the Pacific Rim. And through this global inspiration comes all sorts of local innovation. With their use of spirits as varied as sake, sour beer, and mezcal, and ingredients ranging from seaweed to shiitake mushrooms to spruce tips—and of course, all sorts of market-fresh seafood—we hope the recipes that follow capture some sense of the wildness, diversity, and inventiveness of the West Coast.

West Coaster

Cocktail by Kaitlyn Stewart
Capo & The Spritz
Vancouver, British Columbia

Serves 1

Glassware
1 rocks glass

Garnish
1 oyster
1 Celery Ribbon (page 275)
1 lemon wedge

Rim
2 Tbsp lemon pepper
1 lemon wedge

Cocktail
1½ oz (45 ml) gin (ideally
    Sheringham Distillery Seaside
    Gin)
4 oz (120 ml) Caesar mix, Classic
1 piece nori (4 × 4 inches/10 ×
    10 cm), torn into postage
    stamp–size pieces
¼ oz (7.5 ml) lemon juice
1 tsp fish sauce
2 dashes Vancouver Island Hot
    Sauce Company's Breath of
    Humbaba (see note)
2 dashes Worcestershire sauce
1 turn cracked black pepper

Kaitlyn Stewart knows what she's doing behind the bar. She's earned the title of Diageo World Class Bartender of the Year (a big deal in the bartending world)—the first Canadian and second woman ever to do so. Kaitlyn is also a true ambassador for the beverage scene in Vancouver. This cocktail is a great example of her work, featuring some of her favourite flavours from her home on the West Coast: gin distilled with seaweed, fresh oysters, fish sauce, and nori.

1. Shuck the oyster, keeping it on the half shell and reserving as much of the oyster liquor as possible (see page 238).
2. Pour the lemon pepper onto a small plate. Rub the lemon wedge around half of the rim of your glass and then roll that half of the rim in the lemon pepper.
3. Add the gin, Caesar mix, nori, lemon juice, fish sauce, hot sauce, Worcestershire sauce, and pepper to a cocktail shaker. Fill the shaker with ice to just above the top of the liquid and gently roll all the liquid and ice from this shaker to a second mixing vessel, working back and forth, until the outside of the vessels are very cold to the touch.
4. Fill the rimmed glass three-quarters full with fresh cubed ice. Strain the contents of the shaker into the glass and top with additional ice if desired. Garnish with the shucked oyster, celery ribbon, and lemon wedge.

Note: The Breath of Humbaba hot sauce used in this recipe can be found online and at specialty grocers. It is similar in style to green Tabasco.

Windowsill

Serves 1

Glassware

1 Collins glass

Rim

2 Tbsp Celery Salt (page 288 or
    store-bought)

1 lemon wedge

Cocktail

6 to 8 turns cracked black
    pepper

Small handful celery leaves (see
    note)

Small handful fresh dill (see note)

2 to 3 slices cucumber (each
    ¼ inch/6 mm thick)

3 to 4 slices fresh jalapeño,
    sliced into ⅛-inch (3 mm)
    rounds (seeds removed for
    less heat)

2 lemon wedges

1½ oz (45 ml) vodka

5 oz (150 ml) Caesar mix, Mild

Garnish

1 slice mini cucumber, sliced
    lengthwise (¼ inch/6 mm
    thick), on a skewer

1 or 2 sprigs fresh herbs, such
    as parsley or dill

Muddling, a technique many associate with making a Mojito, also happens to be a simple and effective way to build extra flavour and fragrance into a Caesar. Work slowly and gently to release every last drop of the rich natural oils from the herbs. Basil, rosemary, thyme, cilantro, parsley, dill—whatever you've got growing on the windowsill—will work great in combination with a bit of pepper and citrus in this drink.

1. Pour the celery salt onto a small plate. Circle the rim of your glass with the lemon wedge, then roll the rim in the celery salt.
2. Place the pepper in a cocktail shaker (or other mixing vessel). (We're putting the black pepper on the bottom to act as an abrasive that we're going to muddle our herbs and veggies against to help tear them apart.) Next, layer in the celery leaves, dill, cucumber, and jalapeño (or whatever herbs and veggies you have on your windowsill). Finally, put the lemon wedges on top. (Putting the lemon wedges on top will help protect the herbs and veggies and prevent you from completely shredding and bruising them—see note.)
3. Using a muddler, muddle everything together. Don't over-muddle. You want to extract the flavours and oils from the herbs, veggies, and citrus juice and peel, but you don't want to completely shred everything and emulsify the mixture. If you overdo it, the mixture will lose its bright crisp flavours and taste like soggy greens.
4. Pour the vodka and Caesar mix into the shaker. Fill the shaker with ice to just above the top of the liquid and stir with a bar spoon until the outside of the shaker is the very cold to the touch.
5. Fill the rimmed glass three-quarters full with fresh cubed ice. Strain the contents of the shaker into the glass and top with additional ice if desired. Garnish with the skewer and fresh herbs.

Notes: 1) Everything is muddled and then strained out at the end. Slightly more or less won't make a big difference, so don't worry about a precise measurement. 2) Credit to our friend New York mixologist Eben Klemm here. We adapted the technique of creating a "sandwich" in the shaker with an abrasive on the bottom, herbs in the middle, and citrus on top from Eben's Mojito muddling technique as described in his informative book *The Cocktail Primer*.

Smoked Herb

Cocktail by Trevor Kallies
Brass Fish Tavern
Vancouver, British Columbia

Serves 1

Glassware
1 goblet

Garnish
1 Castelvetrano olive, pitted
1 pickled cocktail onion
1 cucumber spear (3 inches/
    7.5 cm long)
1 lime wedge
1 sprig rosemary (2 to 3 inches/
    5 to 7.5 cm long)
1 sprig thyme (2 to 3 inches/5 to
    7.5 cm long)

Rim
1 Tbsp cracked black pepper
1 Tbsp Celery Salt (page 288 or
    store-bought)
1 lime wedge

Cocktail
2 oz (60 ml) vodka
5 oz (150 ml) Caesar mix, Classic
1 dash Worcestershire sauce
1 dash Tabasco hot sauce
Heavily peated whisky (ideally
    Ardbeg, Laphroaig, or
    Lagavulin)

Trevor Kallies likes to approach cocktail creation from as many angles as possible. He told us he wanted to create a Caesar that appealed to the nose as much as to the eyes and palate. And so the idea of adding smouldering rosemary and thyme sprigs as a garnish was born. While you prepare this drink, smoky aromas from the charred savoury herbs will fill the room, exciting your senses before you've even taken your first sip. And it's pretty amazing to see a trail of smoke curling into the air from your cocktail while it's being served. Pro tip: Fire is hot. Don't touch it with your face.

1. Prepare a skewer with the olive, onion, and cucumber.
2. Mix together the pepper and celery salt and then pour them onto a small plate. Rub the lime wedge around half of the rim of your glass and then roll that half of the rim in the rim spice.
3. Add the vodka, Caesar mix, Worcestershire sauce, and hot sauce to a cocktail shaker (or other mixing vessel). Fill the shaker with ice to just above the top of the liquid and stir with a bar spoon until the outside of the shaker is very cold to the touch.
4. Fill the rimmed glass three-quarters full with fresh cubed ice. Strain the contents of the shaker into the glass and top with additional ice if desired. Garnish with the skewer and lime wedge.
5. Fill an atomizer (or spray bottle) with a wee bit of the whisky, then gently spray a single spritz just above the top of your glass so that the mist floats down into your drink.
6. Nestle the rosemary and thyme sprigs vertically in the glass, leaving as much of the sprigs exposed as possible beyond the rim of the glass. Char these dry portions of the herbs lightly, using a kitchen blowtorch or a lighter. Serve the cocktail immediately while the herbs are still smouldering.

Hot & Sour

Serves 1

Glassware
1 rocks glass

ZS: When we were growing up in Richmond, British Columbia, Aaron and I were both exposed to incredible Asian cuisine—from classic restaurants tucked away in the corners of strip malls, to steaming stalls in the food court of the Richmond Public Market, to many of our friends' family kitchens. A couple of years ago, a piece in the *New York Times* helped to turn the rest of the food-and-beverage world onto something Richmond locals have long known: that some of the best Asian cuisine on the planet can be found in this Vancouver suburb. All of which helps to explain why my go-to comfort food isn't chicken noodle soup but hot and sour soup. And this drink is kinda like hot and sour soup. It's hot, it's sour, it's salty, it's spicy, it's umami, and it reminds me of home—but of course, this version also has alcohol.

Cocktail
½ oz (15 ml) Sesame Fat
    Washed Vodka (page 302)
½ oz (15 ml) gin
¼ oz (7.5 ml) dry (white)
    vermouth
5 oz (150 ml) Caesar mix, Mild
⅓ oz (10 ml) rice vinegar
1 tsp light soy sauce
½ tsp chili bean sauce (toban
    djan) (see note)
⅛ tsp ground ginger
⅛ tsp ground white pepper

Garnish
1 Grilled Tofu Skewer (page 278)

1. Add the vodka, gin, vermouth, Caesar mix, rice vinegar, soy sauce, chili bean sauce, ginger, and pepper to an empty cocktail shaker (or other mixing vessel). Fill the shaker with ice to just above the top of the liquid and stir with a bar spoon until the outside of the shaker is very cold to the touch.
2. Fill the glass three-quarters full with fresh cubed ice. Strain the contents of the shaker into the glass and top with additional ice if desired. Garnish with the skewer.

Note: Chili bean sauce, a.k.a. toban djan, is a Chinese condiment made from fermented beans, chili peppers, soybeans, salt, and flour—and is delicious. It can be found at most specialty Asian markets as well as many mainstream grocery stores. It can also be purchased from Bezos. One of the best-known brands is Lee Kum Kee.

Growshow

Cocktail by Jason Chan
The Village
Victoria, British Columbia

Serves 1

Glassware
1 highball glass

Rim
2 Tbsp Celery Salt (page 288 or
    store-bought)
1 lime wedge

Cocktail
2 oz (60 ml) vodka (ideally
    Sheringham Distillery)
4 oz (120 ml) Caesar mix, Classic
½ oz (15 ml) hot sauce (ideally
    Valentina)
½ oz (15 ml) Worcestershire
    sauce
¼ oz (7.5 ml) lime juice

Garnish
2 to 3 Quick-Pickled Growshow
    Vegetables (page 283), on a
    skewer
1 strip Crispy Bacon (page 275),
    on a skewer (see note)
1 sprig parsley
1 turn cracked black pepper

Ask any one in and around Victoria, British Columbia, where to go for brunch and the Village group of restaurants is likely to come up. Rightfully so. The hospitality is warm, the food is always excellent, and Jason and his team take pride and care in sourcing local ingredients. Case in point: this Caesar is named after their three food gardens—collectively nicknamed The Village Growshow—which are the source of their house-pickled vegetables. Not surprisingly, given their focus on local ingredients, the drink features island-made vodka from Sheringham Distillery in nearby Sooke. Also: bacon.

1. Pour the celery salt onto a small plate. Circle the rim of your glass with the lime wedge, then roll the rim in the celery salt.
2. Add the vodka, Caesar mix, hot sauce, Worcestershire sauce, and lime juice to a cocktail shaker (or other mixing vessel). Fill the shaker with ice to just above the top of the liquid and stir with a bar spoon until the outside of the shaker is very cold to the touch.
3. Fill the rimmed glass three-quarters full with fresh cubed ice. Strain the contents of the shaker into the glass and top with additional ice if desired. Garnish with the skewers of pickled vegetables, bacon, and parsley sprig. Finish with a turn of cracked black pepper.

Note: The Village uses thick-cut double-smoked bacon from Red Barn Market, which has locations across Vancouver Island. If you're not an islander, grab your choice of thick-cut bacon.

Green

Serves 1

Glassware
1 rocks glass

Tomatillos, best known as the base for salsa verde, make for a visually striking and unexpected green Caesar. As the flavours remind us most of Mexican cuisine, we naturally pair our tomatillo-based Caesar with tequila, but you can play around with other spirits. We tend to mix this at a lower alcohol-to-base ratio because of its light, bright profile. With its cheerful hue, crisp sweet-citrusy flavour, and mellow alcohol content, you might find this one becomes your go-to for occasions that call for something refreshing and easy to drink.

Rim
2 Tbsp black lava salt
1 lime wedge

Cocktail
¾ oz (22.5 ml) tequila
6 oz (180 ml) Green Caesar Mix
    (page 69)
4 dashes green hot sauce

Garnish
2 turns cracked black pepper
1 Grilled Prawn (page 277), on a
    skewer

1. Pour the salt onto a small plate. Circle the rim of your glass with the lime wedge, then roll the rim in the salt.
2. Add the tequila, Caesar mix, and hot sauce to a cocktail shaker (or other mixing vessel). Fill the shaker with ice to just above the top of the liquid and stir with a bar spoon until the outside of the shaker is very cold to the touch.
3. Fill the rimmed glass three-quarters full with fresh cubed ice. Strain the contents of the shaker into the glass and top with additional ice if desired.
4. Finish the drink with some cracked black pepper, and garnish with the skewer.

The Merman

Cocktail by Parker Reid
Field House Brewing Co.
Abbotsford, British Columbia

Serves 1

Glassware
1 pint glass

Rim
2 Tbsp Old Bay seasoning
¼ Quick-Pickled Cucumber
(page 282), cut lengthwise

Cocktail
12 oz (360 ml) sour beer (ideally
Field House Brewing's Sour
Wheat Gose)
4 oz (120 ml) Caesar mix, Mild

The crew at Field House Brewing do things very simply, and very well. One visit to their outpost in pastoral Abbotsford will make you a believer. They serve this simple four-ingredient Beer Caesar on Sundays, and Sundays only. Why only Sundays? "Because that's when we serve it, on Sundays." Makes total sense to us. While we've enjoyed many a Beer Caesar, what makes this one unique is the style of beer used: sour beer. In this case, it's Field House's Sour Wheat Gose—but any good quality sour will work perfectly.

1. Pour the Old Bay seasoning onto a small plate. Circle the rim of your glass with the pickled cucumber you're also going to use for your garnish, then roll the rim in the seasoning.
2. Fill your rimmed glass three-quarters full with beer and then top it off by slowly adding the Caesar mix. Garnish with the pickled cucumber.

Vancouver Island Iced Tea

Serves 1

Glassware
1 Collins glass

New York's Long Island on the East Coast is famous for its iconic tea, which contains exactly zero tea but almost all the spirits in the world. As an homage to that arguably ill-conceived but highly effective cocktail, we offer a Vancouver Island version, which also happens to contain zero tea. These should not be consumed unsupervised.

Garnish
1 cherry tomato
1 lemon wedge

Cocktail
½ oz (15 ml) white rum
½ oz (15 ml) tequila blanco
½ oz (15 ml) triple sec
½ oz (15 ml) gin
½ oz (15 ml) vodka
6 oz (180 ml) Caesar mix, Classic
½ oz (15 ml) lemon juice

1. Skewer the cherry tomato and lemon wedge on a sword pick.
2. Pour the rum, tequila, triple sec, gin, vodka, Caesar mix, and lemon juice into a cocktail shaker (or other mixing vessel). Fill the shaker with ice to just above the top of the liquid and stir with a bar spoon until the outside of the shaker is very cold to the touch.
3. Fill the glass three-quarters full with fresh cubed ice. Strain the contents of the shaker into the glass and top with additional ice if desired. Garnish with the sword pick.

Scotch Creek

Cocktail by Chris Whittaker
Quaaout Lodge & Spa at Talking
Rock Resort
Shuswap, British Columbia

Serves 1

Glassware
1 stemless wine glass

Garnish
1 slice cold-smoked salmon
3 to 5 bread and butter pickles
½ Smoky Pickled Egg (page 285)

Rim
2 Tbsp Garlic Scape Salt
    (page 289)
1 lemon wedge

Cocktail
1 oz (30 ml) gin
5 oz (150 ml) Caesar mix, Classic
¼ oz (7.5 ml) Wild Juniper &
    Spruce Tip Vinegar, fine
    strained (page 300)
¼ oz (7.5 ml) bread and butter
    pickle juice (from garnish)
1 tsp Worcestershire sauce
2 dashes hot sauce

Chris Whittaker is a staunch supporter of his local farmers, ranchers, foragers, and fishers. Drawing on his deep knowledge of the region, its people, and its products, he's constantly preserving the best locally grown ingredients each season. With his Scotch Creek Caesar—woody spruce tips, wild juniper vinegar, and a pink salmon garnish—Chris presents the wilds of the Shuswap region, especially the famous Adams River salmon run, one of the world's major salmon spawning sites, in a glass.

1. Skewer the smoked salmon, pickles, and pickled egg.
2. Pour the garlic scape salt onto a small plate. Circle the rim of your glass with the lemon wedge, then roll the rim in the salt.
3. Pour the gin, Caesar mix, vinegar, pickle juice, Worcestershire sauce, and hot sauce into a cocktail shaker (or other mixing vessel). Fill the shaker with ice to just above the top of the liquid and stir with a bar spoon until the outside of the shaker is very cold to the touch.
4. Fill the rimmed glass three-quarters full with fresh cubed ice. Strain the contents of the shaker into the glass and top with additional ice if desired. Garnish with the skewer.

Sangrita

Serves 1

Glassware

2 shot glasses (each 1 to 2 oz/
    30 to 60 ml)

Not to be confused with Sangria, Sangrita ("little blood") is a sweet, spicy, citrusy non-alcoholic juice mixture traditionally served in Mexico alongside a shot of high-quality sipping tequila. Drinking this is the antithesis of the always regretted lick-of-salt, shot-of-cheap-tequila, suck-of-lime ritual. Instead, it's all about enjoying the simplicity of alternating sips of Sangrita and tequila. There are many recipes for Sangrita out there. Most call for orange juice, lime juice, or pomegranate juice, and many add a tomato-clam cocktail to the mix. As you'd expect, the addition of tomato and clam is the way we like ours. We like to drink Sangrita as cold as possible, so we store it in the refrigerator until just before serving, at which point we stir it over ice and strain. This adds some dilution to tamp down the spice level a touch while also brightening up the core flavours.

Sangrita

6 oz (180 ml) Caesar mix, Extra
    Spicy (see note)

3 oz (90 ml) orange juice

2¼ oz (67.5 ml) lime juice

1 oz (30 ml) Pomegranate Syrup
    (page 296)

½ tsp Mexican-style hot sauce
    (such as Cholula or Valentina)

¼ tsp sea salt

¼ tsp cracked black pepper

For Serving

1 to 2 oz (30 to 60 ml) tequila
    blanco

1. Add the Caesar mix, orange juice, lime juice, pomegranate syrup, hot sauce, salt, and pepper to a cocktail shaker (or other mixing vessel). Stir well with a bar spoon to incorporate.
2. Place a fine-mesh sieve over a large bowl and strain the Sangrita into it. Store extra Sangrita in a glass jar or bottle (about 12 oz/360 ml) in the refrigerator for up to 4 days.
3. To serve, pour 1 to 2 oz (30 to 60 ml) of Sangrita into a cocktail shaker (or other mixing vessel). Fill the shaker with ice to just above the top of the liquid and stir with a bar spoon until the outside of the shaker is very cold to the touch.
4. Strain the cold Sangrita into a shot glass. Serve alongside 1 to 2 oz (30 to 60 ml) of tequila in a shot glass. Take a sip of tequila. Take a sip of Sangrita. Repeat.

Note: You can also use Classic or Mild Caesar mix instead of Extra Spicy. As written, this recipe definitely has some kick, but it's not over the top. As always, the spice level is up to you. You can add more or less hot sauce depending on your heat tolerance.

Vampiro

Serves 1

Glassware
1 rocks glass

If Sangrita (page 98) is meant to be a supporting act, sipped alongside tequila, the Vampiro turns it into the main attraction. Think of it as Sangrita's cocktail cousin, the vampire powered by the little blood that is its signature ingredient: hence the name. As with Sangrita, you'll find lots of local variations of this cocktail around Mexico. We prefer the simplest version: Sangrita and tequila mixed into a cocktail rather than served separately.

Rim
1 Tbsp Tajín, classic (see note)
½ Tbsp flaked sea salt
½ Tbsp cane sugar
1 lime wedge

Cocktail
1½ oz (45 ml) tequila
4 oz (120 ml) Sangrita (page 98)

Garnish
1 orange wedge
1 lime wedge

1. Place the Tajín, salt, and sugar in a bowl and mix well. Pour this rim spice onto a small plate. Circle the rim of your glass with the lime wedge, then roll the rim in the rim spice.
2. Add the tequila and Sangrita to a cocktail shaker (or other mixing vessel). Fill the shaker with ice to just above the top of the liquid and stir with a bar spoon until the outside of the shaker is very cold to the touch.
3. Fill the rimmed glass three-quarters full with fresh cubed ice. Strain the contents of the shaker into the glass and top with additional ice if desired. Garnish with the orange and lime wedges.

Note: Tajín is everyone's favourite Mexican spice blend made with chili peppers and a hint of lime. It can be found online or in specialty stores.

Double Double

**Cocktail by Lauren Mote &
Jonathan Chovancek**
Bittered Sling
Okanagan Valley, British
Columbia

Serves 1

Glassware
1 double rocks glass

You'd be hard pressed to find a more dynamic duo in the Canadian hospitality industry than these two. Lauren is the first-ever Diageo Reserve Global Cocktailian and Jonathan is an accomplished chef who's headed up the kitchens of numerous Vancouver institutions. As husband and wife, they own and operate Bittered Sling, crafting premium cocktail bitters. Here, they teamed up to create a drink that combines what they consider, in their words, "two of Canada's most important institutions: Tim Hortons and the Caesar." Uniting these two institutions for Lauren and Jonathan are memories of long summer drives between Vancouver and the Okanagan, filled with "those carefree moments with nothing but the open road and stunning BC countryside ahead of you and a killer playlist to keep you company . . . with a ritual stop at Timmy's for a double-double, a double-toasted everything bagel with cream cheese, tomato, and cucumber. And then a round of Caesars upon arrival, of course."

A note from Jonathan: Stay vigilant when preparing your garnish—there's a fine line between double-toasted (ideal) and burnt to a crisp (not ideal).

Rim
2 Tbsp Everything Bagel Spice
   (page 288 or store-bought)
1 lemon wedge

Cocktail
1 oz (30 ml) Seedlip Garden 108,
   or gin (see note)
6 oz (180 ml) Caesar mix, Classic
¼ oz (7.5 ml) Bagel Shrub
   (page 292)
1 pinch pink Himalayan salt
1 turn cracked black pepper
3 dashes Bittered Sling
   Kensington Aromatic Bitters
   (see note)
2 dashes Tabasco hot sauce
   (optional)

Garnish
1 Bagel Cracker (page 272)

1. Pour the bagel spice onto a small plate. Circle the rim of your glass with the lemon wedge, then roll the rim in the bagel spice.
2. Add the Seedlip, Caesar mix, bagel shrub, salt, pepper, bitters, and Tabasco, if using, to a cocktail shaker. Fill the shaker with ice to just above the top of the liquid and gently roll all the liquid and ice from this shaker to a second mixing vessel, working back and forth until the outside of the vessels are very cold to the touch.
3. Fill the rimmed glass three-quarters full with fresh cubed ice. Strain the contents of the shaker into the glass and top with additional ice if desired. Garnish with the bagel cracker.

Notes: 1) Seedlip is a distilled non-alcoholic spirit. You can substitute gin if you'd prefer an alcoholic version. 2) If you can't get your hands on Bittered Sling Kensington Aromatic Bitters, you can substitute Angostura or any other aromatic bitters.

The Umami One

Serves 1

Glassware
1 rocks glass

Cocktail
1 oz (30 ml) vodka
2 Tbsp Umami Paste (page 299)
½ oz (15 ml) Lillet Blanc (see note)
4 oz (120 ml) Caesar mix, Mild

Garnish
1 Parmesan Tuile (page 280)

The idea behind this cocktail is as straightforward as its name. We wanted to see just how much umami we could pack into a glass without going too far. Drawing on the natural umami of mushrooms, olives, soy sauce, miso, anchovy, fish sauce, balsamic vinegar, and parmesan, this is a very savoury Caesar, all balanced out by a touch of Lillet Blanc, a semisweet and citrusy aperitif wine.

1. Add the vodka and umami paste to a cocktail shaker (or other mixing vessel) and stir until the umami paste is evenly incorporated.
2. Add the Lillet Blanc and Caesar mix to the shaker. Fill the shaker with ice to just above the top of the liquid and stir with a bar spoon until the outside of the shaker is very cold to the touch.
3. Fill the rimmed glass three-quarters full with fresh cubed ice. Strain the contents of the shaker into the glass through a small fine-mesh strainer. (Use a small spatula or spoon to help push it through if your umami paste is on the thicker side.) Top with additional ice if desired. Garnish with the parmesan tuile.

Note: If you don't have Lillet Blanc, you can substitute white vermouth.

The Crescent Caesar

Cocktail by Ryan Reynolds
Co-owner, Aviation American Gin
Vancouver, British Columbia

Serves 1

Glassware
1 coupe, chilled

Cocktail
2½ oz (75 ml) Aviation American Gin
½ oz (15 ml) dry (white) vermouth
½ oz (15 ml) Caesar mix, Mild
¼ oz (7.5 ml) lemon juice, finely strained
1 tsp olive brine

Garnish
1 lemon peel (1 to 2 inches/ 2.5 to 5 cm long)
2 or 3 olives, on a skewer

"To me, the taste of a Caesar is the taste of home. It's the quintessential Canadian cocktail and one of the first drinks I ever had. We lived on Crescent Drive, hence the name," Vancouver native Ryan Reynolds tells us. "My recipe is a Caesar Gin Martini, made dirty. My lawyers said I am contractually obliged to make it with Aviation gin so I did but—don't tell them—I would make it with Aviation regardless because it's delicious. The citrus and floral notes of Aviation balance the savoury flavour of Walter and keep the salty olive brine in check. Enjoy!"

1. Pour the gin, vermouth, Caesar mix, lemon juice, and olive brine into a cocktail shaker. Fill the shaker with ice to just above the top of the liquid and stir with a bar spoon until the outside of the shaker is very cold to the touch.
2. Strain the contents of the shaker into the chilled glass and garnish with the lemon peel and olive skewer.

Steelhead Ceviche

Recipe by Reuben Major
The Belgard Kitchen
Vancouver, British Columbia

Serves 4

Chef Reuben is like family to us. We've been eating his ingredient-driven, globally inspired, flavour-forward food for years. Here he gives us a dish as pretty as it is tasty. It's clear that every ingredient was carefully chosen for what it brings to the dish, from the clean taste of the steelhead salmon, to the freshness of the grape tomatoes, to the textural contrast of the corn and green garbanzo beans—all working to create a whole that is greater than the sum of its well-considered parts. The broth, with just a touch of Caesar flavours—cool, delightfully acidic—is tasty enough to stand on its own. You'll want to have some chips or good crusty bread on hand so as not to miss a drop.

Pickled Shallots

½ cup (120 ml) apple cider
    vinegar
½ cup (120 ml) water
1 Tbsp granulated sugar
1½ tsp kosher salt
1 bay leaf
5 shallots, thinly sliced

Steelhead Ceviche

9 oz (255 g) steelhead salmon,
    skinned and boned
1 lemon, juiced
1 lime, zested and juiced
1 tsp honey
¾ cup (180 ml) green garbanzo
    beans or edamame beans in
    their shells
1 ear of corn, husked
1 cup (240 ml) Caesar mix,
    Holiday (or Classic)
1½ cups (360 ml) rainbow grape
    tomatoes, quartered
1 cup (240 ml) Easter or lipstick
    radishes, cut in ¼-inch (6 mm)
    wedges

Pickled Shallots

1. Combine the vinegar, water, sugar, salt, and bay leaf in a small pot over medium-high heat. Bring to a simmer and continue to simmer for 5 minutes. Remove from the heat and let steep for 30 minutes. Strain through a fine-mesh sieve.
2. Meanwhile, place the shallots in a 2-cup (480 ml) lidded glass jar.
3. Pour the warm brine over the shallots, ensuring they are submerged.
4. Allow to cool to room temperature, then cover and refrigerate for a minimum of 2 hours, but ideally overnight. The shallots will keep for up to 2 weeks in the refrigerator.

Steelhead Ceviche

1. Cut the salmon into ½- to ¾-inch (1 to 2 cm) cubes and place them in a large freezer storage bag.
2. In a medium bowl, whisk together the lemon juice, lime zest, lime juice, and honey until the honey is dissolved. Pour the mixture into the bag, ensuring each piece of fish is nicely coated. Squeeze out any excess air before tightly sealing the bag.
3. Place the bag in the refrigerator until the salmon is cured, approximately 1½ to 2½ hours. Check by breaking a larger piece of fish in half to ensure the cure has penetrated the entire piece of fish. When it's ready it will look more "pink cooked" than "raw red."
4. Shell the beans and cook them for 2 to 3 minutes in a small pot of boiling salted water. Drain and set aside to cool.

– recipe continues

1 Tbsp thinly sliced serrano
   pepper

¼ cup (60 ml) flat-leaf parsley
   leaves

½ cup (120 ml) Pickled Shallots,
   separated into rings

2 Tbsp pickled shallot brine

For Serving

Tortilla chips or crusty bread

5. On a grill pan over high heat, char the corn on the cob, let cool, and then slice off the kernels. Set aside.

6. Once the salmon is fully cured, pour the Caesar mix into the bag to complete the curing broth.

7. In a large mixing bowl, combine the tomatoes, radishes, Serrano pepper, parsley, cooked beans, charred corn kernels, pickled shallots, and pickling brine. Add the cured salmon and broth and fold everything together gently just until evenly distributed.

8. Carefully transfer the ceviche and broth to a deep plate, spread out for even depth. Place the colourful pieces on top for maximum visual appeal. This is best served immediately, with chips or crusty bread.

Seafood Chowder

Recipe by Ned Bell
Naramata Inn
Naramata, British Columbia

Serves 4

In the summer of 2020, Chef Ned and his team opened the Naramata Inn in a century-old hotel in the small, laid-back lakeside community of Naramata, located in the heart of BC's Okanagan Valley—a world-class wine region. His intense focus on hyper-seasonal, hyper-local ingredients runs through everything they do. For instance, they choose to use wild sumac, which grows near the property, as a citrus replacement for lemons and limes, which don't grow in the region. In this chowder, packed with fresh local seafood, Ned adds a touch of Caesar mix, balancing out the richness of the cream with a hint of sweet and acidic tomato. The result is a pink-hued revelation—neither fully New England– nor Manhattan-style but something all its own.

Shellfish & Shellfish Broth

1 lb (450 g) fresh BC clams (Little Neck, Savoury, or Manila)
1 lb (450 g) fresh BC mussels (see note)
¼ cup (60 ml) unsalted butter
½ small white onion, diced
2 cloves garlic, minced
¾ cup (180 ml) dry white wine (see note)
2 cups (480 ml) Caesar mix, Classic

Chowder

3 Tbsp canola oil
1 medium onion, finely diced
1 Tbsp kosher salt
2 cups (480 ml) fresh corn kernels (about 2 cobs)
¼ cup (60 ml) all-purpose flour
¾ cup (180 ml) dry white wine
1 lb (450 g) yellow potatoes, peeled and diced

Shellfish & Shellfish Broth

1. Soak the clams and mussels in fresh cold water for 20 minutes, scrubbing off any residual dirt or sand. Discard any with broken shells or that don't open when tapped. Pull off the beards of the mussels.
2. Melt the butter in a medium-size pot over medium-high heat. Sauté the onions and garlic until just beginning to soften, 2 minutes, then add the clams and mussels and sauté for 1 minute more.
3. Add the wine and Caesar mix and bring to a simmer. Cook for 2 to 4 minutes, until the clams and mussels are cooked and the shells pop open. (Discard any that don't open.)
4. Remove the pot from the heat to halt the cooking. Using a basket strainer, strain the broth from the shells into a large bowl and set aside for the chowder. Keep both the broth and the shellfish.
5. Remove the clams and mussels from their shells and set aside.

Chowder

1. In a large pot over medium heat, warm the oil. Sauté the onions until just beginning to soften, 2 minutes. Add the salt and corn and sauté, stirring occasionally, until the corn has started to soften and the onion is translucent but not brown, about 5 minutes.
2. Add the flour to the pot and cook, stirring constantly, for 2 minutes, then slowly add the wine and whisk until smooth. Cook for 2 minutes more, stirring occasionally.

– recipe continues

1 batch Shellfish Broth

2 cups (480 ml) whole milk

2 cups (480 ml) heavy (35%) cream

2 lb (900 g) wild BC fish, diced into 1-inch (2.5 cm) cubes (see note)

1 batch Shellfish

Cracked black pepper

2 Tbsp finely chopped fresh herbs (like parsley, tarragon, chives)

1 tsp ground sumac, fresh or dried

For Serving

Crusty sourdough

3. Add the potatoes and stir in the shellfish broth. Simmer for 3 minutes. Stir in the milk and cook for 3 minutes, then add the cream. Continue to simmer gently until the potatoes are fork-tender, 10 to 15 minutes.

4. Finally, add the fish and cooked shellfish and simmer for 3 minutes or until the fish is cooked through. Taste and adjust seasoning with more salt and pepper if desired.

5. Ladle the chowder into bowls, and top with the herbs and sumac. Enjoy with some warm, crusty sourdough and wonderful Naramata Bench white wine.

Notes: 1) Ned recommends BC mussels from Outlandish Shellfish Guild (especially the honey mussels) or Salt Spring Island Mussels. 2) Try getting your hands on a bottle of white wine from one of the many wineries in the Naramata Bench sub-appellation in the Okanagan Valley. 3) Depending on your location, wild BC fish might not be readily available. Choose from any of Ned's favourites, including salmon, halibut, hake, sablefish, or ling cod, or whatever your fishmonger says is in season. You can use fresh or frozen but try to find wild and sustainably sourced.

Prairies

One of the perks of working in our industry is that you get invited to a lot of cool things. A couple of years ago, Joshua Linde, a Walter partner, was invited to one of the annual "farm & fish" gatherings of Canadian food-and-beverage industry professionals hosted out on frozen Lake Winnipeg. We've found people in the Prairies to be an inclusive bunch, always game to show a visitor a good time—especially if they can (lovingly) push those visitors out of their comfort zones and introduce them to new experiences along the way.

Josh's day with the group began before dawn, when he helped to fill a pickup with fire logs—thick wedges of wood that he and other guests had pitched in to saw down and soak with kerosene. They drove out to the lake in a caravan, the sky going from black and starry, to light gold, to pink, to magic-hour blue during the drive. The weather was in the minus 40s. Josh's hosts had loaned him a "survival suit." "No bad weather, just bad gear," they told him. The group set up camp far out enough on the ice that they couldn't see the shore, and some of the region's top chefs got to work, laughing together over open flames and cast iron skillets, cooking beer sausage, with potatoes, and cheese curds. But those were only appetizers, supplying the energy needed to get to the main dish: walleye, still swimming below them. After drilling a circle in the ice, and with the help of portable sonar and a lot of patience, they caught some fish, which were cleaned, fried up, and eaten right there on the spot, served with Caesars garnished with handmade sausagettes from Winnipeg chef Tyrone Welchinski.

Living on the Prairies means regularly facing challenges from the natural world. As Josh learned out on Lake Winnipeg, the trick is to embrace these challenges as opportunities for adventure. You get out in the cold and the dark and figure out a way to tackle what nature's dealt you, because the other option is to stay inside for months at a time. When the rewards of getting outside range from walking the emerald circle of Lake Louise, to watching lights dance in the Manitoba sky, to canoeing Saskatchewan's wild country, the choice between outdoors and indoors seems obvious.

Given the importance of the outdoors in the Prairies, it's no surprise how many of our contributors drew inspiration from getting outside, whether to forage fiddleheads in Alberta or pick chanterelles in Saskatchewan, or by visiting independent distilleries and micro-breweries located within walking distance of their bars and restaurants. Their recipes make great use of all sorts of ingredients grown or raised in a region we love for its hearty and approachable food and drink. And, of course, we couldn't write about the Prairies without highlighting Walter Chell, whose original recipe for the Caesar from the Owl's Nest at the Calgary Inn we've attempted to recreate.

Original

Serves 1

Glassware
1 highball glass

There is no definitive record of Walter Chell's original recipe for the clam-and-tomato cocktail he called a Caesar back in 1969 (read the full story on page 4). Through conversations with Walter's daughter, Joan, and by digging through archival material, we've developed the recipe below, which we think is a faithful representation of his original version. Walter mentioned a few surprising things about his Caesar recipe in various interviews over the years. First, he said that he used muddled clams in his original recipe. Second, he apparently *hated* when bartenders used hot sauce in a Caesar (he said he never used the stuff). Third, and maybe most surprising, his secret ingredient was . . . oregano.

To Walter's credit, we really like the oregano (it's unclear if he used fresh or dried), which lends the cocktail a slight earthy and floral fragrance, and a subtle but astringent flavour note. And, since his original wasn't made with a commercial mix, we are calling for our house-made Red Caesar Mix in this recipe. So, get a bit retro, mix up the Original, and give a quick cheers to Walter Chell.

Rim
2 Tbsp Celery Salt (page 288 or store-bought)
1 lime wedge

Cocktail
1 turn cracked black pepper
4 fresh oregano leaves (or ¼ tsp dried)
1 Tbsp whole baby clams or bar clams (see note)
1 lime wedge
1 oz (30 ml) vodka
5 oz (150 ml) Red Caesar Mix (page 68) (or Caesar mix, Mild)
4 dashes Worcestershire sauce

Garnish
1 celery stalk, trimmed
1 lime wedge

1. Pour the celery salt onto a small plate. Circle the rim of your glass with the lime wedge, then roll the rim in the salt.
2. Place the pepper, oregano, clams, and lime wedge (in that order) in a cocktail shaker (or other mixing vessel). Using a muddler, muddle everything together. Don't over-muddle. You want to extract the flavours but you don't want to pulverize the clams or you'll end up with chunks of clam in your drink.
3. Add the vodka, Caesar mix, and Worcestershire sauce to the shaker. Fill the shaker with ice to just above the top of the liquid and stir with a bar spoon until the outside of the shaker is very cold to the touch.
4. Fill the rimmed glass three-quarters full with fresh cubed ice. Strain the contents of the shaker into the glass through a fine-mesh strainer and top with additional ice if desired. Garnish with the celery and lime wedge.

Note: We don't know exactly what kind of clams Walter used. Since he was running a busy bar, we assume he was using commercial clams. Therefore, we recommend you use either store-bought whole baby clams (which typically come canned and packed in water) or bar clams (which typically come bottled and packed in clam juice or brine). The latter will be brinier and add more salinity. Both will make a unique and delicious Caesar.

Banff Springs

Cocktail by Joe Ruhland
Fairmont Banff Springs
Banff, Alberta

Serves 1

Glassware
1 Collins glass

Rim
2 Tbsp Montréal steak spice
1 lemon wedge

Cocktail
1 oz (30 ml) Canadian rye whisky
5 oz (150 ml) Caesar mix, Classic
1 tsp HP Sauce
½ tsp hot sauce
½ tsp fresh lemon juice
2 dashes celery bitters (see note)

Garnish
1 piece Black Pepper Beef Jerky
   (page 273)
1 lemon wheel

There's something about enjoying a well-made cocktail in the lobby of a grand hotel—the experience can often be as luxurious as the surroundings. Enter: Fairmont Banff Springs, perched on the banks of the Bow River and surrounded by trees on a site dating back to 1888, three years after Banff became Canada's first national park. If you're fortunate enough to get there to enjoy an après-ski (or après-hike/canoe/skate/golf) drink, a Caesar is a good bet. This Caesar from Fairmont veteran Joe Ruhland celebrates Canada through the use of rye whisky and gives a nod to our Commonwealth roots with a touch of HP Sauce.

1. Pour the steak spice onto a small plate. Circle the rim of your glass with the lemon wedge, then roll the rim in the steak spice.
2. Add the whisky, Caesar mix, HP sauce, hot sauce, lemon juice, and celery bitters to a cocktail shaker (or other mixing vessel). Fill the shaker with ice to just above the top of the liquid and stir with a bar spoon until the outside of the shaker is very cold to the touch.
3. Fill the rimmed glass three-quarters full with fresh cubed ice. Strain the contents of the shaker into the glass and top with additional ice if desired. Garnish with the beef jerky and lemon wheel.

Note: A few companies make celery bitters. We're biased but we recommend the Cascade Celery Bitters from our friends at Bittered Sling. You can find them online or, better yet, at your local cocktail shop.

The Chucks

Serves 1

Glassware
1 pint glass

If you've ever been in Calgary for any of the ten sweaty, dusty, denim-clad days in July when the whole city gets turned over to Stampede, you'll know that: 1) it's the biggest, rowdiest, craziest party in the country; 2) love it or hate it, you can't escape it; 3) heaping pancake breakfasts are a ubiquitous and glorious tradition. Turns out those pancakes have a history dating back to 1923 (early Stampede days) and a cowboy name Jack Morton, a.k.a. Wild Horse. Legend has it that this southern Albertan was a hulking giant of a man—a horse-trader, a competitive rider, even a wild cow milker, and (allegedly) a horse thief, but only if it was to settle a debt. It is said that Wild Horse Jack was also the person responsible for introducing the chuckwagon races (The Chucks) to Stampede, now its premier event. As to the tradition of the pancake breakfasts—the story goes that Jack and a few of his fellow cowboys welcomed whomever from wherever to share in their pancakes served straight from his chuckwagon stove. So here's a cowboy Caesar with a side of pancakes.

Rim
1 Tbsp flaked sea salt
1 Tbsp cracked black pepper
1 Tbsp maple syrup

Cocktail
2 oz (60 ml) Black Pepper-
 Infused Vodka (page 300)
6 oz (180 ml) Caesar mix, Mild
¾ tsp BBQ sauce
½ tsp maple syrup
½ tsp lime juice
¼ tsp Worcestershire sauce

Garnish
1 strip Maple-Glazed Pepper
 Bacon (page 279)
1 lime wedge

Side Dish
Buttermilk Pancakes (page 273)

1. Mix together the salt and pepper in a bowl and then pour onto a small plate. Drizzle the maple syrup onto a separate plate (the pool of syrup should be at least as wide as your glass). Dip the rim of your glass in the maple syrup, allow any excess to drip back onto the plate, and then roll the rim in the rim spice.

2. Add the vodka, Caesar mix, BBQ sauce, maple syrup, lime juice, and Worcestershire sauce to a cocktail shaker (or other mixing vessel). Fill the shaker with ice to just above the top of the liquid and stir with a bar spoon until the outside of the shaker is very cold to the touch.

3. Fill the rimmed glass three-quarters full with fresh cubed ice. Strain the contents of the shaker into the glass and top with additional ice if desired. Garnish with the bacon and lime wedge. Serve with a side of buttermilk pancakes.

Chanterelle

Cocktail by Adrian Chappell
Primal Pasta
Saskatoon, Saskatchewan

Serves 1

Glassware
1 rocks glass

Rim
2 Tbsp Primal Rim (page 290)
1 lime wedge

Cocktail
1½ oz (45 ml) gin (ideally Black
     Fox #3 gin)
5 oz (150 ml) Caesar mix, Classic
1 oz (30 ml) Chanterelle Purée
     (page 294)
1 tsp Concord Grape Vincotto
     (page 294)
1 dash Tabasco hot sauce
1 tsp freshly grated horseradish

Garnish
2 to 3 Quick-Pickled
     Chanterelles (page 281), on a
     skewer
2 to 3 fresh thyme sprigs

Adrian's cocktail celebrates Saskatchewan's farming and food cultures with some inspiration from Old World Italy. Chanterelle mushrooms, which grow in abundance in the forests of northern Saskatchewan, are used here in two ways: as a paste to add a deep umami boost to the cocktail, and pickled as an elegant garnish. Adrian has added vincotto, the thick syrup Italians traditionally produce by reducing non-fermented grapes. In this case it's made from Concord grapes, a varietal grown in backyards all over Saskatoon. The base spirit is also local, the #3 gin from Black Fox Farm & Distillery near Saskatoon, adding slight notes of rhubarb and calendula that play off the delicate chanterelles.

1. Pour the rim spice onto a small plate. Circle the rim of your glass with the lime wedge, then roll the rim in the rim spice.
2. Add the gin, Caesar mix, chanterelle purée, vincotto, hot sauce, and horseradish to a cocktail shaker (or other mixing vessel). Fill the shaker with ice to just above the top of the liquid and stir with a bar spoon until the outside of the shaker is very cold to the touch.
3. Fill the rimmed glass three-quarters full with fresh cubed ice. Strain the contents of the shaker into the glass and top with additional ice if desired. Garnish with the chanterelle skewer and thyme.

It's a Thing, Man

Serves 1

Glassware
1 double rocks glass

Rim
1 Tbsp cracked black pepper
1 Tbsp Celery Salt (page 288 or
    store-bought)
1 lime wedge

Cocktail
1 oz gin
5 oz (150 ml) Caesar mix, Classic
½ oz (15 ml) Stout Reduction
    (page 298)
1 tsp lime juice
3 dashes hot sauce

Garnish
1 piece Roasted Marrow Bone
    (page 284)

For Serving
1 piece toasted sourdough bread
    (page 284)

AH: Years ago I was at a party in Edmonton where I watched someone pour more than a few ounces of stout into his Caesar. *Interesting move*, I thought. When I asked him about it, all he really had to say was, "Oh, it's a thing, man. It's a thing." Lo and behold, a few years later Zack and I launched a Caesar company. I thought back to that guy and his stout-filled Caesar. I played around with a few stout-and-Caesar combinations before I came up with a stout reduction, intensifying the malty flavour while bringing up the sweetness with some added raw sugar. I added roasted bone marrow as garnish as a nod to Alberta—and because I like it.

1. Combine the pepper and celery salt in a bowl and pour onto a small plate. Circle the rim of your glass with the lime wedge, then roll the rim in the rim spice.
2. Pour the gin, Caesar mix, stout reduction, lime juice, and hot sauce into a cocktail shaker (or other mixing vessel). Fill the shaker with ice to just above the top of the liquid and stir with a bar spoon until the outside of the shaker is very cold to the touch.
3. Fill the rimmed glass three-quarters full with fresh cubed ice. Strain the contents of the shaker into the glass and top with additional ice if desired. Garnish by resting the roasted marrow bone atop. Serve with toasted sourdough bread.

Deep River

**Cocktail by Katy Ingraham &
Jordan Watson**
The Bar at Fleisch
Edmonton, Alberta

Serves 1

Glassware
1 Collins glass

Rim
2 Tbsp Spicy Chartreuse Candy
    (page 291)
1 lemon wedge

Cocktail
2 oz (60 ml) gin (ideally
    Strathcona Spirits Badland
    Seaberry Gin)
3 oz (90 ml) Caesar mix, Mild
½ oz (15 ml) lemon juice
1½ tsp lime juice
1½ tsp Spruce Tip & Saskatoon
    Berry Shrub (page 298)

Garnish
4 brandied Saskatoon berries
    (ideally Mojo Jojo brand), on
    a skewer
1 lemon spiral

Katy and Jordan, the partners behind Fleisch, point to fellow Edmontonian and spirit maker Adam Smith as the inspiration for this lovely and complex Caesar. Adam and his team from Strathcona Spirits travel Alberta foraging for juniper and berries with which to make the Badlands Gin that provides this cocktail's base spirit. And Adam's foraging in turn inspired Jordan to venture out into Edmonton's greenbelt, pocketknife in hand, to nip some spruce tips to add a woody dimension to the drink, while offsetting the bold flavours of this Caesar's Saskatoon berry shrub.

1. Pour the spicy candy onto a small plate. Circle the rim of your glass with the lemon wedge, then roll the rim in the candy.
2. Pour the gin, Caesar mix, lemon juice, lime juice, and shrub into a cocktail shaker (or other mixing vessel). Fill the shaker with ice to just above the top of the liquid and stir with a bar spoon until the outside of the shaker is very cold to the touch.
3. Fill the rimmed glass three-quarters full with fresh cubed ice. Strain the contents of the shaker into the glass and top with additional ice if desired. Garnish with the skewer and lemon spiral.

Chartier

**Cocktail by Sylvie Cheverie &
Sloane Botting**
Chartier
Beaumont, Alberta

Serves 1

Glassware
1 pilsner glass

Garnish
1 to 2 slices farmhouse salami
    (each ¼ inch/6 mm thick)
1 to 2 Quick-Pickled Fiddleheads
    (page 282)

Rim
2 Tbsp Smoked Meat Spice Rim
    (page 291)
1 Tbsp maple syrup

Cocktail
1 oz Garlic-Infused Vodka
    (page 302)
1 tsp Black Pepper Jam
    (page 293) (or hoisin sauce)
6 oz (180 ml) Caesar mix, Mild
1 Tbsp sweet pickling brine (from
    the pickled fiddleheads)
1½ tsp lime juice
4 dashes Worcestershire sauce
3 dashes Tabasco hot sauce

This cocktail from Sylvie and Sloane at Chartier is as enjoyable and perhaps unexpected as the restaurant—a Québec French-style bistro in the heart of Beaumont, Alberta, originally a French farming community. It features foraged fiddleheads, locally crafted charcuterie, garlic-infused vodka, and a punchy black pepper jam. As Sloane says, this one's "prairie to the core" while also giving a nod to the region's French Canadian settlement roots with a Montréal smoked meat–inspired rim applied with a touch of maple syrup.

1. Skewer the salami and pickled fiddleheads.
2. Pour the rim spice onto a small plate. Drizzle the maple syrup onto a separate plate (the pool of syrup should be at least as wide as your glass). Dip the rim of your glass in the maple syrup, allow any excess to drip back onto the plate, and then roll the rim in the rim spice.
3. Add the vodka and jam to a cocktail shaker (or other mixing vessel) and stir until the jam is dissolved. Add the Caesar mix, pickling brine, lime juice, Worcestershire sauce, and hot sauce to the shaker. Fill the shaker with ice to just above the top of the liquid and stir with a bar spoon until the outside of the shaker is very cold to the touch.
4. Fill the rimmed glass three-quarters full with fresh cubed ice. Strain the contents of the shaker into the glass and top with additional ice if desired. Garnish with the skewer.

The Tree House

Cocktail by Elsa Taylor
The Roost
Winnipeg, Manitoba

Serves 1

Glassware
1 rocks glass

Garnish
2 to 4 pieces Crispy Buttermilk
    Calamari (page 275)
1 pickled pepperoncini
1 dill sprig
Pinch black lava salt

Rim
1 Tbsp sea salt
1 Tbsp chopped dill
1 Tbsp Celery Salt (page 288 or
    store-bought)
1 lime wedge

Cocktail
1½ oz (45 ml) gin (ideally Patent 5
    Navy Strength Gin)
1 clove Roasted Garlic (page 297)
1 tsp squid ink (see note)
3 oz (90 ml) Caesar mix, Classic
1½ Tbsp pickled pepper brine
    (from pepperoncini)
1½ tsp Worcestershire sauce
1½ tsp lime juice
3 to 4 dashes Cholula hot sauce

Our friends at The Roost describe themselves as "a couple of kids making treats in a tree house." That's an apt description of what they do, though technically the tree house is an intimate cocktail bar on the second floor of a century-old house overlooking a canopy of green, concrete, and glass in Winnipeg's Little Italy. Their cocktail is indeed a treat, a whimsical concoction that leans into the idea of the Caesar as a meal in a glass, with the unexpected inclusion of muddled roasted garlic, crispy calamari, and rich squid ink to bring depth of flavour while giving the cocktail a cool, mysterious, dark hue.

1. Skewer the calamari, pepperoncini, and dill sprig.
2. Combine the salt, dill, and celery salt in a bowl and pour onto a small plate. Circle the rim of your glass with the lime wedge, then roll the rim in the rim spice.
3. Add the gin, garlic, and squid ink to a cocktail shaker (or other mixing vessel) and muddle to ensure the squid ink and garlic fully combine with the gin. Add the Caesar mix, brine, Worcestershire sauce, lime juice, and hot sauce to the shaker. Fill the shaker with ice to just above the top of the liquid and stir with a bar spoon until the outside of the shaker is very cold to the touch.
4. Fill the rimmed glass three-quarters full with fresh cubed ice. Strain the contents of the shaker into the glass and top with additional ice if desired. Finish the drink with a sprinkle of black lava salt and garnish with the skewer.

Note: You might be familiar with squid ink from its classic use in delicious deeply coloured pasta and risotto. In a Caesar it adds a touch of briny, umami flavour and makes the drink a few shades darker (of course). You can find it online or in specialty grocers.

Ponyboy

Serves 1

Glassware

1 glass for your Caesar

1 large shot glass (2 to 3 oz/
   60 to 90 ml)

You'll find Caesars paired with beer in different spots across Canada, but the practice seems to be most common among folks in the Prairies, traditionally an adventurous bunch. One of our favourite ways of marrying the two elements is also the simplest: serving a Caesar with a shot of beer on the side as a chaser, which some people call a *pony,* while others dub it a *beer back,* or *snit,* or *shorty.* Whatever you call it, it works. Beer makes an ideal palate cleanser to offset a spicy, salty Caesar. Each sip of one makes the other that much tastier. Next time you're making Caesars at the cottage, try pouring your friends a pony each and watch how many people you'll make happy with a single bottle of beer.

PS. Stay gold.

Cocktail

1 Caesar cocktail

2 to 3 oz (60 to 90 ml) ice-cold
   beer

1. Make a Caesar from any of the pages in this book.
2. Pour a tiny little beer in a large shot glass (or any very small glass, for that matter). Serve side by side with your Caesar. Take a sip of Caesar. Take a sip of beer. Repeat.

Calgary Redeye

Serves 1

Glassware

1 pint glass or a sleeve
1 large shot glass (2 to 3 oz/
    60 to 90 ml)

Now that you've experienced the joys of a Caesar with a little beer in the Ponyboy (page 138), try reversing the equation. Unlike with the more complex Michelada (page 142), which has a few more ingredients and is typically served over ice, the only decision you have to make with a Calgary Redeye is how much Caesar mix to add to your beer. This is as basic a concoction as they come. But if you've never tried it, chances are you'll be surprised by how much a touch of Caesar mix—with all of its sweet, salty, sour, bitter, and umami flavours—can transform even the most straightforward beer. We find this combination works best with brews that aren't too hoppy or too dark. Something crisp and refreshing—a lager or pilsner, say—will do the trick.

Cocktail

1 ice-cold beer
2 to 3 oz (60 to 90 ml) cold
    Caesar mix, Mild

1. Pour the beer into a glass. Pour a little bit of Caesar mix into a large shot glass.
2. Take a couple of sips of beer to make some room. Pour the Caesar mix into your beer. Enjoy.

Michelada

Serves 1

Glassware
1 pint glass

AH: The first Michelada I ever had was in Sayulita at a ramshackle beach bar on the Pacific coast of Mexico. Maybe it was the midday heat, mild dehydration, or my general vacation state of mind, but I became an instant convert and have been a fan of this beer cocktail (*cerveza preparada*) ever since. Clearly, I'm not alone. The Michelada is among Mexico's most popular cocktails and is increasingly taking hold in Canada too. What constitutes the "proper" or "authentic" Michelada is a hotly debated topic, and opinions are often regionally divided. I've been lucky enough to sample more than a few variations. Here's my version: simple, savoury, spicy, and very refreshing.

Rim
1 Tbsp Tajín, classic
1 Tbsp kosher salt
1 lime wedge

Cocktail
3 oz (90 ml) Caesar mix, Classic
⅓ oz (10 ml) lime juice
1 tsp Maggi Liquid Seasoning
    (see note)
½ tsp Mexican-style hot sauce
    (such as Cholula or Valentina)
8 oz (240 ml) Mexican lager
    (ideally Modelo Especial)

Garnish
1 lime wedge

1. Combine the Tajín and salt in a bowl and then pour onto a small plate. Circle the rim of your glass with the lime wedge, then roll the rim in the rim spice.
2. Pour the Caesar mix, lime juice, Maggi, and hot sauce into the pint glass and stir to incorporate.
3. Fill the glass with ice and slowly top up with beer. When you're pouring, tilt the glass sideways and pour really slowly to avoid creating a ton of foam. Once the beer is poured, stir gently. Garnish with the lime wedge.

Note: Maggi Liquid Seasoning is delicious and makes pretty much everything taste better. It's sorta like Mexican Worcestershire sauce but more savoury and less sweet. It can be found online or in specialty stores.

Sausagettes

Recipe by Tyrone Welchinski
Welchinski's Meats
Winnipeg, Manitoba

Makes 18 sausagettes

Tyrone Welchinski is serious about the charcuterie he makes. He's damn good at it too, showing us how to make homemade sausagettes. "Manitoba is the largest pig-producing province in the country," he tells us, "so naturally everything I make uses ethically sourced, sustainably raised meat from our local farmers and producers. These make great snacks to pack for a hike or fishing trip, or of course, to garnish your favourite Caesar." You'll need a sausage stuffer and a smoker to make this recipe, and it does take some time and effort. Excellent things often do.

1 Tbsp coriander seed
2 tsp cracked black pepper
1½ tsp celery seed
3½ Tbsp fine kosher salt
⅔ tsp Cure #1 curing salt (see note)
2 tsp chili flakes
1½ tsp granulated sugar
1 tsp minced garlic
¼ cup (60 ml) Caesar mix, Classic
3 lb (1.4 kg) pork leg or shoulder, finely ground (see note)
Natural sheep casings (20/22 mm) or collagen casings (19/21 mm)
Hickory wood chips, soaked

1. Place a stand mixer bowl and paddle attachment in the freezer to chill.
2. In a small pan over medium-high heat, dry-toast the coriander seed, pepper, and celery seed, stirring occasionally until aromatic. Let the spices cool fully and then coarsely grind them with a mortar and pestle. Transfer to a small bowl and mix well with the salt, Cure #1, chili flakes, sugar, garlic, and Caesar mix.
3. Place the ground pork in the ice-cold bowl and add the spice mixture. Secure the bowl and paddle attachment to the stand mixer and mix thoroughly on low speed until the ground pork has legs, meaning it will want to stick to itself, about 3 minutes.
4. Put the meat mixture back in the refrigerator until ready to use. (The meat mixture will separate if it gets too warm, so keep your equipment and meat cold at all times.)
5. Meanwhile, soak the sheep casings in tepid water. Try to use natural casings, as they are porous and will absorb more of the hickory smoke. If you're using collagen casings, there's usually no need to soak them before stuffing (follow the instructions on the package).
6. Set up a sausage stuffer with the stuffing tube gauge appropriate for the diameter of your casing. (For example, for 19 to 21 mm casings, use a 12 to 13 mm stuffing tube. The manual that came with your sausage stuffer will tell you all you need to know about that.)
7. Fill the sausage stuffer with the ground pork mixture, thread the casings on the sausage stuffer tube, and start to stuff the casings. Be careful not to overstuff the casings or they'll burst. (If natural casings are sticking, use a little ice water to lubricate the stuffer tube.) As the casings begin to fill, every 6 to 9 inches (15 to 22 cm), twist the casing seven to eight times to

– recipe continues

create each sausagette link. Alternate the direction that you twist each new link. (Optional: You can also tie some butcher's twine between each link to reinforce your twisted divider.) Then use a sausage pricker or cake tester to remove any air pockets.

8. Allow the sausagettes to rest, uncovered, on a baking rack overnight in the refrigerator. The casings will dry and the smoke will cling more readily to them.

9. The following day, prepare a smoker. Light the charcoal with the dampers fully open. Once it lights, close the dampers almost completely with just enough airflow to keep it lit. Add the soaked hickory wood chips. (Use the appropriate amount of wood chips for your smoker.)

10. Place the sausagettes on the smoker racks. Start with a low temperature, 120°F (50°C), and slowly increase to 180°F (80°C) by opening the dampers just a little more every 30 minutes. Hold the temperature at 180°F (80°C) until the sausagettes' internal temperature reaches 160°F (70°C). The total cook time should be about 4 to 5 hours.

11. At this point, open the dampers and let the sausagettes continue to dry in the smoker for an additional 2½ hours. Or place sausagettes on oven-safe metal baking racks and transfer them to an oven preheated to its lowest possible temperature (no hotter than 180°F/80°C) for an additional 2½ hours. Once they're dry, let cool to room temperature and then store in an airtight container in the refrigerator for up to 4 weeks.

Notes: 1) Cure #1 is a specialty curing salt designed to facilitate food preservation. It's used for curing meats and it can be purchased at butchers or online. 2) You can purchase pork from your local butcher, or better yet, get to know your local farmer. Tyrone sources pork from Zinn Farms in Springstein, Manitoba. They use regenerative farming practices that return nutrients to the soil and provide healthy feed for their heritage Berkshire pigs. Visit your local farmers' market and ask around. You can grind the pork yourself or have your local farmer or butcher grind it for you.

Caesar Can Chicken

Serves 4

Like many Canadians, we'll BBQ all year long—weather be damned. And one of our favourites is beer can chicken. So when we launched our Walter pre-mixed Caesar in a can, trying a Caesar can chicken seemed like a logical move. While a bit goofy-looking (a chicken perched upright with a can of Walter up its backside), this dish is easy to execute, fun to make, and always a crowd-pleaser. The bird gets dry roasted on the outside, yielding crispy skin, while the inside is treated to a Caesar steam bath, resulting in perfectly juicy chicken.

Caesar Can Chicken

1 can (any size) Walter pre-mixed
    Caesar
1 whole chicken (about 4 lb/
    1.8 kg)
Canola oil
2 Tbsp Walter Rim Spice

Caesar Pan Gravy (optional)

1 Tbsp all-purpose flour
Pan drippings from chicken
Leftover Caesar mix from
    roasting can (about 5 to
    7 oz/150 to 210 ml)
3 to 4 Tbsp table (18%) cream
1 Tbsp finely chopped flat-leaf
    parsley

1. Begin by cracking open a can of Walter Caesar Pre-Mixed Cocktail and heating up the BBQ to 375°F (190°C). Alternatively, you can preheat the oven to 425°F (220°C).

2. Empty half of the Caesar into a glass full of ice for yourself to enjoy as you cook and then place the half-full can in the middle of a 10-inch (25 cm) cast iron skillet. (Note: if the Walter can has a shrink sleeve, remove it, as it isn't heat-safe.)

3. Pat the chicken dry, then rub oil all over it. Season the chicken inside and out with the rim spice. Use the entire quantity of spice to coat all the nooks and crannies.

4. With the open end of the seasoned chicken facing down, shimmy the bird right down on top of the Caesar can so it's stable and sitting upright in the skillet. Tuck the wingtips behind the chicken's back to keep them from getting too crispy.

5. Place the skillet on the BBQ on indirect medium heat (meaning, turn off the burners directly under the chicken) and let the chicken roast for 1¼ to 1½ hours with the lid closed. Alternatively, pop the skillet in the oven and roast for 1 to 1¼ hours. The chicken is done when the juices run clear or an instant read thermometer inserted into the thickest part of the thigh (not touching bone) reaches 165°F (75°C).

6. Remove the skillet from the BBQ or oven and then, using heavy-duty tongs, remove the chicken from the can and place it on a cutting board. Be careful: the can and liquid inside will be hot. Let the chicken rest for 10 minutes to allow the juices to distribute. If you intend to make pan gravy, this is the time, so save the roasting can and its contents, otherwise discard. Don't clean your skillet. If gravy isn't on the menu, simply rest the chicken, then slice and serve that tasty bird.

– recipe continues

7. Optional: While the chicken is resting you have exactly 10 minutes to whip up an umami-laced, rich, and tangy pan gravy to accompany the chicken using only a couple of extra ingredients. Donning an oven mitt, place the skillet on the stove over medium-high heat. Create a roux by whisking the flour into the drippings, scraping up any residual flavourful bits from the bottom of the pan. Cook, stirring often, until it begins to smell nutty and starts to brown, 2 minutes.

8. Whisking constantly, very slowly pour the remaining warm Caesar mix from the roasting can into the roux to create a smooth gravy. Bring to a simmer and cook for 3 minutes to thicken, stirring often. Whisk in the cream until your desired taste and viscosity have been achieved. Simmer the gravy for 1 more minute, stir in the parsley, and then serve alongside the roast chicken.

Note: Our Walter Rim Spice also makes a great dry rub for oven-baked chicken wings. Simply toss some wings in olive oil and then season generously with rim spice. Bake at 425°F (220°C) for 30 to 40 minutes, flipping once, until the internal temperature reaches 165°F (75°C) and the wings are deeply golden and crispy.

Spaghetti Alle Vongole

Recipe by Joan Chell
Calgary, Alberta

Serves 4

From conversations with Walter Chell's daughter, Joan, we got a clear sense that her dad was passionate about not just drinks but also food—and he was an exemplary cook in his own right. As an homage to Walter and the dish that inspired the Caesar, we worked with Joan to craft this updated take on the original Chell family Vongole recipe that she told us they would often make with whatever pasta they had on hand. You'll find this is a dish that goes well beyond nostalgia. This pasta is equal parts elegant and comforting, made with just a few choice ingredients.

2¾ lb (1.25 kg) small BC Manila clams
1 lb (450 g) dried spaghetti (or pasta of choice)
½ cup (120 ml) extra virgin olive oil + more for serving
3 cloves garlic, minced
½ tsp crushed pepperoncino + more for serving (optional)
Sea salt and ground black pepper
½ cup (120 ml) dry white wine
2 cups (480 ml) cherry tomatoes, halved
2 Tbsp chopped flat-leaf parsley + 2 Tbsp whole parsley leaves, divided

For Serving
Crusty bread

1. Soak the clams in fresh cold water for 20 minutes, scrubbing off any residual dirt or sand. Discard any with broken shells or that don't open when tapped.
2. Meanwhile, bring a large pot of salted water to a boil over high heat for the pasta. Cook the pasta for 1 to 2 minutes less than the package directions say. The pasta should be slightly underdone when it's added to the sauce so everything finishes cooking together.
3. Place a large saucepan over high heat. When the pasta has about 5 minutes left to cook, it's time to get the clams rolling. Place the oil, garlic, pepperoncino, and a good pinch of salt and pepper in the hot pan. Cook until the garlic is fragrant but not browned, about 1 minute. Add the clams and then the wine.
4. Promptly cover the saucepan with a lid to trap the steam and continuously shake it so the clams cook evenly. The clams will start to open after 3 to 4 minutes. Add the tomatoes and chopped parsley when the clams have just opened. Continue cooking just to soften the tomatoes and heat them through, about 1 minute. Turn the heat to low and discard any clams that are still shut tight.
5. At this point, the pasta should be ready. Drain the nearly cooked spaghetti, reserving ¼ cup (60 ml) of the pasta water.
6. Toss the spaghetti with the clams and tomatoes, allowing the noodles to nestle into the delicate sauce to cook to a perfect al dente, 1 to 2 minutes. Add some of the reserved pasta water if the noodles seem dry. Adjust the salt and pepper to taste.
7. To finish, give the whole parsley leaves a rough tear and fold them into the spaghetti along with a splash of olive oil and sprinkle of extra pepperoncino if desired. Serve immediately. Nice with some crusty bread for soaking up any extra sauce.

Central

While the recipes in this book offer glimpses into many of the country's smaller towns, resort areas, and more remote locations, at heart we're city kids. We love the energy, noise, and diversity of Canada's urban centres. Zack is based in Toronto and Aaron in Vancouver, and our favourite Walter-related travel destination is Montréal. It feels a universe apart from Toronto and Vancouver, and also happens to have more restaurants per capita than anywhere in North America after New York. Damn good restaurants—where the chefs are highly skilled and international in their influences, and work at their craft unapologetically, with an enviable sense of confidence in themselves, no matter what they're doing.

Anyone who's been to Montréal will agree that eating and drinking there is unlike dining anywhere else, not only in Canada but in the world. There's just something about the way Montrealers pride themselves on loving the things that they love. It borders on obsessive. You walk down a cobblestoned street in Old Montréal and you can feel the deep pride in the city's place, culture, and history. It's a pride that permeates the food and drink culture; a bagel seems to mean so much more to a Montrealer than to someone in any other town or city in Canada. And of course, in a place where so many foods are synonymous with the city itself, there are the endless nuanced and passionate debates about who in Montréal does which iconic Montréal thing best: St-Viateur or Fairmount for bagels? Lester's, Snowdon, or Schwartz's for smoked meat? Want your all-dressed hot dog steamé or toasté? And on and on until the end of time. (For the record, our position is St-Viateur, Lester's, toasté—we look forward to your letters).

We're reminded of that Montréal pride—bordering on obsession—anytime we visit Maison Publique in the Plateau. It's a relatively small place, simple and unassuming, with a long bar you notice as soon as you enter, gorgeously weathered wallpaper, patinaed wood-panelled walls, and a tin ceiling, all of which produce a homey atmosphere that makes it feel like a mix of English gastropub and French bistro. You walk in and you just feel warm. The affable, passionate manager, Félix, comes to greet us warmly. Chef Derek's welcome is equally warm. We don't ever order. Felix: "So I'll just start bringing stuff, oui? Oh, and I think you should have the Welsh rarebit. And you will." And so we do. He'll just keep bringing us round after round of food and drink, each one better than the last. At some point, we'll call mercy and then only one or two more things get sent our way.

We could easily have painted the same scene at any number of Montréal institutions where we've felt that same spirit of generosity and exuberance on equally memorable nights—from Chuck Hughes' raucous and delightful Garde Manger to Joe Beef or any one of Frédéric Morin and David McMillan's other spots, where the food and drink on offer reflect the histories of the neighbourhoods so respectfully and suit the needs of the local clientele so skilfully.

The recipes in this section strive to give some sense of the pride of place and culture felt not only in Montréal but across all of Central Canada, which, let's not forget, also includes the globally renowned restaurant city of Toronto, as well as emerging hotspots such as Prince Edward County and others. In the pages that follow you'll witness, for instance, the clam mastery of Bronwen Clark of Toronto's legendary Rodney's Oyster House, an innovative non-alcoholic plant-based Caesar celebrating Ontario's brief but beautiful growing season from Sarah Parniak, and Ottawa chef Stephen La Salle's recipe for a Caesar inspired by our nation's capital, complete with ketchup chip rim.

Cabane à Sucre

Serves 1

Glassware
1 rocks glass

Rim
2 Tbsp flaked sea salt
1 lemon wedge

Cocktail
1 oz (30 ml) gin
½ tsp Pernod (see note)
5 oz (150 ml) Caesar mix, Classic
1 tsp Sugar Pie Syrup (page 298)

Garnish
1 Maple Snow Taffy (page 279)

If you grew up in Québec or Ontario, chances are you took at least one field trip (likely more) out to sugar shack country to see the maple trees getting tapped. No such outing was complete without the quintessentially Canadian experience of making maple taffy lollipops in the snow. In this recipe we use them as a sweet garnish—hard frozen lollipops that yield to soft, chewy, delightful taffy as they warm in your mouth—to complement the botanicals from the gin while the Pernod brings a fragrant and addicting anisette candy subtlety behind each sip. We hope this garnish proves to be a gateway to nostalgia or a whole new, very Canadian experience.

1. Pour the salt onto a small plate. Circle the rim of your glass with the lemon wedge, then roll the rim in the salt.
2. Add the gin, Pernod, Caesar mix, and syrup to a cocktail shaker (or other mixing vessel). Fill the shaker with ice to just above the top of the liquid and stir with a bar spoon until the outside of the shaker is very cold to the touch.
3. Fill the rimmed glass three-quarters full with fresh crushed ice. Strain the contents of shaker into the glass and top with additional ice if desired. Garnish with the taffy.

Note: Pernod is an anise-flavoured French liqueur with a distinctive licorice flavour. Traditionally found in many bouillabaisse recipes, it pairs beautifully with seafood, which is why we find it works really well in a Caesar. It has a very distinct flavour, though, so it's best used in moderation.

Quahog

Cocktail by Bronwen Clark
Rodney's Oyster House
Toronto, Ontario

Serves 1

Glassware
1 Mason jar

If you've visited an oyster bar in Canada at any time in the past quarter century, chances are that it was influenced in some way by the original Rodney's Oyster House, opened more than three decades ago when PEI-born Rodney Clark brought some of the Maritimes to the heart of Toronto. Rodney's daughter, Bronwen Clark, also knows her bivalves—she now runs the family business. "When we at Rodney's think of Caesars, we actually think first of freshly shucked clams," she told us when sharing this recipe. "'Quahog' is Mi'qmak for 'hard shell,' and that's exactly the type of clam this recipe calls for. Littlenecks, Cherrystones, Bull, Topnecks, or Countnecks: all come from the Quahog family, drawn from East Coast Canadian waters."

Rim
2 Tbsp Lemon Dust Rim
    (page 289)
1 lemon wedge

Garnish
8 live littleneck clams
1 tsp Rodney's Back from Hell
    Hot Sauce (page 297) (or any
    scotch bonnet pepper sauce)
½ tsp lemon juice
1 bull quahog shell (to hold the
    clams)
1 thumb peeled fresh
    horseradish, grated

Cocktail
1½ oz (45 ml) vodka (ideally
    Iceberg)
6 oz (180 ml) Caesar mix, Classic
5 dashes Worcestershire sauce
1 oz (30 ml) lemon juice
½ oz (15 ml) fresh clam liquor,
    from the clams

1. Pour the lemon dust rim onto a small plate. Circle the rim of your Mason jar with a lemon wedge, then roll the rim in the rim spice.
2. Shuck the clams and place them in a fine-mesh strainer set over a small bowl to catch the clam "liquor." Pour the liquor through a fine-mesh strainer again to catch any sand or grit, then set the liquor aside. Check the clam meat to be sure you have removed any grit or shell.
3. In a bowl, mix together the clam meat, hot sauce, and ½ tsp of lemon juice. Stir gently until the clam meat is well coated. Try to keep the pieces of meat intact. Leave to marinate at room temperature while you prep the rest of your cocktail.
4. Pour the vodka, Caesar mix, Worcestershire sauce, lemon juice, and reserved clam liquor into a cocktail shaker (or other mixing vessel). Fill the shaker with ice to just above the top of the liquid and stir with a bar spoon until the outside of the shaker is very cold to the touch.
5. Fill the rimmed Mason jar three-quarters full with fresh crushed ice. (If you don't have crushed ice, you can smash regular cubed ice in a tea towel to crush it.) Strain the contents of the shaker into the glass and top with additional ice if desired.
6. Garnish the cocktail with the clam shell. It will sit over the top of the mouth of the Mason jar. Spoon your marinated clams into the shell and top with the horseradish. If you can't get your hands on a large quahog shell, you can put your clam mixture in a 2 oz (60 ml) shot glass and serve beside your Caesar. Serve with a long wooden skewer or a cocktail fork.
7. You can also dump your marinated clams into the drink before taking your first sip, but be sure to use your skewer as you make your way through your beverage.

Tomato Water Last Word

Serves 1

Glassware
1 coupe, chilled

The Last Word is one of the great classic cocktails of the 20th century. Invented in Detroit during the Prohibition era, there is likely a Canadian connection, since bootlegged booze from across the border almost certainly featured in the original incarnation. The drink was re-popularized in the 21st century thanks in large part to the Zig Zag Café in Seattle (just a couple of hours' drive from Vancouver down the I5), where we've had the pleasure of enjoying a few. In our version, which was inspired by our pal Nick Paton, we replace the traditional maraschino liqueur with fresh tomato water. The brightness of the tomato water complements the sweet slightly vegetal notes from the Green Chartreuse and the botanicals offered by the gin. And side note: tomato water is easy to make, but it does need to be prepped at least 24 hours in advance, so plan ahead.

Cocktail
1 oz (30 ml) gin
1 oz (30 ml) Green Chartreuse
2 oz (60 ml) Tomato Water
    (page 299)
½ oz (15 ml) lime juice, finely
    strained
2 tsp clam juice (page 71 or
    store-bought)

Garnish
1 cherry tomato, on a skewer

1. Pour the gin, Chartreuse, tomato water, lime juice, and clam juice into a cocktail shaker. Fill the shaker with cubed ice to just above the top of the liquid and shake vigorously until well chilled.
2. Strain the contents of the shaker into the chilled glass and garnish with the skewer.

Garde Manger

Cocktail by Jess Midlash &
Chuck Hughes

Garde Manger

Montréal, Québec

Serves 1

Glassware

1 highball glass

June 2006, opening night of Garde Manger in cobblestoned Old Montréal. For partners Chuck and Tim and their team, tensions are high, the scene is hectic, nerves are frayed—in other words, the standard chaos experienced by restaurateurs on opening night since the beginning of time. Mid-evening, Tim (holding down the bar), gets a request for a Caesar and realizes they don't yet have one on their carefully crafted cocktail list, so he quickly puts one together. But what to use for garnish? He runs over to the packed raw bar, grabs a Gaspé steamed crab claw, and plunks it into the drink. From the kitchen, Chef Chuck watches. He realizes they have a classic in the making. The Garde Manger Caesar has evolved over the years as other team members (most recently GM Jess Midlash) put their marks on it, but one thing has remained constant: a single enticing piece of crab poking out from the top of an expertly crafted cocktail—a nod to that chaotic opening night thousands of Caesars ago.

Garnish

1 snow crab leg (or claw), thawed
   overnight in the refrigerator
   (see note)
1 lemon wedge

Rim

2 Tbsp Celeriac Rim (page 287)
1 lemon wedge

Cocktail

1½ oz (45 ml) vodka
6 oz (180 ml) Caesar mix, Mild
1 tsp freshly grated horseradish
¼ oz (7.5 ml) olive brine
3 to 4 dashes Chuck Hughes
   Jalapeño Hot Sauce
   (see note)
3 dashes Worcestershire sauce

1. Carefully run a sharp paring knife through one side of the snow crab leg or claw to score the shell and allow easier access to the meat. Garde Manger serves its Caesar with crab crackers and forks. Guests are expected to work for it!

2. Pour the rim spice onto a small plate. Circle the rim of your glass with the lemon wedge, then roll the rim in the rim spice.

3. Pour the vodka, Caesar mix, horseradish, olive brine, hot sauce, and Worcestershire sauce into a cocktail shaker (or other mixing vessel). Fill the shaker with ice to just above the top of the liquid and stir with a bar spoon until the outside of the shaker is very cold to the touch.

4. Fill the rimmed glass three-quarters full with fresh cubed ice. Strain the contents of the shaker into the glass and top with additional ice if desired. Garnish with the snow crab leg (or claw) and the remaining lemon wedge.

Notes: 1) The hot sauce in this recipe is Chuck Hughes' own brand. You can find it online and at specialty grocers. It's similar in style to green Tabasco. 2) In Canada, snow crabs are typically caught, cooked, and blast frozen right on the boat to preserve their freshness. Look for them at your local fishmonger or in the seafood section of your grocery store. In a pinch, you can thaw the crab quickly by running it under cold water for 20 minutes.

Rebuttal

Serves 1

Glassware
1 rocks glass

Rim
2 Tbsp kosher salt
1 Tbsp Honey Syrup (page 295)

Cocktail
1 oz (30 ml) vodka
5 oz (150 ml) Caesar mix, Classic
1 tsp lemon juice
1 tsp lime juice
1 tsp orange juice
1 tsp grapefruit juice
1 tsp Honey Syrup (page 295)

Garnish
2 Dehydrated Citrus Wheels
    (page 276), made with the
    citrus of your choice

There are some self-proclaimed Caesar purists who'll tell you the only citrus fruit that belongs in a Caesar is lime. We disagree. To make our case, we've used four different citrus fruits (lemon, lime, orange, and grapefruit) in this cocktail. Each one lends something slightly different to the equation and, when balanced with a good dose of honey, the end result is a bright, sunshiny Caesar—and bonus, it packs a heavy dose of vitamin C.

1. Pour the salt onto a small plate. Drizzle the honey syrup onto a separate plate (the pool of honey syrup should be at least as wide as your glass). Dip the rim of your glass in the honey syrup, allow any excess to drip back onto the plate, and then roll the rim in the salt.
2. Pour the vodka, Caesar mix, lemon juice, lime juice, orange juice, grapefruit juice, and honey syrup into a cocktail shaker (or other mixing vessel). Fill the shaker with ice to just above the top of the liquid and stir with a bar spoon until the outside of the shaker is very cold to the touch.
3. Fill the rimmed glass three-quarters full with fresh cubed ice. Strain the contents of the shaker into the glass and top with additional ice if desired. Garnish with the citrus wheels.

Vegeta

Cocktail by Julien Vézina

Honō Izakaya

Québec City, Québec

Serves 1

Glassware

1 Collins glass

Rim

2 Tbsp Roasted Rice Rim
    (page 290)

1 lime wedge

Cocktail

¾ oz (22.5 ml) gin (ideally Nikka
    Coffey Gin)

5 oz (150 ml) Caesar mix, Classic

1 tsp Tare (page 298)

1 tsp sriracha

½ Tbsp Worcestershire sauce

Garnish

6 to 8 Taro Chips (page 286)

1 Dehydrated Citrus Wheel
    (page 276), made with lime

We think this is probably the only Caesar in existence named for the cold-blooded warrior Vegeta from the Japanese manga *Dragon Ball*. Julien, co-owner of Honō Izakaya, Québec City's first proper izakaya, offers a simple explanation for the name: "The garnish looks like his hair." Fair enough. Name and garnish aesthetics aside, this low-alcohol cocktail is a beauty, making expert use of carefully considered Japanese ingredients—Nikka Coffey gin, tare marinade, togarashi, dashi, and taro chips, among others.

1. Pour the rim spice onto a small plate. Circle the rim of your glass with the lime wedge, then roll the rim in the rim spice.
2. Pour the gin, Caesar mix, tare, sriracha, and Worcestershire sauce into a cocktail shaker (or other mixing vessel). Fill the shaker with ice to just above the top of the liquid and stir with a bar spoon until the outside of the shaker is very cold to the touch.
3. Fill the rimmed glass three-quarters full with fresh cubed ice. Strain the contents of the shaker into the glass and top with additional ice if desired. Garnish with the taro chips and the lime wheel.

K-Pop

Serves 1

Glassware
1 rocks glass

Rim
2 Tbsp K-Pop Rim (page 289)
1 lime wedge

Cocktail
1 oz (30 ml) tequila
¼ cup (60 ml) kimchi
½ tsp gochujang (see note)
5 oz (150 ml) Caesar mix, Mild

Garnish
2 or 3 Tteokbokki (page 286), on
    a skewer (see note)
1 lime wedge

We eat out quite a bit and tell ourselves it's "research." Canada has lots of amazing food neighbourhoods, and while we've had the chance to check out many of them over the years, we find ourselves coming back time and again to Toronto's Koreatown, a great strip of restaurants along Bloor Street West (RIP Honest Ed's). It was here, over a meal of spicy kimchi Jjagae (kimchi stew), tteokbokki (soft rice cakes in a spicy gochujang sauce), and banchan (Korean side dishes), when the obvious hit: these spicy, deep flavours would make for an excellent Caesar cocktail. This is that cocktail, and it is excellent—and spicy and deep. The research paid off.

1. Pour the rim spice onto a small plate. Circle the rim of your glass with the lime wedge, then roll the rim in the rim spice.
2. Add the tequila, kimchi, and gochujang to a cocktail shaker (or other mixing vessel). Using a muddler, muddle everything together. Don't over-muddle. You want to extract the flavours from the kimchi but not shred it into pieces.
3. Add the Caesar mix to the shaker. Fill the shaker with ice to just above the top of the liquid and stir with a bar spoon until the outside of the shaker is very cold to the touch.
4. Fill the rimmed glass three-quarters full with fresh cubed ice. Strain the contents of the shaker into the glass and top with additional ice if desired. Garnish with the warm skewered tteokbokki and lime wedge.

Notes: 1) Gochujang is a fermented Korean red chili paste that is sweet and savoury and packs some kick. It can be found at most Asian markets or, if you're lucky, the specialty aisle of your local grocery store. 2) The tteokbokki garnish in this recipe comes without the spicy gochujang sauce it is almost always served with. In this instance, it's meant to be dunked into the Caesar, where gochujang and kimchi flavours abound, thereby referencing the traditional preparation.

Garden

This non-alcoholic, plant-based Caesar by drinks and travel writer Sarah Parniak celebrates Ontario's bountiful growing season. She was inspired by childhood memories of summer afternoons spent wandering through her family's generous garden plot, snacking on sun-warmed veggies. "I love this Caesar's simplicity," she says. "To me, the best drinks are made from quality ingredients that have ample room to breathe and shine through." Here, the fresh, verdant notes of Seedlip Garden (a non-alcoholic spirit with distilled botanicals like sweet peas, herbs, and hops) complements the piquancy of the Caesar mix. Everything is tied together by an herbal snap from the infused vinegar, a bit of heat, and a hit of citrusy umami.

Cocktail by Sarah Parniak
Toronto, Ontario

Serves 1

Glassware
1 chalice

Rim
2 Tbsp Lemon Pepper Sea Salt
    (page 290)
1 lemon wedge

Cocktail
2 oz (60 ml) Seedlip Garden 108
4 oz (120 ml) Caesar mix, Vegan
1 tsp Herb-Infused White Wine
    Vinegar (page 295)
1 dash Cholula green pepper
    sauce
Pinch Lemon Pepper Sea Salt
    (page 290)

Garnish
Seasonal garden veggies (like
    heirloom cherry tomatoes,
    snap peas, and cucumbers),
    on a skewer
1 Castelvetrano olive, pitted, on
    a skewer
1 lemon twist

1. Pour the lemon pepper sea salt onto a small plate. Circle the rim of the glass with the lemon wedge, then roll the rim in the salt.
2. Add the Seedlip Garden 108, Caesar mix, vinegar, green pepper sauce, and a pinch of lemon pepper sea salt to a cocktail shaker and gently "roll" all the ingredients from the shaker to a second mixing vessel, back and forth, to mix. Fill the shaker with ice to just above the top of the liquid and roll again to chill until the outside of the shaker is very cold to the touch.
3. Fill the rimmed glass three-quarters full with fresh cubed ice. Strain the contents of the shaker into the glass and top with additional ice if desired. Garnish with the two skewers and the lemon twist.

Eye of the Tiger

Serves 4

Glassware
4 double shot glasses (each
    2 oz/60 ml)

Garnish
4 eggs

Cocktail
3 oz (90 ml) vodka
3 oz (90 ml) Caesar mix, Classic
½ oz (15 ml) hot sauce
1 tsp lemon juice
5 turns cracked black pepper

Our good buddy Chris Frankowski likes to call the Caesar "The Evening Mixer and the Morning Fixer." We designed this recipe with the *fixer* part in mind. We make this pretty spicy to fight the previous evening's demons with a little fire of our own.

1. Bring a small pot of water to a hard boil and prepare an ice bath. Coddle the eggs by placing them in the boiling water for 1 minute, then submerging immediately in the ice bath. (See safety note on page 55.) Once they're cool, shell them, remove the yolks and place each yolk on 4 spoons. Set aside for garnish.

2. Add the vodka, Caesar mix, hot sauce, lemon juice, and pepper to a cocktail shaker (or other mixing vessel). Fill the shaker with ice to just above the top of the liquid and stir with a bar spoon until the outside of the shaker is very cold to the touch.

3. Strain the contents of the shaker equally into the four shot glasses. Garnish each shooter with an egg yolk on a spoon. Drop the egg yolk into the shot glass and down the whole lot in one gulp. Conquer the world. (Substitution: take Tylenol, have a nap.)

The Diplomat

Cocktail by Stephen La Salle
Ottawa, Ontario

Serves 1

Glassware
1 Collins glass

Rim
2 Tbsp Ketchup Chip Rim
    (page 289)
1 lemon wedge

Cocktail
1 oz (30 ml) vodka
8 oz (240 ml) Caesar mix, Classic
¼ oz (7.5 ml) lemon juice
4 dashes hot sauce
4 dashes Worcestershire sauce

Garnish
1 large ketchup chip
1 piece Roasted Dulse
    (page 284)
1 celery stalk, trimmed

If it were up to us, we'd have Parliament move to name Chef Stephen La Salle an ambassador. He's already doing the job unofficially, welcoming visitors from around the world to the capital with his disarming Canadian charm and very Canadian food and drink. He talks proudly about Ottawa as a place of confluence: a place where three rivers meet, a place where Ontario borders Québec, and a place where so much energy is devoted to helping people from across the country and farther afield come together to try to solve the problems of the day. So it's fitting that Stephen should suggest a drink with a ketchup chip rim (a delight for Canadians, a surprise for the uninitiated) and seasoning that evokes the flavours of Montréal steak spice, offset by a traditional base and a simple garnish. A bit of diplomacy in a glass.

1. Pour the rim spice onto a small plate. Circle the rim of your glass with the lemon wedge, then roll the rim in the rim spice.
2. Pour the vodka, Caesar mix, lemon juice, hot sauce, and Worcestershire sauce in a cocktail shaker (or other mixing vessel). Fill the shaker with ice to just above the top of the liquid and stir with a bar spoon until the outside of the shaker is very cold to the touch.
3. Fill the rimmed glass three-quarters full with fresh cubed ice. Strain the contents of the shaker into the glass and top with additional ice if desired. Garnish with the biggest ketchup chip you can find, the piece of roasted dulse, both resting on the rim, and the celery stalk.

Oaxaca

Serves 1

Glassware
1 Collins glass

Around 2007, Phil Ward of New York's Death & Co introduced the Oaxaca Old-Fashioned, one of the finest drinks to come out of the modern cocktail movement. It was also a major contributor to making mezcal—once a relatively rare item outside of Mexico—a must-have in bars around the world. The genius of the Oaxaca Old-Fashioned lies in the mixing of tequila and mezcal and then using them in a surprising way to completely reimagine a classic cocktail. Through our own experimentation we've found that amplifying that tequila-mezcal combination with some pineapple juice yields an equally surprising and delicious result. With a nod to Phil and the crew at Death & Co, here's our Oaxaca Caesar.

Rim
2 Tbsp kosher salt
1 lime wedge

Cocktail
1 oz (30 ml) tequila blanco
¼ oz (7.5 ml) mezcal joven
5 oz (150 ml) Caesar mix, Extra
    Spicy
½ oz (15 ml) pineapple juice
    (fresh or canned)
½ tsp lime juice

Garnish
1 Grilled Pineapple Skewer
    (page 277)

1. Pour the salt onto a small plate. Circle the rim of your glass with the lime wedge, then roll the rim in the salt.
2. Pour the tequila, mezcal, Caesar mix, pineapple juice, and lime juice into a cocktail shaker (or other mixing vessel). Fill the shaker with ice to just above the top of the liquid and stir with a bar spoon until the outside of the shaker is very cold to the touch.
3. Fill the rimmed glass three-quarters full with fresh cubed ice. Strain the contents of the shaker into the glass and top with additional ice if desired. Garnish with the pineapple skewer.

Bingo

Cocktail by Trevor Burnett
Toronto, Ontario

Serves 1

Glassware
1 highball glass

Garnish
2 pieces Roasted Duck Sausage
(page 284)
1 lemon wedge

Rim
2 Tbsp Bingo Rim (page 287)
1 lemon wedge

Cocktail
1 oz (30 ml) Duck Fat Washed
Gin (page 301)
4 oz (120 ml) Caesar mix, Smoky
Maple
1 tsp lemon juice

A true bon vivant, Trevor Burnett works tirelessly to advance the cocktail culture here in Canada through his many lectures, tastings, and (really fun) parties. He's the architect of The Incredible Project Drink Chariot, a mobile cocktail unit that brings some of that fun wherever it's needed. His Boozy Bingo pop-up nights are something to behold, as is the exquisitely tailored gold sequined blazer he dons while doing his duty as bingo caller. Unsurprising then, that Trevor's recipe is distinctive and delicious, and employs a bit of fancy cocktail-making technique to boot. If you're already familiar with fat washing, you'll likely know this Caesar is not one to be missed. And if you're new to the concept, give it a go—Trevor has you covered here.

1. Place the sausage on a parchment-lined baking sheet under the broiler on high until reheated and slightly caramelized, 3 to 5 minutes. Watch closely so it doesn't burn. Remove from the oven and slice into 2-inch (5 cm) pieces. Prepare a skewer with the duck sausage and set aside.

2. Pour the rim spice onto a small plate. Circle the rim of your glass with the lemon wedge, then roll the rim in the rim spice.

3. Pour the gin, Caesar mix, and lemon juice into a cocktail shaker (or other mixing vessel). Fill the shaker with ice to just above the top of the liquid and stir with a bar spoon until the outside of the shaker is very cold to the touch.

4. Fill the rimmed glass three-quarters full with fresh cubed ice. Strain the contents of the shaker into the glass and top with additional ice if desired. Garnish with the skewer and lemon wedge.

Untitled (The Amaro One)

Serves 1

Glassware
1 rocks glass

As we discussed at length in Nerding Out (pages 16 to 55), when we're creating well-balanced cocktails we're always looking for ways to heighten the tension between our various flavours with the goal of making something as exciting and unexpected as it is comforting and easy to drink. This cocktail, perhaps more than any other in the book, pushes the envelope of bitterness, with the addition of just ¼ oz (7.5 ml) of amaro (the catch-all name for bittersweet Italian digestifs). We're using Montenegro because we like its distinctive hints of orange peel, coriander, and nutmeg, but any good quality amaro would do nicely. The bracing herbal notes are balanced out through the use of two sweeter spirits: pisco, distilled from grapes, and rum, from sugar cane. A healthy amount of sour lemon juice ties it all together. If you are a Negroni drinker, this Caesar should be right up your alley. Serve it super cold and well stirred, as the cocktail benefits greatly from the additional dilution.

Rim
2 Tbsp kosher salt
1 lemon wedge

Cocktail
½ oz (15 ml) pisco
½ oz (15 ml) white rum
¼ oz (7.5 ml) amaro (ideally
    Montenegro)
5 oz (150 ml) Caesar mix, Classic
½ oz (15 ml) lemon juice

Garnish
2 or 3 Quick-Pickled Pearl Onions
    (page 283), on a skewer

1. Pour the salt onto a small plate. Circle the rim of your glass with the lemon wedge, then roll the rim in the salt.
2. Pour the pisco, rum, amaro, Caesar mix, and lemon juice into a cocktail shaker (or other mixing vessel). Fill the shaker with ice to just above the top of the liquid and stir with a bar spoon until the outside of the shaker is very cold to the touch.
3. Fill the rimmed glass three-quarters full with fresh cubed ice. Strain the contents of the shaker into the glass and top with additional ice if desired. Garnish with the skewer.

The Fed

Cocktail by Zach Slootsky
The Federal
Toronto, Ontario

Serves 1

Glassware
1 rocks glass

Rim
2 Tbsp Fed Rim (page 288)
1 lemon wedge

Cocktail
1 oz (30 ml) vodka
4 oz (120 ml) Caesar mix, Mild
¼ oz (7.5 ml) pickle brine (from
    gherkins)
¼ oz (7.5 ml) lemon juice
½ oz (15 ml) Worcestershire
    sauce
4 dashes Marie Sharp's Original
    Hot Habanero Pepper Sauce
    (see note)
1 dash Maggi Liquid Seasoning
    (see note on page 142)

Garnish
2 or 3 gherkins, on a skewer
1 Cool Ranch Dorito
1 tsp freshly grated horseradish
1 lemon wedge

We hope you're lucky enough to have a place like The Federal near you. A few dozen tables, a few seats at the bar, and just the right amount of noise coming from the speakers, the chatter of other patrons, and the clinking of dishes and glasses. Every detail is carefully considered here, from the species of succulent in the planters to how they plate their omelettes for service. Their Caesar packs a pretty decent kick and uses a gherkin-and-Doritos garnish. As owner Zach Slootsky explains, "The Federal runs on three essentials: pickles, Cool Ranch Doritos, and the tears of our haters."

1. Pour the rim spice onto a small plate. Circle the rim of your glass with the lemon wedge, then roll the rim in the rim spice.
2. Pour the vodka, Caesar mix, pickle brine, lemon juice, Worcestershire sauce, hot sauce, and Maggi into a cocktail shaker (or other mixing vessel). Fill the shaker with ice to just above the top of the liquid and stir with a bar spoon until the outside of the shaker is very cold to the touch.
3. Fill the rimmed glass three-quarters full with fresh cubed ice. Strain the contents of the shaker into the glass and top with additional ice if desired. Garnish with the skewer, one single glorious Cool Ranch Dorito, freshly grated horseradish, and the lemon wedge.

Note: Marie Sharp's is a classic Caribbean hot sauce from Belize. Their Original Hot Habanero Pepper Sauce is made with red habanero peppers and carrots and is addictively sweet and spicy. It can be found online or in specialty stores.

Clam Bake!

Recipe by Nicole & Nathan Hynes
Sand and Pearl
Prince Edward County, Ontario

Serves 4 to 6

Our friends Nicole and Nathan are the owners of Sand and Pearl, an oyster bar and fish shack in Ontario's gorgeous Prince Edward County, known simply as The County to locals. Sand and Pearl is open from May to mid-October, which allows them to cook with the freshest seasonal ingredients. Out back in the restaurant's expansive yard, local bands play, yoga people do yoga, and the Sand and Pearl team cook over hot coals in their firepit, including this take on an old-fashioned clam bake. Repeat in your own backyard or at a campfire-friendly beach for a dose of summer County vibes. If you don't know how to build a campfire for cooking, you should probably learn—there's most likely someone on YouTube who can help.

Clam Bake

20 littleneck clams

2 lb (900 g) new potatoes, halved

1 Tbsp salt

1 Tbsp olive oil

1 red onion, roughly sliced

1 head garlic, cloves individually peeled and left whole

1 lb (450 g) pork sausage (approximately 2 to 4 links)

4 ears fresh Ontario corn, husked and quartered

1 lb (450 g) colossal shrimp, shell on (6/8 count)

2 lb (900 g) snow crab legs (ideally Fogo Island Fish)

12 cherry tomatoes

1 jalapeño, stemmed and sliced

¼ cup (60 ml) flat-leaf parsley, roughly chopped

1 cup (240 ml) unsalted butter, cubed

Clam Bake

1. Build a hot campfire set up with a large cooking grate. Alternately, preheat your BBQ to 500°F (260°C) or oven to 450°F (230°C).

2. Soak the clams in fresh cold water for 20 minutes. Scrub off any residual dirt or sand. Discard any clams with broken shells or that don't open when tapped.

3. Place the potatoes in a large pot of boiling water with the salt and parboil until almost cooked through (the tip of knife should go in with slight resistance), 10 to 15 minutes. Drain and set aside.

4. In a medium pan, warm the oil. Sauté the onions and garlic until softened, and set aside.

5. Preheat a skillet large enough to hold the whole sausages without crowding. Par-cook the sausages, no oil required, giving the links a nice sear on all sides but taking them off the heat before they are fully cooked, about 5 minutes. Cut each link into quarters widthwise.

6. In a large deep-sided roasting pan (approximately 12 × 20 inches/30 × 50 cm, or the biggest that will fit in your oven), start to build the clam bake in layers, spreading the ingredients evenly in the whole pan. Onions and garlic first, then the potatoes, sausage pieces, corn, shrimp, crab, clams, cherry tomatoes, jalapeño, and finally, the parsley.

7. Dot the top layer with the cubed butter and squeeze the lemon juice on top and toss the lemon halves in for extra flavour. Dust evenly with the rim spice. Pour the beer over the clam bake.

– recipe continues

4 lemons, halved

3 Tbsp Walter Rim Spice

16 fl oz (480 ml) lagered ale
(ideally Sweetgrass Golden
Ale)

Caesar Drawn Butter

1 cup (240 ml) unsalted butter

⅓ cup (80 ml) Caesar mix, Extra
Spicy

For Serving

1 loaf crusty bread

8. Cover with a lid, or tightly with aluminum foil, and cook according to the
following guidelines:
   - Approximately 20 minutes over a hot fire
   - Approximately 20 minutes in a 500°F (260°C) BBQ over direct heat
   - Approximately 25 minutes in a 450°F (230°C) oven

Caesar Drawn Butter

1. Melt the butter slowly in a small saucepan over medium heat until it begins
   to foam. Remove from the heat and set aside to cool for 10 minutes. This
   will separate the butter into three parts: foamy milk solids on top, clear
   butterfat in the middle (the good stuff), and watery whey on the bottom.

2. Once the butter has settled and cooled slightly, skim off and discard the
   foamy milk solids that have risen to the top. Carefully pour the golden
   clarified drawn butter into a fresh small saucepan. Pour slowly, being
   careful to leave behind and discard the white watery whey from the bottom
   of the original saucepan.

3. Whisk the Caesar mix into the drawn butter until well incorporated and
   keep warm until ready to serve.

Final Assembly

The clam bake is ready to take off the heat when the shrimp are pink, the
clams have opened, and the potatoes are fork-tender. Serve family-style with
individual dishes of warm Caesar drawn butter for dipping and crusty bread for
mopping up the juices.

Butter Baked Alaskan Cod

Recipe by David McMillan
Joe Beef
Montréal, Québec

Serves 4

Joe Beef is a Montréal institution. But you already know that. What you might not know is that Chef David is a veritable encyclopedia of Québécois food and drink. Which is why we asked if we could pick his brain while we were doing some research for this book. During our chat, in typical David fashion, he casually mentioned that he just so happens to have a recipe for a baked cod dish inspired by the Caesar cocktail's signature flavours, but with each of the components deconstructed. It should be noted here that David immediately added, "I hate the word 'deconstructed.'"

Fresh Caesar Coulis

1½ lb (680 g) plum tomatoes
1 tsp kosher salt
1 clove garlic, minced
2 Tbsp finely grated fresh horseradish
⅛ tsp celery salt
2 Tbsp extra virgin olive oil
1 Tbsp Worcestershire sauce
3 dashes Tabasco hot sauce
Cracked black pepper

Butter Baked Alaskan Cod

1 cup (240 ml) unsalted butter
4 portions (each 8 oz/225 g) fresh Alaskan cod, or a similar white fish
½ tsp Celery Salt (page 288 or store-bought)
Kosher salt and cracked black pepper

Fresh Caesar Coulis

1. To skin and seed the plum tomatoes, start by bringing a large pot of water to a boil and setting up an ice bath close by. Remove the stem of each tomato and, using a sharp knife, cut a shallow "x" through the skin on the bottom of each tomato. Place the tomatoes carefully into the boiling water until their skins just start to loosen, about 30 seconds, then remove and plunge immediately in the ice bath.
2. Peel off and discard the tomato skins. Cut each peeled tomato into quarters and then scrape out and discard the seeds. Roughly chop the remaining tomato flesh.
3. Place the chopped tomatoes in a fine-mesh strainer set over a bowl and sprinkle with the kosher salt. Allow the tomatoes to drain for 1 hour and discard (or enjoy) the resulting tomato water.
4. Blitz the tomato pulp in a blender until smooth, then add the garlic, horseradish, celery salt, oil, Worcestershire sauce, and hot sauce and give it another quick blitz just to combine. Adjust the flavouring levels to your preference, and season with salt and pepper to taste. This coulis should be kept at room temperature in the blender until ready to serve. Give it one more quick blitz in the blender before plating.

Butter Baked Alaskan Cod

1. Preheat your oven to 375°F (190°C).
2. Melt the butter and pour it into a shallow baking dish just large enough to accommodate all the fish portions comfortably (approximately 11 × 7 inches/ 28 × 18 cm). The butter should form a nice deep pool in which to place the fish.

– recipe continues

Celeriac Salad with Lemon Vinaigrette

1 lemon, juiced

2 Tbsp extra virgin olive oil

½ tsp Worcestershire sauce

Kosher salt and cracked black
    pepper

1 small (or ½ large) celeriac
    (celery root)

2 cups (480 ml) celery heart
    leaves (see note)

3. Pat the fish dry. Season both sides with the celery salt, kosher salt, and pepper. Place the fish in the melted butter. Spoon some melted butter over each piece before baking.

4. Cook the cod, basting once or twice again during the bake, until the flesh is opaque and flakes easily with a fork, 15 to 20 minutes. The cooking time will vary according to the thickness of the fish. The internal temperature of the fish should read between 140°F and 145°F (60°C and 63°C) on an instant read thermometer.

5. Baste with butter one last time right before serving.

Celeriac Salad with Lemon Vinaigrette

1. While the fish is in the oven, make the lemon vinaigrette by whisking together the lemon juice, oil, and Worcestershire sauce. Season with salt and pepper to taste.

2. Clean and trim the celeriac. Using a ribbon blade Microplane, shave about 2 cups' (480 ml) worth, so that it's in equal proportion to the celery leaves.

3. Toss the celery leaves and celeriac together. Lightly dress the salad with the vinaigrette right before serving.

Final Assembly

To plate the dish family-style, spoon the coulis into a nicely sized puddle in the base of a large platter before nestling in the butter-basted cod. Top each piece of fish with a tennis ball–size serving of celeriac salad and hit with an extra turn of freshly cracked black pepper.

Note: For celery leaves, pick the tender bright green leaves from the ribs in the heart of the celery.

Caesar Wedge Salad with Grilled Jerk Shrimp

Recipe by Craig Wong
Patois Restaurant & Bar
Mignonette
Toronto, Ontario

Serves 4

Born and raised in Scarborough after his parents emigrated from Jamaica, Chef Craig Wong draws from a variety of cuisines while respecting the ingredients he uses and cultures from which he draws inspiration. This ethos is in keeping with the rigorous training he received working at restaurants such as Alain Ducasse au Plaza Athénée and Heston Blumenthal's Fat Duck. Versatile chefs come up with versatile recipes. Chef Craig crafted this one with flexibility in mind, ideal for making outdoors on the grill while your friends pepper you with their various requests. "Feel free to swap the grilled chicken for shrimp," Craig advises. "Or cold soba noodles for lettuce." The core flavours can accommodate all sorts of quick changes on the fly using ingredients you happen to have on hand.

Jerk Seasoning
¼ cup (60 ml) light soy sauce
1½ tsp over-proof rum
1½ tsp ground pimento (allspice)
2 scotch bonnet peppers, stemmed
1½ bunches green onions
½ head garlic, cloves peeled
¼ cup (60 ml) chopped fresh pineapple
¼ cup (60 ml) sliced fresh ginger
5 sprigs thyme, leaves picked and chopped
2 tsp packed brown sugar
1½ tsp kosher salt
⅛ tsp freshly grated nutmeg

Jerk-Marinated Shrimp
1 lb (450 g) black tiger shrimp (16/20 count), peeled and deveined
¼ cup (60 ml) Jerk Seasoning

Jerk Seasoning

1.   Place the soy sauce and rum in a blender. Add the pimento, peppers, green onions, garlic, pineapple, ginger, thyme, sugar, salt, and nutmeg. Blitz until a smooth paste forms.

2.   Transfer to an airtight container and store in the refrigerator for up to 1 week.

Jerk-Marinated Shrimp

1.   Toss the shrimp and ¼ cup (60 ml) jerk seasoning in a medium bowl until the shrimp are evenly coated. Cover and marinate in the refrigerator for 1 to 4 hours.

Creamy Bloody Caesar Dressing

1.   Place the sour cream, Caesar mix, mayonnaise, vinegar, coriander seed, paprika, salt, and pepper in a medium bowl. Whisk until evenly incorporated. Adjust to taste with salt and pepper. Transfer to an airtight container and store in the refrigerator for up to 1 week.

– recipe continues

Creamy Bloody Caesar Dressing

1¼ cups (300 ml) sour cream

¾ cup (180 ml) Caesar mix, Classic

½ cup (120 ml) mayonnaise

1 Tbsp red wine vinegar

1 tsp ground coriander

1 tsp Spanish paprika

1 tsp kosher salt

½ tsp cracked black pepper

Wedge Salad with Grilled Jerk Shrimp

Canola oil

1 batch Jerk-Marinated Shrimp

Kosher salt

½ lemon

1 head iceberg lettuce, cut into four wedges and cored

3 red radishes, thinly sliced into rounds

½ head fennel, thinly sliced

½ to 1 batch Creamy Bloody Caesar Dressing

10 fennel fronds, picked

¼ cup (60 ml) fresh dill, picked

10 fresh mint leaves, roughly chopped

Wedge Salad with Grilled Jerk Shrimp

1. Once the shrimp are marinated, preheat your BBQ on high for 10 minutes and oil the grill.

2. Season the shrimp with a sprinkle of salt and place on the hot grill. Cook, turning occasionally, until the shrimp are just cooked through and well charred, 3 to 5 minutes. (Alternatively, you can cook them in a lightly oiled skillet or grill pan over medium-high heat.) Transfer the shrimp to a plate and top with a liberal squeeze of lemon juice.

3. To start building the salad, divide the iceberg lettuce wedges, radish, and fennel on to individual plates or arrange on a family-style platter. Pour the dressing over the wedges, ensuring it makes its way into all the small nooks and crannies between the lettuce leaves. Place the grilled shrimp on top of the lettuce and garnish with the fennel fronds, dill, and mint.

Cottage Burger with Caesar Ketchup and Jalapeño Dill Potatoes

Recipe by Lora Kirk
Little Chefs in the Garden
Kawartha Lakes, Ontario

Serves 4

When Chef Lora and her partner, Chef Lynn Crawford, think about Caesars, they think about weekends at the cottage, which means burgers. But don't be fooled into thinking this is just another burger. This is *the* burger. With patties made with beef, sausage, and parmesan cheese, and the addition of Caesar ketchup (a revelation), Lora builds on the classic bistro-style burger to create something altogether new and yet totally familiar. Not to mention a legendary potato salad recipe that will make you realize you never really knew what potato salad was supposed to taste like.

Cottage Burgers

1 lb (450 g) mild Italian sausage
    meat, removed from casings

1 lb (450 g) ground beef

1 clove garlic, finely minced

1 egg

¼ cup (60 ml) chopped flat-leaf
    parsley

½ cup (120 ml) grated parmesan
    cheese

½ cup (120 ml) bread crumbs

1 tsp kosher salt

1 tsp cracked black pepper

2 tsp Worcestershire sauce

½ tsp sriracha

Canola oil

Caesar Ketchup

1 cup (240 ml) Caesar mix, Classic

1 cup (240 ml) strained tomatoes
    (passata)

¼ cup (60 ml) balsamic vinegar

1 Tbsp packed brown sugar

¾ tsp kosher salt

Cottage Burgers

1. Place the sausage meat, ground beef, garlic, egg, parsley, parmesan, bread crumbs, salt, pepper, Worcestershire sauce, and sriracha in a medium bowl and gently mix it all together by hand. Try not to over-work the mixture or the burgers will be dense.
2. Form four 8 oz (225 g) patties, plate, cover, and refrigerate for at least 1 hour.

Caesar Ketchup

1. While the patties chill, combine the Caesar mix, strained tomatoes, balsamic, sugar, and salt in a medium pot over medium heat. Bring to a boil, stirring occasionally, and then turn the heat to low.
2. Simmer the mixture until reduced by half and nicely thickened, 25 to 35 minutes. Stir frequently to prevent burning.
3. Remove from the heat and let cool to room temperature. Store in an airtight container in the refrigerator for up to 2 weeks.

Pickled Jalapeño Dill Potato Salad

1. Place the halved potatoes in a large pot of cold, salted water. Bring to a boil over medium-high heat, turn the temperature to low, and simmer until the potatoes are fork-tender, 12 to 15 minutes. Drain the potatoes well and let cool for 10 minutes.

– recipe continues

Pickled Jalapeño Dill Potato Salad

2 lb (900 g) tri-coloured mini
  potatoes, halved

Salt (any type)

1 Tbsp extra virgin olive oil

1 Tbsp unsalted butter

2 small white onions, thinly
  sliced

2 Tbsp fresh thyme leaves

⅓ cup (80 ml) mayonnaise

⅓ cup (80 ml) chopped fresh dill

1 Tbsp finely chopped pickled
  jalapeños

1 Tbsp pickled jalapeño brine

1 Tbsp Walter Rim Spice

For Serving

Sliced provolone cheese

Butter lettuce leaves

Sliced pickles

Sliced tomatoes

Sliced sweet onion

4 toasted brioche buns

2. Meanwhile add the oil and butter to a medium skillet over medium-low heat. Once the butter is melted, add the onions and thyme. Cook, stirring occasionally, until the onions are golden brown, about 15 minutes. Transfer the onion mixture to a plate and let cool slightly.

3. In a large bowl, mix together the mayonnaise, dill, pickled jalapeños, and brine. Gently fold in the reserved potatoes and onion mixture, then season to taste with the rim spice.

Final Assembly

1. Heat your BBQ or grill pan on high heat and brush the burgers lightly with canola oil on both sides.

2. Grill the burgers, flipping minimally, until their internal temperature is 160°F (70°C), 10 to 12 minutes. The burgers should be nicely charred on the outside and no longer pink in the middle.

3. Set out burger toppings such as sliced provolone cheese, butter lettuce leaves, sliced pickles, sliced tomatoes, and sliced sweet onion on a serving tray. Tuck the burgers into toasted brioche buns, slather with Caesar ketchup, and finish with preferred toppings. Serve with the potato salad.

Clam Shack Shuka

**Recipe by Donna Dooher &
Megan DeHaas**
Mildred's Temple Kitchen
Toronto, Ontario

Serves 3 to 4

1 tsp ground cumin

½ tsp coriander seeds

¼ cup (60 ml) extra virgin olive oil

2 large yellow onions, sliced

2 red bell peppers, sliced into
    ¾-inch (2 cm) strips

2 yellow bell peppers, sliced into
    ¾-inch (2 cm) strips

6 ripe Roma tomatoes, roughly
    chopped

6 thyme sprigs, leaves picked
    and chopped

2 bay leaves

2 Tbsp chopped parsley

½ tsp saffron threads

Pinch cayenne pepper

Kosher salt and cracked black
    pepper

1 cup (240 ml) + ½ cup (120 ml)
    Caesar mix, Classic, divided

2 Tbsp honey

6 to 8 eggs

1 Tbsp cilantro, chopped

Mildred's Temple Kitchen, and its previous iteration Mildred Pierce, have been among Toronto's favourite brunch spots for over 30 years. Their legendary shakshuka has been our go-to brunch order for years. In this recipe, Donna and Megan have incorporated Caesar flavours into the classic North African/Middle Eastern dish of eggs poached in tomato sauce with peppers, onion, garlic, and spices. If you're like us, and the only thing you love more than brunch is Caesars at brunch, this dish is for you.

1. Place a 10- or 12-inch (25 or 30 cm) well-seasoned cast iron skillet in the oven and set the oven to preheat to 400°F (200°C).

2. In a separate small pan over medium heat, dry-roast the ground cumin and coriander seeds for 2 to 3 minutes, shaking the pan often to prevent the spices from burning. Remove from the heat.

3. Carefully remove the hot cast iron skillet from the oven and add the oil, onions, and bell peppers. Return the pan to the oven and roast until the vegetables begin to soften and take on some colour, 15 to 20 minutes.

4. Remove the skillet from the oven again and add the toasted spices, tomatoes, thyme, bay leaves, parsley, saffron, cayenne, salt, pepper, 1 cup (240 ml) of Caesar mix, and honey. Stir together.

5. At this point the vegetable mixture can either be returned to the oven (turn it down to 350°F/175°C) or transferred to the stovetop on medium-high heat.

6. Whether in the oven or on the stovetop, cook for approximately 45 minutes, stirring occasionally to prevent sticking. If it's starting to look a little dry, add up to ½ cup (120 ml) Caesar mix a couple of tablespoons at a time until the mixture has a pasta sauce–like consistency.

7. When your desired consistency is reached, remove from the heat and discard the bay leaves. Taste and adjust seasoning—it should be potent and flavourful. (This sauce component of the shakshuka can be done up to 2 days in advance, stored in the refrigerator in an airtight glass container, and warmed when needed. Just bring the sauce back to a simmer in the cast iron pan before proceeding to the next step.)

– recipe continues

For Serving

Sourdough bread

Salted butter, room temperature

8. Make six to eight gaps in the mixture and carefully break an egg into each one. Sprinkle each egg with salt and pepper and place the skillet back into the 350°F (175°C) oven for 10 to 12 minutes, or until the egg whites are just set but yolks are still runny. (If you opted to do step 6 on the stovetop, remember to preheat your oven for this step.)

9. Remove the pan from the oven and sprinkle the cilantro evenly over top. Serve alongside slices of toasted sourdough bread and butter.

Albacore Tuna Tostada

Recipe by Derek Dammann
Maison Publique
Montréal, Québec

Serves 6

Chef Derek Dammann is a real chef's chef. He opened his much-loved gastropub in the Plateau with business partner Jamie Oliver after they'd cooked together in London. But his roots are out West. He grew up in the small Vancouver Island town of Campbell River, self-proclaimed "Salmon Capital of the World." But when we started to talk about recipes for this book, he told us that lately his true obsession was Mexican cuisine and that he'd been making tuna tostadas nonstop. So he decided we needed a Caesar-inspired tostada. And here it is: a dish packed with fresh, bold flavours and contrasting textures. It also happens to pair perfectly with a Michelada (page 142).

Chipotle Mayonnaise
1 egg
1 Tbsp lime juice
1 clove garlic, minced
¼ cup (60 ml) chipotle peppers in adobo, chopped
½ tsp kosher salt
½ cup (120 ml) canola oil
Cracked black pepper
Adobo sauce (from the chipotles), to taste

Caesar Marinade
½ cup (120 ml) Caesar mix, Mild
½ cup (120 ml) white soy sauce (see note)
½ cup (120 ml) lime juice

Tuna Tostada
1 lb (450 g) albacore tuna, centre-cut
Kosher salt and cracked black pepper
Canola oil

Chipotle Mayonnaise

1. Bring a small pot of water to a hard boil and prepare an ice bath. Coddle the egg by placing it in the boiling water for 1 minute, then submerging it immediately in the ice bath. (See safety note on page 55.) Once cool, separate out the egg yolk to use in the mayo and discard the white (or set it aside for another use).
2. Using a mortar and pestle, pound the egg yolk, lime juice, garlic, chipotle peppers, and salt to a smooth paste.
3. Slowly drizzle in the oil, constantly whisking with the pestle until you have a smooth, emulsified mayonnaise.
4. Season to taste with salt and pepper, then stir in some of the adobo sauce from the chilies until you have your desired spice level. Store in an airtight container in the refrigerator for up to 4 days.

Caesar Marinade

1. Add the Caesar mix, soy sauce, and lime juice to a medium bowl and mix together. Set aside at room temperature.

Tuna Tostada

1. Season the tuna with salt and pepper. Place a small sauté pan on the stove over high heat and add a few drops of oil. When the oil starts to smoke, quickly sear the tuna on all sides. Do not cook it through. Sear the outside quickly and keep the interior ultra-rare and cold. Transfer the tuna to a plate to rest and come to room temperature.

– recipe continues

¼ head green cabbage, very
 thinly sliced

1 tsp ground cumin, divided

6 fresh corn tortillas

2 small avocados, diced

4 radishes, thinly sliced

3 serrano chilies, thinly sliced,
 divided

2 Lebanese or mini cucumbers,
 thinly sliced

1 small white onion, thinly sliced

8 cherry tomatoes, quartered

½ cup (120 ml) cilantro, roughly
 chopped

2 Tbsp extra virgin olive oil

1 lime, juiced

6 lime wedges

Dried chamomile leaves

2. While the tuna is resting, add 3 inches (7.5 cm) of oil to a tall, heavy, wide-bottomed pot and place over medium heat. (You need a tall pot, as the oil will expand and double in volume when you add the cabbage.) Once the oil reaches 375°F (190°C) (use a candy thermometer to check the temperature), add the cabbage in batches and gently fry, stirring often, until it is golden brown and crispy, about 1 minute. Don't crowd the pot. You may need to let the oil come back to temperature between batches.

3. Drain the crispy cabbage on paper towels and season immediately with salt and ground cumin to taste.

4. Using the same oil, fry the corn tortillas one at a time until stiff and crispy (the goal is to have a big corn chip), 1 minute per side. Once they're crunchy and golden, transfer to paper towels and season lightly with salt and a dusting of ground cumin to taste.

5. To prepare the salad, add the avocado, radishes, 2 chilies, cucumber, onions, tomatoes, and cilantro to a medium mixing bowl. Dress with the oil, lime juice, salt, and pepper and toss together gently.

6. Using a very sharp knife, slice the tuna about the width of a pinky finger and place the slices in the marinade for 2 minutes.

7. Start assembling the tostadas by spreading a generous schmear of the chipotle mayo on one side of a tostada. Place 3 to 4 slices of marinated tuna on each tostada, then a generous pinch of fried cabbage, and finally, top the cabbage with a large spoonful of the salad. Garnish each tostada with a lime wedge for an extra squeeze of lime juice, a pinch of dried chamomile leaves, and more sliced chilies, to taste. Serve immediately.

Note: White soy sauce (or shiro) is lighter in flavour and colour, due to a higher wheat-to-soy ratio, than traditional soy sauce. It provides a delicate taste without adding colour to a dish and can be found online or at most Asian grocers.

Crawfish Boil

Recipe by Rich Francis
Seventh Fire Dinners
Six Nations Reserve, Ontario

Serves 4

"Long before crawfish were popular in Louisiana, the Indigenous peoples of Turtle Island were consuming these little crustaceans, over hundreds of years, for survival, feasts, and ceremonies," writes Chef Rich Francis. "Times have changed, and other cultures have influenced our Indigenous foods. I've adapted the popular Southern crawfish boil into my Indigenous catering menus, keeping the tradition alive."

12 lb (5.5 kg) live crawfish (see note)
1 lb (450 g) blue cultured mussels
6 heads garlic, halved
3 onions, quartered
6 celery stalks, roughly chopped
4 lemons, halved
4 limes, halved
4 jalapeños, sliced in rounds
2 Tbsp grated fresh horseradish
1 cup (240 ml) Old Bay seafood seasoning
2 bottles (1.9 L total) Caesar mix, Classic
2 quarts (1.9 L) water
½ cup (120 ml) Worcestershire sauce
Tabasco hot sauce
Kosher salt and cracked black pepper
4 ears corn, husked and quartered widthwise
4 Andouille sausage links, cut into 1-inch (2.5 cm) pieces
1 lb (450 g) shrimp, shell on (16/20 count)

For Serving
Cornbread
Lemon wedges
Hot sauce

1. Soak the crawfish in a large container filled with fresh water, swish them around for 5 minutes, then transfer to a colander and rinse under fresh running water. Discard the dirty soaking water in the container and start again. Repeat this purging process until the water in the container remains clear. Throw out any dead or damaged crawfish.
2. Soak the mussels in fresh cold water for 20 minutes, scrubbing off any residual dirt or sand. Discard any mussels with broken shells or that don't open when tapped.
3. In the largest pot you can find, minimum 20 quarts (19 L), mix together the garlic, onions, celery, lemons, limes, jalapeños, horseradish, Old Bay seasoning, Caesar mix, water, Worcestershire sauce, hot sauce, salt, and pepper.
4. Bring this spicy Caesar liquid to a boil over high heat and then add the corn and sausages. Cover, turn down the heat to medium-low, and let simmer for 8 to 10 minutes.
5. At the 10-minute mark, crank up the heat to high to bring the cooking liquid back to a full, rolling boil and then stir in the crawfish, mussels, and shrimp. Cover the pot. Boil until the mussels are opened (discard any that don't open), the shrimp are pink, and the crayfish are bright red with antennas that pluck off easily, 4 to 5 minutes.
6. Depending on the size of pot, you may need to cook the seafood in two batches. Once the first batch is cooked, use a large spider strainer to lift out all of the cooked seafood, corn, and sausage. Leave the aromatics in the pot to continue flavouring the boiling liquid for the second batch.
7. Serve immediately on a newspaper-covered table with lots of cornbread, lemon wedges, and hot sauce.

Note: If you can't find fresh crawfish, you can use frozen. Simply thaw overnight in the refrigerator. Frozen crawfish will already be cleaned, so you can skip step 1.

East Coast

Zack's wife, Amanda, comes from a long line of Nova Scotia Smiths from Cape Breton and the South Shore. There's plenty of maritime lore in her family tree. One of her great-grandfathers, Captain "Dynamite" Smith, was a sea captain, and one of her grandfathers, Norman, went to sea as a teenager on his dad's ships, including as part of the Merchant Navy during the Second World War.

Almost a century old and simply built, the Smith family cottage on the South Shore, three hours' drive from Halifax, is a special place for the family. For a city boy like Zack—"come from away," as they say—it's a refreshing change of pace and scenery. He once naively asked Grandfather Norman if he could maybe take his rowboat out for a spin. Norman turned and looked at him severely and said "Boy"—Zack was 30 years old at the time—"that's the North Atlantic out there. It'll swallow you up and spit you out if you don't know what you're doing."

Out front of the cottage the tide goes out for what feels like a mile, and kids run down to play in the warm tide pools and to dig for treasures like razor clams and quahogs left behind by the sea. Here at the water's edge the villagers host lobster feeds, which have become the highlight of annual trips to the cottage for Zack, Amanda, and their kids. The feed works like so: after settling on what day to hold it, the call goes out to see who among the locals has fresh lobsters, and whoever does delivers them to the beach in a giant cardboard box. A few of the burlier neighbours haul a giant pot down to the ocean to fill it with sea water and then set it to boil over an open fire. Next, the lobsters are taken from where they've been resting on beds of wet seaweed and dropped into the pot to be steamed, as an assembly line of people of all ages gather to work on the crustaceans as they come out of the pot, gone from bluish green to bright red.

In our home cities of Vancouver and Toronto, lobster is an indulgence, most often something we'd eat out, with an elegant presentation, fancy lobster crackers, and a price tag to match. A lobster feed on the South Shore of Nova Scotia, 10 feet from where the fishers live and work, is not a fancy affair. This is everyday food. Butcher blocks and cutting boards are set out helter-skelter on the table alongside hatchets, cleavers, and machetes. As soon as the lobsters hit the table, everyone gets to work. Hacking and cracking, peeling and dipping, while the locals show you how to do it and point out all the good parts you're missing (turns out that green lobster goo is actually a "delicacy," known as tomalley). For sides there are big baskets of freshly baked brown bread and bowls of melted butter (so much butter). If you're looking for vegetables, there's maybe some potato salad. Some wine. Some beer. Some rum. Buckets on the ground for shells. And there's all sorts of talk, and music, and laughter.

What we've learned from our times out East is that clichés are clichés for a reason. East Coasters really are among the friendliest and most joyful folks in the world, certainly the easiest to talk to, in our experience. And it takes nothing away from their generosity of spirit to acknowledge the practical role it has played in the history of Atlantic Canada, especially in the island communities. As eighth-generation Fogo Islander Anthony Cobb told us, "The people you invited over for 'a time'—people you have business with, people you fish with—become your extended family. These are small groups, gathering in small houses. Everyone chips in with bringing the food and doing the prep. It's a way to celebrate, for sure, but also forged by necessity, cementing community bonds."

No surprise that lobster features among the cocktails and food that follow—but so too do freshly shucked oysters, cultured mussels, bar clams, and dried capelin, giving a small glimpse into the range of possibilities provided by Eastern waters. These recipes showcase the ingenuity that people in the region have used to preserve, prepare, and serve their ingredients with true Atlantic warmth and hospitality, each step of the process accompanied by a great story, of course.

The Land & Seasar

Cocktail by Anthony Cobb
Fogo Island Fish Inc.
Fogo Island, Newfoundland and
Labrador

Serves 1

Glassware
1 highball glass

Like many folks from his part of Canada, Anthony Cobb is a true storyteller. Through all the stories and memories he's shared with us, one message shines through: be thoughtful and humble about your relationship to the natural world. Long before it became trendy or cool to be a locavore, he'd been quietly setting an example for how to do farm-and-sea-to-table in a sustainable way. As an eighth-generation Fogo Islander, Anthony's recipe honours the long traditions of farming and fishing—what he calls the "terroir and merroir"—of the small island off Newfoundland's northeast coast that he calls home, a few dozen kilometres from the easternmost point in Canada.

The Land & Seasar offers a glimpse into local history through the use of pickled beets and molasses (land) and capelin and sea salt (sea). Every Fogo Island home would grow and pickle beets for the long winter, Anthony explains, while molasses was traded for fish as part of the salt cod trade that linked this small island to the Americas, Africa, and Europe. Capelin is a keystone species in the waters around Fogo Island and vital to the fabric of a healthy ocean. Its presence ensures the well-being of cod, whales, sharks, seabirds, and many other species. And of course, there's some Newfoundland screech rum in there for good measure.

Rim
2 Tbsp sea salt

Cocktail
2 oz (60 ml) Newfoundland
   screech rum (see note)
1 oz (30 ml) pickled beet juice
   (see note)
1 tsp blackstrap molasses
8 oz (240 ml) Caesar mix, Classic

Garnish
1 dried capelin (see note)

1. Pour the sea salt onto a small plate.
2. Fill a shallow dish with the rum and dip the top of your glass into it. (You're going to use this rum in the cocktail, so don't throw it away!) Dip the rim in the salt to give it a generous coating.
3. Pour the beet juice and molasses into a cocktail shaker (or other mixing vessel) and stir until the molasses is dissolved.
4. Pour the rum from the shallow dish (that you used to rim your glass) and the Caesar mix into the shaker. Fill the shaker with ice to just above the top of the liquid and stir with a bar spoon until the outside of the shaker is cold to the touch.
5. Fill the rimmed glass three-quarters full with fresh cubed ice. Strain the contents of the shaker into the glass and top with additional ice if desired. Garnish with a dried capelin. Long may your big jib draw!

Notes: 1) Sorry, but you must use Newfoundland screech rum to make this drink properly. There are no substitutes. 2) Pickled beet juice is the brine from a jar of pickled beets. 3) You can find dried capelin at some specialty grocers or online (like: arcticafood.ca).

Consider the Lobster

Serves 1

Glassware

1 stein

Rim

1 Tbsp Walter Rim Spice

1 Tbsp Old Bay seasoning

1 Tbsp grated lemon zest

1 lemon wedge

Cocktail

1½ oz (45 ml) Citrus Brown Butter
Washed Vodka (page 301)

6 oz (180 ml) Caesar mix, Mild

1 oz (30 ml) lemon juice

¼ tsp sea salt

¼ tsp cracked black pepper

Garnish

1 Lobster Tail (page 278)

1 lemon wedge

By no means do we think a rich brown-butter fat washed Caesar capped by sweet and tender lobster tails also basted in brown butter is going to enter your regular cocktail rotation. But that's the point. Sometimes life calls for a little indulgence. Here we wanted to create a drink worthy of the prized place that lobster holds in the history and culture of Atlantic Canada. While there are a few moving parts to this garnish—lobster, butter, a bit of lemon, salt and pepper, olive oil, parsley, and heat—the result is something worth celebrating.

Lobster fishing is a complex issue in the region, and we would like to express our belief in the rights of the Indigenous peoples of Canada to participate in a sustainable livelihood fishery, as established by the Supreme Court of Canada.

1. Combine the rim spice, Old Bay seasoning, and lemon zest in a bowl and mix well. Pour it onto a small plate. Circle the rim of your glass with the lemon wedge, then roll the rim in the rim spice.
2. Add the vodka, Caesar mix, lemon juice, salt, and pepper to a cocktail shaker (or other mixing vessel). Fill the shaker with ice to just above the top of the liquid and stir with a bar spoon until the outside of the shaker is very cold to the touch.
3. Fill the rimmed glass three-quarters full with fresh cubed ice. Strain the contents of the shaker into the glass and top with additional ice if desired. Garnish with the just-cooked lobster tail and lemon wedge.

Note: If you want to learn a ton about lobsters and read an excellent piece of food writing that even includes a philosophical debate over the nature of consciousness, check out David Foster Wallace's 2004 essay whose title lends this cocktail its name.

Yellow

Serves 1

Glassware
1 rocks glass

Owning a Caesar mix company means spending a lot of time with the colour red: looking at it, drinking it, cleaning it out of your clothes. Day in, day out. Honestly, it can all be a bit much sometimes. Enter the Yellow Caesar. While this drink could easily coast along on its stunning looks alone, its roasted yellow heirloom tomatoes, habaneros, and yellow peppers yield a taste that more than lives up to its inviting appearance. And to tie all this yellowness together, Jessica Smith helped us adapt her Grandma Shirley's classic Nova Scotian mustard pickle recipe.

Rim
2 Tbsp kosher salt
1 lemon wedge

Cocktail
1 oz (30 ml) vodka
5 oz (150 ml) Yellow Caesar Mix
   (page 70)
2 dashes habanero pepper sauce
   (such as Marie Sharp's)

Garnish
2 or 3 Grandma Shirley's
   Mustard Pickles (page 276),
   on a skewer

1. Pour the salt onto a small plate. Circle the rim of your glass with the lemon wedge, then roll the rim in the salt.
2. Pour the vodka, Caesar mix, and pepper sauce into a cocktail shaker (or other mixing vessel). Fill the shaker with ice to just above the top of the liquid and stir with a bar spoon until the outside of the shaker is very cold to the touch.
3. Fill the rimmed glass three-quarters full with fresh cubed ice. Strain the contents of the shaker into the glass and top with additional ice if desired. Garnish with the skewer.

Boardwalk

**Cocktail by Jesse Vergen &
Adele Moriarty**
Saint John Ale House
Saint John, New Brunswick

Serves 1

Glassware
1 rocks glass

Rim
2 Tbsp Celery Salt (page 288 or
     store-bought)
1 lime wedge

Cocktail
1½ oz (45 ml) gin
6 oz (180 ml) Caesar mix, Mild
½ oz (15 ml) bar clam brine
     (see note)
½ tsp hot sauce
½ tsp Worcestershire sauce
2 drops liquid smoke
Celery Salt (page 288 or
     store-bought)
Cracked black pepper

Garnish
3 to 6 bar clams (see note), on a
     skewer, liquid reserved
1 lime wedge
1 tsp freshly grated horseradish

For more than a decade, Saint John Ale House has been featuring freshly caught seafood from the Bay of Fundy at its popular destination on the Boardwalk in uptown Saint John, a scenic section of the country's oldest incorporated city. We love this recipe for how effectively it showcases clams as the central ingredient. Think of it as clams three ways: in the Caesar mix, in the bar clam brine, and in the unfussy, straight-to-the-point skewer of bar clams, finished with a touch of liquid smoke to provide some tension against all those salty, mineral flavours.

1. Pour the celery salt onto a small plate. Circle the rim of glass with the lime wedge, then roll the rim in the rim spice.
2. Combine the gin, Caesar mix, clam brine, hot sauce, Worcestershire sauce, liquid smoke, and a pinch each of celery salt and pepper into a cocktail shaker (or other mixing vessel). Fill the shaker with ice to just above the top of the liquid and stir with a bar spoon until the outside of the shaker is very cold to the touch.
3. Strain the contents of the shaker into the glass and top with additional ice if desired. Garnish with the skewer, lime wedge, and horseradish.

Note: Bar clams are usually packed in jars and ready to eat right out of the jar. They're typically packed in a vinegar and salt brine solution, which is different from regular clam juice, which is really the broth from cooking clams. You can find bar clams at your local fishmonger or online. Or better yet, make your own using the recipe on page 272.

Waltermelon

Serves 1

Glassware
1 rocks glass

AH: I'd love to be able to tell you how the inspiration for this dish came from Zack's annual summer trip to the family cottage in the Maritimes, where, in the rolling yard, he and his young family eat al fresco in the warm summer air surrounded by generations of Nova Scotian in-laws, and that during one such meal at magic hour, a refreshing watermelon salad with feta and lemon was served, paired with a round of ice-cold Caesars. But I can't. The real story behind this cocktail starts with Zack's food nerdery, and his complete and total obsession with *The Flavor Bible*, Karen Page and Andrew Dornenburg's influential book, loved by chefs and bartenders the world over. It has a quote from Chef José Andres: "Tomatoes with watermelon is a simple, refreshing, and perfectly balanced combination. The acidity of the tomatoes is a counterpoint to the sweetness of the watermelon." Zack knew right away that this passage was a drink that needed making. (And once the name Waltermelon popped into his head there was really no stopping him.) We tried a bunch of different versions (we're talking dozens) until we fixed on the recipe here. We think you'll be as delighted as we were by how well the flavours work together, just as The Bible foretold.

Garnish
1 piece watermelon (2 inch/5 cm wedge)
1 chunk feta cheese (1 inch/ 2.5 cm cube)

Rim
2 Tbsp kosher salt
1 lemon wedge

Cocktail
1½ oz (45 ml) tequila reposado
2 oz Watermelon Juice (page 300)
2 oz Caesar mix, Mild
¼ oz (7.5 ml) Simple Syrup (page 297)
¼ oz (7.5 ml) lemon juice

1. Prepare your garnish by skewering the watermelon and feta.
2. Pour the salt onto a small plate. Circle the rim of your glass with the lemon wedge, then roll the rim in the salt.
3. Pour the tequila, watermelon juice, Caesar mix, simple syrup, and lemon juice into a cocktail shaker (or other mixing vessel). Fill the shaker with ice to just above the top of the liquid and stir with a bar spoon until the outside of the shaker is very cold to the touch.
4. Fill the rimmed glass three-quarters full with fresh cubed ice. Strain the contents of the shaker into the glass and top with additional ice if desired. Garnish with the skewer.

Oyster Shooter

Serves 4

Glassware

4 double shot glasses (each
　　2 oz/60 ml)

Garnish

4 oysters

Cocktail

3 oz (90 ml) vodka
3 oz (90 ml) Caesar mix, Mild
1 tsp freshly grated horseradish
1 tsp lemon juice
½ tsp hot sauce

Whenever we serve up these throwback party treats at a gathering, our guests typically have one of two reactions:

Reaction 1: I'm out.
Reaction 2: I'm in!

For the record, reaction 2 is the only acceptable one.

1. Shuck the oysters, keeping them on the half shell and reserving as much of the oyster liquor as possible. (See page 238.)
2. Pour the vodka, Caesar mix, horseradish, lemon juice, and hot sauce into a cocktail shaker (or other mixing vessel). Fill the shaker with ice to just above the top of the liquid and stir with a bar spoon until the outside of the shaker is very cold to the touch.
3. Strain the contents of the shaker equally into the shot glasses. Top each shooter with an oyster on the half shell.
4. To drink, drop the oyster and oyster liquor into your shot glass and discard the shell. Cheers your friends and down the entire thing in one gulp. Chewing optional.

Dear Friend

**Cocktail by Matthew Boyle &
Jeffrey Van Horne**
Dear Friend Bar
Dartmouth, Nova Scotia

Serves 1

Glassware
1 goblet

Nova Scotians Matthew Boyle and Jeffrey Van Horne, the duo behind the admirable Dartmouth cocktail bar Dear Friend, are known for putting a lot of thought into creating cocktails that are as sophisticated as they are unorthodox. This Caesar is a case in point. The use of low-ABV dry vermouth and Green Chartreuse for the cocktail's base, rather than a single strong spirit, makes for a light, silky, herbaceous drink. We love how the recipe pushes against the standard definitions of a Caesar, showing how you can expand a drink's possibilities through a simple shift in ingredients. And if you're looking for an endorsement, when Zack tried this for the first time, his response was, "Uh . . . this might be the best Caesar I've ever had . . . like, ever."

Garnish
1 oyster
½ tsp Horseradish Mignonette
    (page 295)
1 lemon wedge

Rim
1 Tbsp sea salt
1 Tbsp cracked black pepper
1 lemon wedge

Cocktail
2 oz (60 ml) dry (white) vermouth
    (ideally Dolin Dry)
½ oz (15 ml) Green Chartreuse
6 oz (180 ml) Caesar mix, Vegan
½ oz (15 ml) Celery Juice
    (page 293)
¼ oz (7.5 ml) Horseradish
    Mignonette (page 295)

1. Shuck the oyster, keeping it on the half shell and reserving as much of the oyster liquor as possible. (See page 238.)
2. Mix together the salt and pepper in a bowl and then pour it onto a small plate. Circle the rim of your glass with the lemon wedge, then roll the rim in the rim spice.
3. Pour the vermouth, Chartreuse, Caesar mix, celery juice, and horseradish mignonette into a cocktail shaker. Fill the shaker with ice to just above the top of the liquid and gently roll all the liquid and ice from this shaker to a second mixing vessel, working back and forth, until the outside of the vessels are very cold to the touch.
4. Fill the rimmed glass three-quarters full with fresh cubed ice. Strain the contents of the shaker into the glass and top with additional ice if desired. Garnish with the shucked oyster and top with the horseradish mignonette and lemon wedge.

Friend of the Devil

Serves 1

Glassware
1 rocks glass
1 large shot glass (2 to 3 oz/
    60 to 90 ml)

Garnish
1 slice of baguette
1 pat of salted butter

Rim
1½ Tbsp cane sugar
½ Tbsp kosher salt
2 Tbsp Agave Syrup (page 292)

Cocktail
1½ oz (45 ml) Chili Pepper-
    Infused Vodka (page 300)
5 oz Caesar mix, Extra Spicy
½ oz (15 ml) Agave Syrup
    (page 292)
½ oz (15 ml) lemon juice
¼ oz (7.5 ml) Stargazer hot
    sauce (see note)

For Serving
2 to 3 oz (60 to 90 ml) ice-cold
    whole milk

Sometimes inspiration comes from unexpected places. In this case, a late night spent listening to the Grateful Dead, and the realization that Friend of the Devil is the perfect name for a cocktail. A spicy cocktail. A diabolically spicy cocktail. You can, of course, make any Caesar hotter just by adding more hot sauce, but that also means adding the sauce's salt, vinegar, and other flavours. While this drink doesn't skimp on the hot sauce, we get even more straight heat (without piling on the flavour) by also using a hot chili pepper-infused vodka.

1. Prepare your garnish by smearing a nice thick piece of baguette with some good salted butter. The bread and butter will help temper the heat of the cocktail.
2. Mix together the sugar and salt in a bowl and then pour it onto a small plate. Drizzle the agave syrup onto a separate plate (the pool of syrup should be at least as wide as your glass). Dip your glass rim in the agave syrup, allow any excess to drip back onto the plate, and then roll the rim in the sugar and salt.
3. Pour the vodka, Caesar mix, agave syrup, lemon juice, and hot sauce into a cocktail shaker (or other mixing vessel). Fill the shaker with ice to just above the top of the liquid and stir with a bar spoon until the outside of the shaker is very cold to the touch.
4. Fill the rimmed glass three-quarters full with fresh cubed ice. Strain the contents of the shaker into the glass and top with additional ice if desired. Garnish with the buttered baguette slice.
5. Pour some ice-cold milk in a large shot glass (or maybe a bigger glass if you think you're going to need it). Serve alongside your Caesar and sip to cool your palette as needed.

Note: Stargazer is a sriracha-inspired hot sauce made in Ontario. Made famous on *Hot Ones*, it touts a blazing 182,000 Scoville rating. Its makers, Pepper North, rate it a 9/10, which means we don't want to know what a 10/10 is. You can find it at select grocers or buy it via Pepper North's website. If you can't find (or tolerate) Stargazer, use the hottest hot sauce you can handle.

César Cubano

**Recipe by Julio Cabrera &
Michelle Bernstein**
Cafe La Trova
Miami, Florida

Serves 1

Glassware
1 rocks glass

Garnish
1 Serrano Ham & Blue Cheese
    Croqueta (page 284)
1 green olive, pitted

Rim
2 Tbsp Salted Coffee Rim
    (page 291)
1 lime wedge

Cocktail
1½ oz (45 ml) white rum (ideally
    Bacardi Superior)
4 oz (120 ml) Caesar mix, Classic
½ oz (15 ml) lime juice

ZS: I got to know Julio Cabrera when I lived in Miami for a few years. I'd see him at the Regent Cocktail Club, where he'd already gained a national reputation for his skills behind the bar and as a proud champion of his native Cuba and its *cantinero* culture. Being a homesick expat, I would ask him if he could make me a Caesar, but he never had the ingredients on hand. Julio now runs Cafe La Trova with Chef Michelle Bernstein in Miami's Little Havana, to the acclaim of locals and critics alike. When I told him about this book, he finally agreed to make me a Caesar, by way of Miami and Cuba. Not surprisingly, it's made with rum and a good amount of lime juice. More surprising, and totally original, is the coffee-based rim spice. Michelle provides the perfect Little Havana–inspired garnish with a grown-up ham and cheese croqueta, whose crispy exterior gives way to a creamy core of béchamel and Serrano ham accented by funky blue cheese.

1. Prepare the garnish by skewering the croqueta and green olive.
2. Pour the rim spice onto a small plate. Circle the rim of your glass with the lime wedge, then roll the rim in the rim spice.
3. Pour the rum, Caesar mix, and lime juice into a cocktail shaker (or other mixing vessel). Fill the shaker with ice to just above the top of the liquid and stir with a bar spoon until the outside of the shaker is very cold to the touch.
4. Fill the rimmed glass three-quarters full with fresh cubed ice. Strain the contents of the shaker into the glass. Top with additional ice if desired. Garnish with the skewer.

Caesar Ice with Fresh Shucked Oysters

Recipe by Michael Smith
Inn at Bay Fortune
Bay Fortune, Prince Edward
Island

Makes enough to top 6 dozen
oysters

Chef Michael Smith and his wife, Chastity, run the historic Inn at Bay Fortune on a rambling stretch of land at the eastern edge of Prince Edward Island, about an hour's drive from Charlottetown. Long ago, it served as an artists' colony frequented by Broadway actors and silent film stars seeking to escape New York. Along with harvesting the produce from the eight acres of the property they've devoted to their culinary farm, Michael and Chastity draw on the fresh bounty of Bay Fortune on their doorstep, and Colville Bay just down the way. As you might expect, that means luscious Atlantic oysters are in abundance. They've served thousands of freshly shucked Malpeque oysters with their signature topping, a dollop of icy-but-not-too-spicy grown-up Caesar-flavoured slushie.

Caesar Ice

2 cups (480 ml) Caesar mix, any
    flavour (any flavour Caesar
    mix can be substituted based
    on taste)
1 cup (240 ml) vodka, gin, or
    aquavit
½ cup (120 ml) granulated sugar
2 lemons, zested with a
    Microplane and juiced

Oysters

72 oysters, washed and rinsed

Caesar Ice

1. Add the Caesar mix, your spirit of choice, sugar, lemon zest, and lemon juice to a medium bowl. Stir well to dissolve the sugar and combine.
2. Split the mixture evenly between two 16 oz (500 ml) Mason jars. Screw the lids on tightly, then place in the freezer.
3. Every 30 minutes to an hour, give the jars a good shake to form ice-crystal slush. Repeat for up to 8 hours until fully slushified. You can store leftovers in the freezer for up to 6 months.

Oyster Shucking

1. Place an oyster on a cutting or oyster board with the hinge facing toward you. Hold in place with a clean dry cloth.
2. Using an oyster knife, twist into the hinge of the oyster in a repeating "key in the lock" motion until open. (Do not attempt to lever the shell open, as this will invariably break it.) Once the top shell is loosened, wipe the oyster knife, as it may have dirt or bits of shell. Before you attempt to remove the top shell, scrape the oyster knife along the inside of the top shell to sever the muscle that is holding the oyster shut, starting at the hinge end. Now remove the top shell. Lastly, carefully scrape the oyster knife along the inside of the bottom shell to release the oyster. The liquor (the briny liquid) in the oyster is delicious and precious. Try not to spill even a single drop.

– recipe continues

Final Assembly

1. Layer crushed iced on a festive platter. Steady the shucked oysters as you go by alternating upside-down empty top shells with fully laden bottoms on top of the ice. Keep refrigerated until ready to serve.

2. When you're ready to serve, top each oyster with a chilly dollop of the Caesar ice. Shuck, slurp, chew, and swallow!

Skillet Rolls

Jessica Smith

Barrington Passage, Nova Scotia

Makes 16 to 20 small rolls

Our first employee at Walter was Jessica Smith, an award-winning pastry chef who also happens to be Zack's sister-in-law. While Jessica no longer works full-time for Walter, she was instrumental in helping us test and refine many of the recipes in this book, and here shares one of her own. Jess spends summers at the family cottage on the South Shore of Nova Scotia where, as a child, her grandmother first taught her to bake. "My grandmother from Cape Breton was, and always will be, the best baker in the family, and I've been working through her crumbling, butter-stained, burnt-edged recipe pages for years now. I used three of these well-loved recipes as inspiration for these rolls," she told us. "With my pastry background I wanted to figure out a way to use Walter unconventionally by baking with it. Marrying the richness of a buttery, eggy bread with the sweetness of tomatoes and lobster seemed promising." The result is a fluffy, sweet, and savoury dinner roll that subtly conjures the essence of a Caesar.

Oven-Dried Tomatoes

2 cups (480 ml) grape tomatoes, halved

Kosher salt

½ cup (120 ml) extra virgin olive oil

Skillet Rolls

¾ cup (180 ml) Caesar mix, Holiday

½ cup (120 ml) unsalted butter, divided

3 Tbsp white sugar + a pinch, divided

1 Tbsp tomato paste

¼ cup (60 ml) warm water at 110°F (40°C)

1 packet (7 g/¼ oz/2¼ tsp) active dry yeast

Oven-Dried Tomatoes

1. Preheat your oven to 250°F (120°C) and line a baking sheet with parchment paper.
2. Place the tomatoes cut-side up on the prepared baking sheet and sprinkle lightly with kosher salt. Bake until the tomatoes are shrunken and no longer juicy, 2 to 3 hours. The timing depends on the size of the tomatoes, so expect some differences in level of chew and sweetness within the same batch.
3. Let the tomatoes cool completely and then transfer to a 1-cup (240 ml) lidded glass jar. Add the oil, making sure the tomatoes are submerged. Seal the jar and store in the refrigerator for up to 1 week.

Skillet Rolls

1. Place the Caesar mix and ¼ cup (60 ml) of the butter in a small pot. Heat until the butter is melted, and then whisk in the 3 Tbsp of sugar and tomato paste until combined. Remove from the heat.
2. In a small bowl, dissolve a pinch of sugar in the warm water and then sprinkle the yeast on top. Allow to bloom until foamy, 10 minutes.
3. Remove half of the oven-dried tomatoes from the oil and finely dice.

– recipe continues

1 batch Oven-Dried Tomatoes,
    divided

4 cups (960 ml) + ¼ cup (60 ml)
    all-purpose flour, divided

2 Tbsp finely chopped fresh
    tarragon, divided

2 Tbsp finely chopped fresh
    sage, divided

1 tsp kosher salt

2 large eggs, room temperature

Extra virgin olive oil

Large-flaked sea salt

3 to 6 sage leaves

2 to 3 tarragon leaves

4. In a stand mixer fitted with the dough hook, combine 4 cups (960 ml) of flour, 1 Tbsp of tarragon, 1 Tbsp of sage, and salt. Add the diced tomatoes. Mix on low speed until the dry ingredients are well distributed.

5. With the mixer still running on low speed, pour in the cooled Caesar butter mixture, the bloomed yeast, and the eggs. Increase the speed to medium and allow the dough to come together, scraping down the sides of the bowl as needed. If the dough is too sticky, spoon in an additional ¼ cup (60 ml) flour by the tablespoon until a soft smooth ball forms.

6. Reduce the speed to medium-low and knead for 3 minutes. The dough should be smooth, soft, and no longer tacky.

7. Transfer the dough to a large, lightly oiled bowl, cover loosely, and let proof in a warm area until doubled in size, 1 hour.

8. Once the dough is proofed, melt the remaining ¼ cup (60 ml) butter in a small saucepan over low heat. Gently mix in the remaining 1 Tbsp each of tarragon and sage. Remove from the heat.

9. Punch down the dough, then portion into 16 to 20 equal pieces. Form each piece into a smooth, round, compact bun by rolling it against the counter with a cupped hand.

10. Roll each bun in the saucepan of melted sage tarragon butter to coat, then place them smooth side up, evenly spaced, in concentric circles in a large 10- or 12-inch (25 or 30 cm) cast iron skillet. Reserve the remaining herb butter for a final baste of your rolls once they come out of the oven.

11. Cover the skillet loosely and let proof once more in a warm area until doubled in size again, 30 to 40 minutes. Preheat your oven to 350°F (175°C) when the dough is nearly proofed.

12. Bake the rolls until golden brown on top, 25 to 30 minutes.

13. Remove the skillet from the oven and brush the rolls with the remaining melted herb butter. Remove the remaining oven-dried tomatoes from the oil, then use them to garnish the rolls along with a liberal sprinkle of flaked sea salt, and the sage and tarragon leaves. Serve the warm, glistening rolls right from the skillet.

Mussels Escabeche

Recipe by Charlotte Langley
Scout Canning
Abrams Village, Prince Edward Island

Serves 4

Escabeche

5 lb (2.25 kg) PEI blue cultured mussels
1 Tbsp canola oil
2 cloves garlic, minced
1 leek, white and tender green parts only, finely diced
1 red bell pepper, finely diced
1 yellow bell pepper, finely diced
1 jalapeño, finely diced
1 cup (240 ml) Caesar mix, Extra Spicy
½ cup (120 ml) extra virgin olive oil
¼ cup (60 ml) sherry vinegar
1 mini cucumber (or ¼ English cucumber), finely chopped
3 green onions, finely chopped
¼ cup (60 ml) flat-leaf parsley, roughly chopped
¼ cup (60 ml) basil, roughly chopped
Kosher salt and cracked black pepper

For Serving

1 lime, cut into wedges
Salted butter, room temperature
1 loaf fresh bread

Chef Charlotte Langley cares intensely about where food comes from—not just geographically but also historically. In PEI, she grew up hearing stories about catching and canning seafood. One day, after coming face-to-face with an antique canning machine gathering dust in the back of an old warehouse, she was inspired to start her craft seafood cannery, Scout Canning. Small wonder that she presented us with a recipe so clearly steeped in history. Escabeche—the catch-all term for dishes cooked from meat, fish, or veggies marinated in a spicy vinegary sauce—has centuries-old roots stretching from the Middle East to the Iberian Peninsula to Latin America, and can differ wildly in ingredients and taste. Charlotte's packs both a bright, flavourful punch and vibrant colouring.

1. Clean the mussels under cold running water and remove all of their beards. Discard any mussels with shells that are damaged or that don't open when tapped.

2. Pour 1 to 2 inches (2.5 to 5 cm) of water into a large stockpot fitted with a stainless steel colander for steaming. Bring the water to a boil over high heat.

3. Drop the mussels into the steamer, cover with a lid, and steam until the shells open, 7 to 10 minutes. Remove from the heat to cool slightly. Discard any mussels whose shells have not opened.

4. Place a large saucepan over medium-low heat and add the canola oil, followed by the garlic, leeks, red and yellow bell peppers, and jalapeño. Sweat until soft and translucent, 7 to 10 minutes.

5. Transfer this mixture (known as soffritto) to a medium bowl. Shell the mussels and place the meat on top, keeping the tender morsels as intact as possible.

6. Pour the Caesar mix, olive oil, and vinegar into the bowl, then give the mixture a gentle stir. Let rest for a few minutes to allow the flavours to marry.

7. Add the cucumber, green onions, parsley, and basil to the mixture. Fold together until evenly distributed. Taste and adjust seasoning with the salt and pepper. The escabeche is best enjoyed at room temperature in individual dishes with lots of the tasty liquid, lime wedges for squeezing, and buttered fresh bread.

Note: You can prep this dish a couple of days in advance, but add the fresh herbs at the last moment, just before serving.

North

The Words of Tiffany Ayalik
Inuk performer born and raised in Yellowknife, NWT.

I have one of the coolest jobs in the world. As the host of the TV show *Wild Kitchen*, I get to travel around the North and meet interesting people who hunt, forage, trap, and grow their own food. The North has some interesting characters, from the commercial to the kooky, but something unites us up here despite our differences. It's hard to put your finger on why, and many long-time Northerners have their own theories. Perhaps it's the breathtaking cold of a January winter when temperatures can plummet to minus 50°C, or the brilliant pink winter afternoon sunsets when cold steals all the moisture from the air that can cloud the view. Or maybe it's our summers of midnight sun and 2 a.m. BBQs. Whatever that magic is, I think the extremes we experience bring us together. And, when we do come together, no gathering is complete without—you guessed it—food!

Now, when I say "The North," it probably conjures up images of igluit (plural of iglu), ice fishing, aurora borealis, barren, treeless landscapes, and frost-bitten toes in Klondike bars—all somewhat correct but certainly not a uniform experience across the North. We have three distinct territories: Yukon, Northwest Territories, and Nunavut, and between the three lie thousands of kilometres, dozens of Indigenous groups and languages, and several climates and ecosystems. Each of these landscapes offers many challenges and rugged terrain, but also an opportunity for some amazing ingenuity if you're willing to think outside the box. Being so far away from commercial agriculture means that shipping food up North is unbelievably expensive (not to mention the large carbon footprint of shipping an avocado from Mexico to Inuvik), and by the time it gets to us, food with labels boasting "farm fresh" bring an eye-roll and a chuckle to Northern shoppers. So how do we meet these challenges? How do we keep ourselves fed, interested, and responsible to the planet? We take a cue from the Indigenous people, who've been not only surviving but thriving in the North. A big part of that is feasting.

I am Inuit and my family is from Kugluktuk, NU, but I grew up in the bustling northern metropolis of Yellowknife, NWT (don't ever confuse Whitehorse and Yellowknife in our presence—you will be publicly scorned with regional wrath). One of my favourite memories as a kid was when family would come "down south" to Yellowknife to see the doctor, get their wisdom teeth pulled, or go on a shopping spree (including loading up on fresh groceries for a fraction of the cost). When family made that long journey "south," we would find, packed in their luggage, frozen Arctic char caught the previous day, caribou from a recent hunting trip, or—wonder of wonders—beluga whale muktuk (the outer layer of skin and fat) caught by one cousin or another. Tea would be made and the table set. The Inuit table is

much different than most, especially when eating traditional foods. We sit on the floor, open up a cardboard box to use as a cutting board, and set out our favourite flavour enhancers— soy sauce and salt. Then the feast begins. We would catch up on what was happening with the weather back home, where the caribou were, who was out hunting, who was having luck with fish nets, and whether the berries were coming out yet. I loved these meals together. The frozen fare would chill my tummy and a cup of hot tea warmed me up again.

I have learned so much about Northern abundance from the people I've met through *Wild Kitchen*. All of them in one way or another are striving for connection to their food. Some live completely off the grid and harvest most of what they eat, some have hunting camps that they take their kids to in order to pass on Indigenous knowledge. Others have commercial operations and employ hunters and harvesters and provide food back to their own communities. There may not be orchards in the North but there is abundance if you know where to look.

Harvesting Northern abundance is tricky; it means listening to the land and making the most of what is available for those brief moments before a sudden and usually extreme change of season launches us into the next chapter. It means keeping an eye on the trees in the spring to catch the tender spruce tips at the perfect moment when they offer a delicious burst of citrus zest. It means walking slowly through a trail, eyes down looking for the asparagus-shaped fireweed shoots once the snow has melted. In summer it means spending hours out fishing when the sun doesn't set and, in the fall, working with the weather to dry your fish for winter. And it means, in the depths of what feels like an endless winter, delighting in the work you did to preserve the summer's abundance to tide you over until the sun comes back. Northern abundance is also best served with company. When you haven't seen the sun for weeks and you break out the last jar of rosehip-raspberry jam for your visitors, the pleasure of tasting preserved sunshine spread on toast is a gentle reminder of the plentiful offerings of the North.

Contemporary food in the North is an exciting blend of local and international inspirations and reflects the people who call the North home. Reindeer chili cheese fries, caribou curry, char ceviche, fireweed grenadine, spruce tip potato salad, and Szechuan ginger moose are all dishes that you can find up here. Working with what we have locally helps us to think creatively and allows for some pretty exciting fare. I hope you can come and taste it for yourself.

One request: when you come up North, please don't call it "barren." Our land is far from it.

Miner's Daughter

Cocktail by John Pan
Miner's Daughter/Dirty Northern
Public House
Whitehorse, Yukon

Serves 1

Glassware
1 rocks glass

Rim
2 Tbsp Wild Yarrow Rim
    (page 292)
1 Tbsp Honey Syrup (page 295)

Cocktail
1½ oz (45 ml) vodka (ideally
    Klondike)
½ oz (15 ml) Yukon Jack liqueur
4 oz (120 ml) Caesar mix, Classic
½ oz (15 ml) lime juice
4 dashes Tabasco hot sauce
3 dashes Worcestershire sauce

Garnish
1 to 2 pieces Elk Jerky
    (page 276)
1 lime wedge

When John first sent us his recipe, we had to double-check the numbers with him: was one part booze to two parts mix the right ratio? "Of course," John answered, "that's how we do it here . . . we have to stay warm somehow!" John's cocktail features a spirit that is unique to the region: Yukon Jack, an 80-proof liqueur made from Canadian whisky and honey and named for famed Yukon gold prospector Leroy Napoleon "Jack" McQuesten. This is paired with Klondike Vodka, the first spirit to be legally produced in Yukon Territory, made with gold flakes to allude to Yukon's gold rush past. And while this cocktail has some bite to be sure, the strength and sweetness of the liquor is well balanced by the lime, the wild yarrow rim, and the elk jerky garnish. Seems like a pretty good way to stay warm.

1. Pour the rim spice onto a small plate. Drizzle the honey syrup onto a separate plate (the pool of syrup should be at least as wide as your glass). Dip the rim of your glass in the honey syrup, allow any excess to drip back onto the plate, and then roll the rim in the rim spice.

2. Pour the vodka, Yukon Jack, Caesar mix, lime juice, hot sauce, and Worcestershire sauce into a cocktail shaker (or other mixing vessel). Fill the shaker with ice to just above the top of the liquid and stir with a bar spoon until the outside of the shaker is very cold to the touch.

3. Fill the rimmed glass three-quarters full with fresh cubed ice. Strain the contents of the shaker into the glass and top with additional ice if desired. Garnish with the elk jerky and lime wedge.

Nunavut Country Food Arctic Caesar

Recipe by Ranjit "Ray" Pieres
Frobisher Inn
Iqaluit, Nunavut

Serves 1

Glassware
1 highball glass

Garnish
2 to 3 pieces Candied Arctic
    Char (page 274)
2 to 3 Arctic blueberries or
    crowberries (substitute local
    blueberries or blackberries)

Rim
2 Tbsp Caribou Jerky Rim
    (page 287)
2 Tbsp maple syrup

Cocktail
1½ oz (45 ml) gin (ideally
    Ungava)
6 oz (180 ml) Caesar mix, Smoky
    Maple
½ oz (15 ml) Cloudberry Syrup
    (page 294)

Iqaluit's Frobisher Inn stands sentinel on a hill at the southern end of Baffin Island, the largest island in Canada. "Iqaluit" means "place of many fish" in Inuktitut, the language spoken by the majority of Nunavut's inhabitants. Fresh seafood naturally figures prominently in the local cuisine, as do the wild berries from the Arctic Tundra. This recipe features both. The star, though, is the Arctic char from the region's deep alpine lakes and cold coastal waters. This fish has managed to thrive farther north than any other, sometimes growing to enormous sizes. When you're preparing your candied char (substitute salmon if necessary) be sure to cut up your fish into garnish sizes before you brine it. Doing this maximizes the surface area that provides the sweet, chewy edges that come from smoking the char in pieces rather than as a whole.

1. Prepare the garnish by skewering the candied char and berries.
2. Pour the rim spice onto a small plate. Drizzle the maple syrup onto a separate plate (the pool of syrup should be at least as wide as your glass). Dip the rim of your glass in the maple syrup, allow any excess to drip back onto the plate, and then roll the rim in the rim spice.
3. Pour the gin, Caesar mix, and syrup into a cocktail shaker (or other mixing vessel). Fill the shaker with ice to just above the top of the liquid and stir with a bar spoon until the outside of the shaker is very cold to the touch.
4. Fill the rimmed glass three-quarters full with fresh cubed ice. Strain the contents of the shaker into the glass and top with additional ice if desired. Garnish with the skewer.

Nordic

Serves 1

Glassware
1 rocks glass

This drink represents a marriage of two Norths: Canadian and Scandinavian. We use dill-infused aquavit (a traditional Scandinavian spirit) and a caraway-dill rim to deliver spicy, herby, anise-forward flavours, which pair elegantly with a garnish of salty, silky salmon roe from our own Northern waters. Serve this cocktail very cold, because the North is generally very cold.

Rim
2 Tbsp Nordic Rim (page 290)
1 lemon wedge

Cocktail
1½ oz (45 ml) Dill-Infused
　　Aquavit (page 301)
¼ cup (120 ml) diced Simmered
　　Beet (page 297)
5 oz (150 ml) Caesar mix, Mild
1 tsp freshly grated horseradish
⅛ tsp white pepper
⅓ oz (10 ml) lemon juice

Garnish
1 tsp Canadian salmon roe
1 sprig fresh dill

1. Pour the rim spice onto a small plate. Circle the rim of your glass with the lemon wedge, then roll the rim in the rim spice.
2. Add the aquavit and beets to a cocktail shaker (or other mixing vessel) and muddle until the beets are well infused into the spirit. Add the Caesar mix, horseradish, pepper, and lemon juice to the shaker. Fill the shaker with ice to just above the top of the liquid and stir with a bar spoon until the outside of the shaker is very cold to the touch.
3. Fill the rimmed glass three-quarters full with fresh cubed ice. Strain the contents of the shaker into the glass and top with additional ice if desired. Garnish with the salmon roe and dill.

Bug Repellent

Cocktail by Mel Leonard
NWT Brewing Company
Yellowknife, Northwest Territories

Serves 1

Glassware
1 pilsner glass

Rim
2 Tbsp NWT Rim (page 290)
1 lemon wedge

Cocktail
1½ oz (45 ml) vodka
1 lemon wedge
½ small (approximately
    2-inch/5 cm piece) dill pickle,
    roughly chopped
6 oz (180 ml) Caesar mix, Mild
3 dashes Tabasco hot sauce
2 dashes Worcestershire sauce
2 oz (60 ml) India pale ale (ideally
    NWT Brewing Bug Repellent
    IPA) (see note)

Garnish
2 or 3 Quick-Pickled Chaga
    Vegetables (page 281), on a
    skewer

Between the 60th parallel and the Arctic Circle stands the sharp-angled outpost of wood, glass, and corrugated steel housing the NWT Brewing Company and its adjoining pub, the Woodyard. Inside they brew quality ale with water from the nearby Great Slave Lake. Here, the crisp citrus and bitter hops from a splash of their flagship Bug Repellent IPA plays off the intensity of a cocktail base infused with muddled pickles, making this a thoughtful example of how to take a spirit-based Caesar in a totally new direction by incorporating beer as a modifier. And while it won't actually repel any bugs, it's perfect for sipping on a patio in any part of the country.

1. Pour the rim spice onto a small plate. Circle the rim of your glass with the lemon wedge, then roll the rim in the rim spice.
2. Add the vodka, lemon wedge, and dill pickle to a cocktail shaker (or other mixing vessel) and muddle to infuse the pickle and lemon juices. Pour the Caesar mix, hot sauce, and Worcestershire sauce into the shaker. Fill the shaker with ice to just above the top of the liquid and stir with a bar spoon until the outside of the shaker is very cold to the touch.
3. Fill the rimmed glass three-quarters full with fresh cubed ice. Strain the contents of the shaker into the glass. Top with the India pale ale and garnish with the skewer.

Note: If you can't get your hands on NWT Brewing Company's Bug Repellent IPA, use an IPA from your favourite local craft brewery.

The Fashion Caesar

**Cocktail by Fashion Santa
(a.k.a. Paul Mason)**
The North Pole
(and sometimes Toronto)

Serves 1

Glassware
1 stylish glass

Rim
2 Tbsp Fashion Rim (page 288)
1 lemon wedge

Cocktail
1½ oz (45 ml) gin
6 oz (180 ml) Caesar mix,
    Holiday
⅓ oz (10 ml) lemon juice
¼ tsp sea salt
¼ tsp cracked black pepper

Garnish
1 Ocean Water Steamed Lobster
    Claw (page 279)
1 sprig tarragon
1 sprig sage
1 lemon wheel

To celebrate the launch of our seasonal Holiday Caesar Mix made with sage, tarragon, and lobster stock, we teamed up with Paul Mason, better known as Fashion Santa, to be our Holiday Caesar spokesman. The thinking was simple: Walter is the premium Caesar mix for the holidays. Paul is the premium Santa. He worked with us to create this stylish lobster-garnished recipe, unquestionably fashionable and something worth celebrating.

1. Pour the rim spice onto a small plate. Circle the rim of your glass with the lemon wedge, then roll the rim in the rim spice.
2. Add the gin, Caesar mix, lemon juice, salt, and pepper to a cocktail shaker (or other mixing vessel). Fill the shaker with ice to just above the top of the liquid and stir with a bar spoon until the outside of the shaker is very cold to the touch.
3. Fill the rimmed glass three-quarters full with fresh cubed ice. Strain the contents of the shaker into the glass and top with additional ice if desired. Garnish with the lobster claw, tarragon, sage, and lemon wheel.
4. Make it fashion.

Sweet & Sour Caribou Meatballs

Recipe by JenniLee Vaneltsi

Fort McPherson, Northwest Territories

Makes 18 meatballs

Meatballs

½ cup (120 ml) bread crumbs

½ cup (120 ml) Caesar mix, Smoky Maple

½ cup (120 ml) quick oats

2 Tbsp dried onion flakes

1½ tsp kosher salt

1 tsp garlic powder

½ tsp onion powder

½ tsp dried parsley

½ tsp paprika

½ tsp celery seed

½ tsp cracked black pepper

2 eggs

2 lb (900 g) ground caribou meat (or elk, venison, or beef)

Sweet and Sour Sauce

1 cup (240 ml) ketchup

½ cup (120 ml) packed brown sugar

¼ cup (60 ml) Caesar mix, Smoky Maple

¼ cup (60 ml) white vinegar

¼ cup (60 ml) soy sauce

For Serving

Cooked rice

"Sharing" was a word that came up a lot when we spoke with JenniLee, who often cooks for as many as two dozen workers in Fort McPherson, located in the Inuvik region of the Northwest Territories. Frozen roads and highways can sometimes make it hard to stay connected to food suppliers from far away, so "most families have at least one freezer going so that there's always something ready on hand to share with someone who might need it," she tells us. JenniLee also tells us how the communal hunts organized through her band are all about sharing knowledge, duties, and resources among the elders and younger hunters as well as the rest of the community. It's no surprise then that this dish is meant to be enjoyed with others and can easily be doubled or tripled. JenniLee makes these meatballs with her region's traditional staple of caribou, but elk, venison, or even beef work nicely as well.

1. Preheat your oven to 350°F (175°C). Line a baking sheet with aluminum foil and lightly oil the foil.
2. Stir together the bread crumbs and Caesar mix in a small bowl. Set aside to soak for a couple minutes until the bread crumbs are fully moistened.
3. Meanwhile, in a large bowl, mix together the oats, onion flakes, salt, garlic powder, onion powder, dried parsley, paprika, celery seed, black pepper, eggs, and soaked bread crumb mixture until combined.
4. Gently stir in the caribou to make a homogenous mixture. Avoid overworking the meat, to keep the meatballs as light and tender as possible.
5. Form the mixture into 2-inch (5 cm) meatballs (approximately 3 tablespoons), rolling lightly between your palms to bind them together. (Oil your hands if the meat is sticking to them.) Evenly space the meatballs on the prepared baking sheet as you work.
6. For the sweet and sour sauce, whisk together the ketchup, sugar, Caesar mix, vinegar, and soy sauce in a medium bowl. Pour the sauce over the meatballs on the baking sheet, ensuring each one is well coated.
7. Bake until the meatballs are no longer pink inside and the internal temperature is 160°F (70°C), 25 to 30 minutes.
8. Enjoy the meatballs on a bed of rice, scooping up the extra sauce to provide a finishing glaze.

Seared Scallops with Beurre Blanc Greens & Caesar Vinaigrette

Recipe by Robin Wasicuna

Twin Pine Diner

Yellowknife, Northwest Territories

Serves 4

Seasoned pro Chef Robin Wasicuna may be the only classically French-trained chef who's also a certified cannabis sommelier. Perhaps that explains this dish, which is equal parts refined and playful, in terms of both looks and taste. The Caesar vinaigrette serves as the ideal accent to the buttery heart of golden seared scallops and sweet and crunchy vegetables blanched to bright green, all coated with a velvety gin-based beurre blanc.

Caesar Vinaigrette

1 egg

⅓ cup (80 ml) Caesar mix, Mild

1½ tsp lemon juice

½ tsp Dijon mustard

½ tsp anchovy paste

½ tsp Worcestershire sauce

½ clove garlic, minced

2 Tbsp finely grated parmesan
    cheese

¼ tsp kosher salt

¼ tsp cracked black pepper

2 Tbsp extra virgin olive oil

Tender-Crisp Blanched Vegetables

12 green beans, trimmed and cut
    into 2½-inch (6 cm) batons

4 celery stalks, cut on the bias
    into ¼-inch (6 mm) slices,
    leaves reserved for garnish

12 thick asparagus spears,
    woody ends trimmed, tips
    separated, and stems thinly
    ribboned

Caesar Vinaigrette

1. Bring a small pot of water to a hard boil and prepare an ice bath. Coddle the egg by placing it in the boiling water for 1 minute then submerging it immediately in the ice bath. (See safety note on page 55.) Once cool, separate out the egg yolk to use in the vinaigrette and discard the white (or save it for another use).

2. Add the coddled egg yolk, Caesar mix, lemon juice, mustard, anchovy paste, Worcestershire sauce, garlic, cheese, salt, and pepper (in that order) to a small food processor or the mixing jar of an immersion blender. Process ingredients until smooth.

3. While the food processor or blender is running, slowly drizzle in the oil until the vinaigrette is smooth and emulsified. Store in an airtight container in the refrigerator for up to 4 days.

Tender-Crisp Blanched Vegetables

1. Bring a large pot of water to a boil and set up an ice bath.

2. Blanch the green beans, celery, and asparagus tips and ribbons in the boiling water for 30 seconds, then plunge immediately in the ice bath. Once they're cool, drain well on paper towel and set aside.

Beurre Blanc

1. Place the diced shallot in a small, heavy saucepan and add the gin, vinegar, and a pinch of pepper. Cook over medium heat until reduced by half and syrupy, about 5 minutes.

– recipe continues

Beurre Blanc

1 shallot, finely diced

¼ cup (60 ml) gin

1 tsp champagne vinegar

Cracked black pepper

½ cup (120 ml) cold salted
    butter, cubed

Seared Scallops

1 lb (450 g) sea scallops (10/20
    count)

Kosher salt and cracked black
    pepper

2 Tbsp salted butter

2 Tbsp grapeseed oil

Final Assembly

½ batch Caesar Vinaigrette

Reserved celery leaves

1 tsp freshly cracked black
    pepper

1 tsp crushed dried juniper
    berries

2. Once the mixture is reduced, start whisking in the butter, one cube at a time, until the sauce is emulsified and smooth. Beurre blanc should be the consistency of hollandaise sauce.

3. Set aside on very low heat to keep warm. (If it gets too hot or too cold, it will separate, so prepare the sauce as close to plating as possible and whisk every so often to maintain the emulsion.)

Seared Scallops

1. Preheat a large, well-seasoned cast iron skillet over high heat. While it's heating, pat the scallops dry and season with salt and pepper.

2. When the pan is hot, add the butter and oil. Once the fat starts to smoke, quickly drop in the scallops. You might have to work in batches to avoid overcrowding the pan. If working in batches, repeat the process, adding additional butter and oil as needed.

3. Sear the scallops so the exterior develops a golden crust but the meat is just translucent in the middle, about 2 minutes per side. Only move the scallops once to turn them.

Final Assembly

1. While the scallops are searing, turn the blanched vegetables in the saucepan of warm beurre blanc to coat and heat gently.

2. Serve the seared scallops on a bed of beurre blanc-coated vegetables. Dapple with the vinaigrette and garnish with the reserved celery leaves, pepper, and juniper berries.

Appendix

Sauces, Syrups, Shrubs, Vinegars & More

Infusions & Fat Washes

272

Garnishes

Bagel Cracker

Used in Double Double (page 102)

Makes 1 cracker

1 bagel, any kind (except cinnamon raisin)

1 to 2 tsp plain cream cheese

2 to 3 thin slices of fresh veggies (such as tomato, shallot, cucumber)

Pinch of Everything Bagel Spice (page 288)

1. Slice a bagel vertically into thin ¼-inch (6 mm) rounds. Toast a slice twice until crispy like a cracker.

2. Spread the bagel cracker with a layer of cream cheese (better for sticking stuff to it) and top with the thinly sliced vegetables and a pinch of everything bagel spice. While you're at it—you should have 4 or 5 more bagel slices—you might as well toast up the slices and make some snacks. Leftover double-toasted bagel slices can be stored in an airtight container at room temperature for up to 1 week.

Bar Clams, Chili Garlic

Makes about 3 cups (720 ml)

1 lb (450 g) freshly shelled cooked BC clam meat (from making clam juice, page 71)

2 cloves garlic, thinly sliced

1 to 2 red Fresno chilies, stemmed, thinly sliced in rounds, and seeded

3 thick ribbons of lemon peel, white pith removed, each 4 inches (10 cm) long

2 Tbsp flat-leaf parsley, roughly chopped

½ tsp kosher salt

10 turns cracked black pepper

1 cup (240 ml) + ½ cup (120 ml) fresh clam juice (page 71), divided

For Serving

Extra virgin olive oil

Lemon wedges

Slices of grilled crusty bread, drizzled with olive oil

1. In a medium bowl, mix together the clams, garlic, chili rounds, lemon peel, parsley, salt, pepper, and the 1 cup of clam juice. Season with additional chilies, salt, and pepper to personal taste.

2. Transfer to a large airtight glass jar and top up with an additional ½ cup clam juice if required to just cover the clams. Marinate in the refrigerator, covered, for at least 6 hours but ideally 12.

3. Right before serving, stir in a generous glug of olive oil and squeeze in the juice from the lemon wedges to taste. Present the clams alongside grilled crusty bread drizzled with olive oil—or simply place the jar on the table with a handful of toothpicks alongside for skewering. Store it in an airtight container in the refrigerator for up to 2 days.

Bar Clams, Orange Fennel

Makes about 3 cups (720 ml)

1 lb (450 g) freshly shelled BC clam meat (from making clam juice, page 71)

4 thick ribbons of orange peel, white pith removed, each 4 inches (10 cm) long

¼ cup (60 ml) thinly sliced fennel stalks

2 Tbsp fennel fronds, picked

2 Tbsp finely diced red onion

½ tsp kosher salt

¼ tsp chili flakes

10 turns cracked black pepper

1 cup (240 ml) + ½ cup (120 ml) fresh clam juice (page 71), divided

For Serving

Extra virgin olive oil

Orange wedges

Grilled crusty bread, drizzled with olive oil

1. In a medium bowl mix together the clams, orange peel, fennel fronds and stalks, onions, salt, chili flakes, pepper, and 1 cup of clam juice. Season with additional salt, pepper, and chili flakes to personal taste.

2. Transfer to a large glass jar with a lid and top up with an additional ½ cup clam juice if required to just cover the clams. Marinate in the refrigerator, covered, for at least 6 hours but ideally 12.

3. Right before serving, stir in a generous glug of olive oil and squeeze in the juice from the orange wedges to taste. Present the clams alongside grilled crusty bread drizzled with olive oil—or simply place the jar on the table with a handful of toothpicks alongside for skewering. Store the clam mixture in an airtight container in the refrigerator for up to 2 days.

Black Pepper Beef Jerky

Used in Banff Springs (page 122)

Makes 20 to 25 pieces

1 lb (450 g) lean beef (eye of round, top round, or bottom round)

1½ Tbsp packed brown sugar

2 tsp cracked black pepper

⅓ cup (80 ml) low-sodium soy sauce

1½ Tbsp Worcestershire sauce

1. Place the cut of beef in the freezer for 30 minutes to partially freeze and make slicing easier.

2. In the meantime, prepare the marinade by mixing together the sugar, pepper, soy sauce, and Worcestershire sauce in a small bowl.

3. When the meat is chilled and firm, slice it into ⅛- to ¼-inch (3 to 6 mm) thick strips, ensuring all the fat

is removed, as it will cause jerky to go rancid more quickly. You can slice with the grain for a chewier jerky, or against the grain for a more tender result.

4. Drop the meat strips into a large freezer bag and pour in the marinade, massaging the meat to ensure all the pieces are evenly coated. Refrigerate for 12 to 24 hours, giving the bag a little massage a few times throughout the marinating process.

5. Once the meat is marinated, preheat your oven to 160°F (70°C) and arrange oven racks to provide as much air flow around the racks as possible to promote even drying. Line two baking trays with aluminum foil and place oven-safe metal baking racks on top.

6. Lay the meat strips out in an even layer on the baking racks and hit each piece of meat with a couple of extra grinds of black pepper.

7. Bake for 3 to 5 hours, flipping the jerky once after 1½ hours. The total drying time will depend on the thickness of the meat and humidity levels, so check every half hour or so after the first couple of hours. To test jerky for doneness, take one piece out to cool. It should look leathery and be pliable when bent with a few cracks but not break fully.

8. When the jerky is finished and completely cool, store it in an airtight container in the refrigerator. Apparently jerky will keep for up to 2 weeks in the refrigerator but, in our homes, it's usually gone in a few days.

Buttermilk Pancakes

Makes about 12 pancakes

2 cups (480 ml) all-purpose flour

2 Tbsp granulated sugar

2 tsp baking powder

1 tsp baking soda

½ tsp kosher salt

2 cups (480 ml) + ¼ cup (60 ml) buttermilk, room temperature, divided

2 large eggs, room temperature

3 Tbsp unsalted butter, melted

Canola oil

For Serving

Butter pats

Maple syrup

1. In a large mixing bowl, sift together the flour, sugar, baking powder, baking soda, and salt. Set aside.
2. In a second mixing bowl, whisk together the 2 cups (480 ml) of buttermilk, eggs, and melted butter.
3. Pour the wet ingredients into the dry ingredients and whisk just until incorporated, adding the additional ¼ cup (60 ml) buttermilk gradually if needed to loosen the batter a bit. Do not overmix. Some small lumps are fine. (This is quite a thick batter.)
4. Let the pancake batter rest for 10 minutes. (Resting the batter gives the leavening agents time to activate and results in a high rise on the pancakes.)
5. Preheat your oven to 250°F (120°C). Heat a large non-stick pan or griddle over medium heat. Grease the pan with oil, then ladle in about ¼ cup (60 ml) of batter for each pancake. Do not crowd the pan.
6. The pancakes are ready to be flipped when bubbles form on the surface. Flip carefully to protect the rise, and continue cooking on the other side until golden brown and fluffy, about 2 minutes.
7. Repeat with the remaining batter. Place the cooked pancakes on a plate and keep warm in the oven. Serve with pats of butter and maple syrup.

Candied Arctic Char

Used in Nunavut Country Food Arctic Caesar (page 254)

Makes about 12 strips

1½ cups (360 ml) water

2 Tbsp kosher salt

¼ cup (60 ml) packed brown sugar

½ cup (120 ml) gin (or vodka or water)

½ cup (120 ml) + 3 Tbsp maple syrup, divided

½ tsp cracked black pepper

1 lb (450 g) Arctic char, cleaned, skinned, and cut into 1-inch (2.5 cm) strips

1 Tbsp canola oil

Maplewood smoker chips (as required by smoker), soaked

Cracked black pepper

1. To make the brine, pour the water into a large bowl. Add the salt and brown sugar to dissolve and then add the gin, ½ cup (120 ml) maple syrup, and pepper.
2. Place the char in a large freezer bag and pour in the brine. Place the bag in a deep baking tray (to contain any leaks) and ensure each piece of fish is submerged. Refrigerate for 8 hours.
3. Once it's brined, place the fish in a colander, rinse under fresh cold water, and then pat each piece dry.
4. Use the oil to grease an oven-safe metal baking rack with narrow enough spacing to support the fish, then evenly space each piece, flesh-side up, on it. Place a baking sheet underneath to catch any drips.
5. Refrigerate to air-dry for 2 hours so that a tacky thin skin will form and help the smoke flavour adhere.
6. Set up your smoker (or BBQ with smoker unit) with the pre-soaked maplewood chips, and preheat to 225°F (110°C). Remove the rack from the baking sheet and place it directly in the smoker. Depending on the thickness and size of the char morsels, the smoking process will take 30 to 60 minutes. Varying thicknesses will give a nice variety of chewy, jerky-like pieces and tender, flakier ones. Leave the fish on the smoker even longer if you prefer a drier finished product.
7. As the fish cooks, baste the pieces with the maple syrup every 10 to 15 minutes.
8. Once the fish has reached 140°F (60°C), is firm enough to your liking, and is nicely lacquered, remove from the smoker, baste one last time with maple syrup, and then hit it with a grind of pepper. Move the morsels to a parchment-lined baking tray while still warm to prevent sticking, and let cool to room temperature.

9. Candied char can be served at room temperature or chilled. Store it in an airtight container in the refrigerator for up to 3 days.

Celery Ribbons

Used in West Coaster (page 78)
Makes 6 to 10 ribbons

1 celery rib
1 squeeze lemon juice

1. Run a vegetable peeler lengthwise along the outer side of the celery stick to create long thin ribbons.
2. Submerge the ribbons in an ice bath and add a squeeze of lemon juice. Let them crisp up for at least an hour in the refrigerator. Ribbons can be stored in cold water overnight in the refrigerator. Remove the celery from the water and air dry before using as a garnish.

Crispy Bacon

Used in Growshow (page 86)
Makes 4 to 6 pieces

4 to 6 pieces thick-cut smoked bacon

1. Preheat your oven to 375°F (190°C). Place a baking rack on top of an aluminum foil–lined baking sheet.
2. Cook the bacon until nice and crispy, 20 to 30 minutes. Oven temperatures and bacon thicknesses vary, so keep a close eye on the bacon in the last few minutes of cooking.
3. Remove the bacon slices from the rack when they're still warm to prevent sticking and transfer to a paper towel–lined plate. Let cool to room temperature prior to using them as a garnish.
4. Store extra bacon (if you have any, which you won't) in an airtight container in the refrigerator for up to 4 days.

Crispy Buttermilk Calamari

Used in The Tree House (page 136)
Makes 20 to 40 pieces

1 lb (450 g) calamari, cleaned
1 lemon, zested and juiced
2 cups (480 ml) all-purpose flour
2 tsp sea salt
¼ tsp cracked black pepper
¾ cup (180 ml) buttermilk
Canola oil
2 tsp Old Bay seasoning

1. Cut the calamari tubes into 1-inch (2.5 cm) rings and leave the tentacles (if you have them) whole. Place them in a medium bowl.
2. Pour the lemon juice over the calamari pieces, cover, and let tenderize for 30 minutes in the refrigerator.
3. In the meantime, prepare two dredging stations by mixing together the flour, salt, and pepper in one large bowl and pouring the buttermilk into another.
4. Heat 2 to 3 inches (5 to 7.5 cm) of canola oil to 375°F (190°C) in a heavy, wide, deep-sided pot (use a candy thermometer to check the temperature).
5. Once the calamari is marinated, work in small batches to dredge and cook the morsels. Toss the calamari in the flour mixture to coat, then in the buttermilk, then back in the flour mixture, shaking off any extra flour by sifting in a colander.
6. Still working in batches, fry the calamari until golden and crisp, 2 to 3 minutes in total, carefully turning once or twice in the hot oil for even browning. Let oil come back to temperature between batches.
7. Drain the calamari on paper towel and immediately season with the Old Bay and lemon zest. Repeat with the remaining calamari and skewer when just cool enough to do so.

Dehydrated Citrus Wheels

Used in Rebuttal (page 168) and Vegeta (page 170)

Makes 8 to 10 wheels per fruit

1 lemon

1 lime (or other citrus fruit)

1. Preheat your oven to 170°F (75°C). Slice the lemon and lime into wheels ¼ inch (6 mm) thick. A mandolin works well, but a sharp knife will do the trick too.
2. Arrange the citrus wheels on an oven-safe metal baking rack set on top of a baking sheet.
3. Let the citrus dehydrate in the oven for 4 to 6 hours, flipping after 2 hours. You'll know they're done when all the moisture is fully evaporated and they're almost brittle to the touch. Check by removing a citrus wheel from the oven and letting it cool. It should feel crisp and completely dry. Store in an airtight container in your pantry for up to 1 month.

Elk Jerky

Used in Miner's Daughter (page 252)

Makes 20 to 25 pieces

1 lb (450 g) lean elk meat, top round or other lean cut (or caribou or beef) (see note)

1 tsp + 1 Tbsp juniper berries, finely crushed, divided

1½ tsp salt

¼ cup (60 ml) Worcestershire sauce

2 Tbsp Canadian wildflower honey

2 Tbsp apple cider vinegar

½ tsp hickory liquid smoke

1. Place the meat in the freezer for 30 minutes to partially freeze and make slicing easier.
2. In the meantime, prepare the marinade by mixing together the 1 tsp of juniper berries, salt, Worcestershire sauce, honey, vinegar, and liquid smoke in a small bowl.
3. When the meat is chilled and firm, thinly slice into ⅛- to ¼-inch (3 to 6 mm) thick strips, ensuring all fat is removed, as it will cause the jerky to go rancid more quickly. You can slice the meat with the grain for a chewier jerky, or against the grain for a more tender result.
4. Drop the meat into a large freezer bag and pour in the marinade, massaging to ensure all pieces are coated. Refrigerate for 12 to 24 hours, giving the bag a massage a few times throughout the marinating process.
5. Once marinated, preheat your oven to 160°F (70°C) and arrange oven racks to provide as much air flow around the racks as possible to promote even drying. Line two baking sheets with aluminum foil and place an oven-safe metal baking rack on top of each one.
6. Lay the meat strips out in an even layer on the baking racks and dust the jerky strips with the remaining 1 Tbsp juniper berries.
7. Bake for 3 to 5 hours, flipping the jerky once after 1½ hours. The total drying time will depend on the thickness of the meat and humidity levels, so check every half hour or so after the first couple of hours. To test the jerky for doneness, take one piece out to cool. It should look leathery and be pliable when bent with a few cracks, but not break fully.
8. When the jerky is finished and completely cool, refrigerate it in an airtight container for up to 2 weeks.

Note: Elk roam throughout Yukon, and elk sausages, steaks, and delicious jerky feature on almost all menus in the region. Substitute your own local favourite if elk isn't readily available wherever you may be.

Grandma Shirley's Mustard Pickles

Used in Yellow (page 222)

Makes 8 cups (2 L)

3½ cups (840 ml) water

6 Tbsp (90 ml) pickling salt

4 cups (960 ml) sliced pickling or mini cucumbers (½-inch/
1 cm rounds)

½ lb (225 g) white pearl onions, peeled

1 small onion, finely diced

2 celery stalks, finely diced

¼ large cauliflower head, separated into florets

1 green bell pepper, finely diced

½ red bell pepper, finely diced

1¼ cups + ¼ cup (300 ml + 60 ml) granulated sugar,
divided

1 cup + ¼ cup (240 ml + 60 ml) white vinegar, divided

1½ tsp mustard seed

1 tsp celery seed

¼ cup (60 ml) all-purpose flour

1 Tbsp dry mustard

½ tsp ground turmeric

1. Make a brine by pouring the water into a medium
saucepan over high heat. Add the pickling salt, bring
to a boil, and boil until the salt is fully dissolved.
2. Place the cucumbers, pearl onions, onions, celery,
cauliflower, and bell peppers in a large bowl. Pour the
hot brine over the vegetables and place a heavy plate
on top to keep the vegetables submerged. Cover the
bowl and let stand at room temperature overnight
(10 to 12 hours).
3. In the morning, drain the vegetables in a colander,
then rinse under cold running water and set aside.
4. In a pot large enough to hold all the brined vegetables,
bring the 1¼ cups (300 ml) of sugar, 1 cup (240 ml) of
vinegar, mustard seed, and celery seed to a boil. Add
the vegetables and bring to a boil again.
5. Meanwhile, whisk together the flour, dry mustard,
turmeric, the remaining ¼ cup (60 ml) sugar, and the
remaining ¼ cup (60 ml) vinegar in a small bowl until
smooth and homogenous. Stir this mixture into the pot.
6. Stir gently to coat all the vegetables and prevent the
sauce from sticking to the bottom of the pot. Continue
to boil for 3 to 5 minutes until sauce thickens enough
to coat the back of spoon.
7. Carefully divide up the hot pickles and accompanying

sauce into two 4-cup (960 ml) glass jars. Cover with
the lid while still hot. (There's no need to sterilize the
jars first.) Let cool to room temperature, then store in
the refrigerator for up to 2 months.

Grilled Pineapple Skewer

Used in Oaxaca (page 182)

Makes 1 skewer

1 pineapple spear (6 × 1 inches/15 × 2.5 cm)

½ tsp honey

Pinch Tajín

1 long wooden or steel skewer

1. Place the pineapple spear on the skewer. (If you're
using a wooden skewer, soak it in advance so it
doesn't burn.) Get a BBQ (or grill pan) screaming
hot and grill the pineapple on all sides until nice char
marks develop, approximately 5 minutes per side.
2. Remove the pineapple skewer from heat and, while
it's still hot, brush with the honey and dust with a
pinch of Tajín.

Grilled Prawns

Used in Green (page 88)

Makes 8 prawns

8 head-on, tail-on prawns (16/20 count), deveined

2 Tbsp olive oil

½ tsp sea salt

½ tsp cracked black pepper

1 lemon wedge

1. Toss the prawns in the oil, salt, and pepper.
2. Preheat a pan or grill to medium-high. Once it's hot,
add the prawns, turning occasionally, until they turn
bright red, about 5 minutes.

3. Remove from the heat and squeeze the juice from the lemon wedge on top. These can be served warm off the grill or stored in an airtight container in the refrigerator for up to 3 days and served cold.

Grilled Tofu Skewers

Used in Hot & Sour (page 84)

Makes 8 pieces

1 block (12 oz/350 g) extra-firm tofu
3 Tbsp soy sauce
1 Tbsp rice vinegar
1 Tbsp granulated sugar
¼ tsp red pepper flakes
Canola oil

1. Press the block of tofu for 30 minutes by wrapping it loosely in a clean tea towel and sandwiching it between two flat surfaces such as baking trays. Place a heavy item—like a cast iron skillet—evenly on the top baking tray to help press the tofu block.

2. Prepare the marinade by mixing together the soy sauce, rice vinegar, sugar, and red pepper flakes in a small bowl until the sugar is dissolved.

3. Slice the pressed tofu into eight long, evenly sized strips. Place them in a shallow-sided dish and pour the marinade evenly over top to coat each strip. Marinate in the refrigerator for at least 30 minutes, turning the strips occasionally for even coverage.

4. Once the tofu is marinated, start heating a BBQ or grill pan over high heat. While it heats, carefully thread a skewer lengthwise through the middle of each tofu strip. (If you're using wooden skewers, soak them in advance so they don't burn.)

5. When the grill pan is hot, brush it liberally with oil to prevent sticking and grill the tofu skewers for 10 to 12 minutes, turning to achieve beautifully caramelized grill marks on all four sides. The leftover marinade can be brushed on top throughout cooking for extra flavour and colour.

6. These are best served warm. If not used immediately as a garnish, they can be stored in an airtight container in the refrigerator for up to 4 days.

Lobster Tail

Used in Consider the Lobster (page 220)

Makes 2 servings

1 lobster tail
1 tsp olive oil
3 Tbsp Citrus Brown Butter, melted (page 294), divided
1 tsp chopped flat-leaf parsley
1 tsp lemon zest

1. Preheat your BBQ for direct medium-high heat. (You can also use a grill pan over medium-high heat.)

2. Cut the lobster tail in half lengthwise (through the "belly" side) with a sharp chef's knife and insert a metal skewer lengthwise along each half to stop them from curling during grilling. Brush the lobster meat with the oil to help protect the delicate meat and prevent sticking.

3. When the grill is hot and ready, grill the lobster tails flesh-side down for 5 minutes and then turn over to expose the caramelized grill marks. At this point, baste the lobster meat with half of the butter. Cook shell-side down until the meat is opaque and the internal temperature is 135°F (60°C), 4 to 6 minutes.

4. Take the lobster tail halves off the heat to prevent overcooking and carefully remove the metal skewers. Brush generously with the remaining butter and finish with a dusting of parsley and lemon zest. Store extra in an airtight container in the refrigerator for up to 2 days.

Maple-Glazed Pepper Bacon

Used in The Chucks (page 124)

Makes 10 to 12 slices

1 lb (450 g) thick-cut smoked bacon
2 Tbsp Canadian maple syrup
Cracked black pepper

1. Preheat your oven to 375°F (190°C).
2. Place two oven-safe metal baking racks on top of two aluminum foil–lined baking trays and lay the bacon strips out on a single layer.
3. Cook the bacon until the slices just start to brown and bubble, 15 to 20 minutes, and then carefully remove the trays from the oven.
4. Brush the top of each piece of bacon with maple syrup and season with a few turns of pepper to taste. Return the trays to the oven until the bacon is nice and crispy, 5 to 15 minutes. (You want the bacon to be crisp enough to stand up in a glass.) Oven temperatures and bacon thicknesses vary, so keep a close eye on the bacon in the last few minutes of cooking.
5. Remove the bacon from the racks when still warm to prevent sticking and transfer to a parchment-lined baking tray in a single layer. Let cool to room temperature before using as a garnish. Store extra in an airtight container in the refrigerator for up to 4 days.

Maple Snow Taffy

Used in Cabane à Sucre (page 160)

Makes 10 lollipops

4 cups (960 ml) freshly fallen snow or finely crushed ice
½ cup (120 ml) pure Canadian maple syrup
10 Popsicle sticks
Flaked sea salt

1. Gather fresh clean snow in a deep-sided baking tray and pack down evenly. When clean snow isn't available, use a blender to pulverize ice cubes and create homemade snow. Keep the snow-packed tray in the freezer until you're ready to go.
2. In a small saucepan, bring the maple syrup to a boil over medium-high heat. Once the syrup reaches soft ball stage (see note), or 235°F to 240°F (112°C to 115°C) measured with a candy thermometer, remove from the heat and let sit for 2 to 3 minutes while the bubbles dissipate and the syrup cools slightly.
3. Carefully drizzle the maple syrup along the packed snow in 6-inch (15 cm) strips, one line at a time. When the syrup just starts to firm up on the snow, 20 to 30 seconds, place a Popsicle stick at one edge and start rolling up the maple taffy. Sprinkle each lollipop with a pinch of salt to finish.
4. If the maple syrup starts to cool and thicken too much to drizzle, gently reheat on the stove until it's liquid again. The lollipops can be stored, uncovered, in the freezer on parchment paper or a silicone mat in an even layer until ready to serve but are best eaten immediately by eager onlookers.

Note: To test the soft ball stage without using a candy thermometer, fill a glass with cold water and a little bit of ice. Take a teaspoon and drop a little bit of the maple syrup in the ice water. Let it cool completely and remove the syrup. If it forms a ball and is sticky and pliable so that it can be moulded by your fingers, it's ready. In other words, it forms a "soft ball" of candy.

Ocean Water Steamed Lobster Claws

Used in The Fashion Caesar (page 262)

Makes 2 claws

1 lemon, quartered
4 bay leaves
10 black peppercorns
2 fresh tarragon sprigs
1 live Atlantic lobster (1½ lb/680g)

1. Fill a large stock pot that will fit a steamer rack about one-quarter full with fresh ocean water (or use fresh water and add 1 Tbsp salt for every 2 cups/480 ml of water to get a similar salinity level). Turn the heat to high, add the lemon, bay leaves, peppercorns, and tarragon and then bring to a vigorous boil for 5 minutes. Carefully drop in the steamer rack. It should sit right above the water line.

2. Before steaming the lobster, stun it by putting it in the freezer or a large ice bath for 20 minutes. Put the stunned lobster on its back on a cutting board. Plunge the tip of a sharp chef's knife about 2 inches (5 cm) from the tip of the head on the underside (along the longitudinal midline between the front legs) and pivot the knife down to split the head. If you're unsure how to dispatch a lobster, there are lots of videos online.

3. Place the lobster on top of the steamer rack. Cover the pot and steam on high heat for 12 to 15 minutes. One sign of doneness is when an antenna or small leg pops off easily when tugged or an instant read thermometer inserted into the thickest part of the tail meat through the underside reads 135°F to 140°F (57°C to 60°C). The lobster meat will be opaque white when fully cooked and the shell a bright red.

4. Remove the lobster from the pot and, using clean tea towels for a better grip, twist the claws off the lobster body (careful, it will be hot!). Remove the claws from the knuckles and reserve the remaining lobster meat in an airtight container in the refrigerator for up to 2 days. Perfect for impromptu lobster rolls. (Method: Grill split top hot dog buns on both sides with butter. Warm the shelled lobster meat in melted butter, season with salt, pepper, and a squeeze of lemon juice. Serve in the hot dog buns.)

5. Refrigerate the claws until chilled and serve cold along with a lobster cracker and bib. For ease of eating with the Caesar, crack the claws halfway (across) with the cracker and remove the shell from the bottom half. Skewer the exposed claw meat to balance as a garnish.

Parmesan Tuile
Used in The Umami One (page 104)
Makes two 4-inch (10 cm) round tuiles

½ cup (120 ml) grated parmesan cheese

1. Preheat your oven to 400°F (200°C). Line a baking sheet with a silicone baking mat or parchment paper.
2. Divide the grated cheese into two well-spaced piles on the prepared baking sheet. Pat down gently so the piles are flat and even.
3. Bake until crisp, lacy, and golden, 4 to 6 minutes. Let cool completely before removing from the baking tray. Store in an airtight container at room temperature and eat within 1 day. But they won't last that long.

Quick-Pickle Basic Recipe
Makes 4 cups (960 ml)

1¼ cups (300 ml) water
1¼ cups (300 ml) vinegar (white, apple cider, rice, red wine, white wine, etc.)
3 Tbsp granulated sugar
2 Tbsp kosher salt
3 tsp dried spices (peppercorns, mustard seed, coriander seed, fennel seed, red pepper flakes, sumac, bay leaf, etc.)
1 lb (450 g) vegetables, sliced (cucumber, carrot, radish, cauliflower, green bean, onion, fennel, etc.)
2 garlic cloves, smashed (optional)
2 to 3 sprigs fresh herbs (dill, thyme, tarragon, chives, etc.)

1. To prepare the brine, place the water, vinegar, sugar, salt, and spices of your choice in a medium saucepan and bring to a boil over medium-high heat. Boil for 1 minute, or until the sugar and salt are dissolved. Meanwhile pack your vegetables, garlic, and fresh herbs tightly into two 2-cup (480 ml) Mason jars.

2. Carefully pour the boiling-hot pickling brine over the vegetables, ensuring they are fully immersed. Seal with the lids and allow to come to room temperature before storing in the refrigerator.

3. Allow a minimum of 24 hours before serving. The flavours will continue to intensify for 5 or 6 days. Store in the refrigerator for up to 6 weeks.

Notes: 1) This basic recipe can be customized in any number of ways by changing (or combining) the type of vinegar, increasing the vinegar to water ratio (i.e., more vinegar), adding a bit more sugar if you like a sweeter pickle (or vice versa), changing the herbs and spices, and of course, changing the vegetables. 2) Because quick pickles are kept in the refrigerator, there is no need to sterilize the jars.

Quick-Pickled Chaga Vegetables

Used in Bug Repellent (page 258)
Makes 4 cups (960 ml)

1½ cups (360 ml) water
¾ cup (180 ml) white vinegar
¼ cup (60 ml) balsamic vinegar
½ cup (120 ml) granulated sugar
¼ cup (60 ml) kosher salt
1 Tbsp powdered chaga (see note)
1 Tbsp fennel seed
1 tsp peppercorn medley
1 tsp whole coriander seed
8 oz (225 g) baby garden carrots, peeled and halved lengthwise
8 oz (225 g) pickling cucumber, quartered lengthwise

1. To prepare the brine, place the water, both vinegars, sugar, salt, chaga, fennel seed, peppercorns, and coriander seed in a medium saucepan, bring to a boil, then boil for 1 minute. Meanwhile, pack your vegetables into two 2-cup (480 ml) Mason jars.

2. Carefully pour the boiling-hot pickling brine over the vegetables in the jars, ensuring they're fully immersed. Close the lids and allow to come to room temperature before storing in the refrigerator.

3. Refrigerate for a minimum of 24 hours before serving. The flavours will continue to intensify for 5 or 6 days. Store in the refrigerator for up to 6 weeks.

Note: Chaga is a mushroom that grows at the base of birch trees in the northern hemisphere. It is purported to have the highest antioxidant properties of any food. You can find it online in powdered or whole dried form.

Quick-Pickled Chanterelles

Used in Chanterelle (page 126)
Makes 4 cups (960 ml)

2 cups (480 ml) water
1 cup (240 ml) rice vinegar
¾ cup (180 ml) granulated sugar
3 Tbsp kosher salt
1 Tbsp mustard seeds
1 Tbsp finely chopped ginger root
1 Tbsp chopped fresh jalapeño (with seeds)
1½ tsp cloves
1½ tsp black peppercorns
8 oz (225 g) chanterelle mushrooms, cleaned

1. Place the water, vinegar, sugar, salt, mustard seeds, ginger, jalapeño, cloves, and peppercorns in a medium pot over high heat. Bring to a rolling boil and then keep at a boil for 5 minutes to incorporate the flavours. Strain through a fine-mesh strainer or cheesecloth.

2. Meanwhile, pack the chanterelles into two 2-cup (480 ml) Mason jars and carefully pour the hot liquid over top until the mushrooms are fully submerged. Seal with the lids and allow to come to room temperature before storing in the refrigerator.

3. Leave to pickle for at least 24 hours before serving. The flavours will continue to intensify for 5 or 6 days. These will keep well for up to 6 weeks in the refrigerator. Extra pickled chanterelles can be served on toast spread with chèvre and fresh herbs.

Quick-Pickled Cucumber

Used in The Merman (page 90)
Makes 4 cups (960 ml)

1¼ cups (300 ml) water
1¼ cups (300 ml) white vinegar
3 Tbsp granulated sugar
2 Tbsp kosher salt
1 bay leaf
2 tsp mustard seeds
1 tsp black peppercorns
1 lb (450 g) pickling (Kirby) cucumber, quartered lengthwise
10 to 12 fronds fresh dill
2 garlic cloves, smashed

1. To prepare the brine, place the water, vinegar, sugar, salt, bay leaf, mustard seeds, and peppercorns in a medium saucepan over high heat. Bring to a boil and keep at a boil until the sugar and salt are dissolved, 1 minute. Meanwhile pack your cucumber, dill, and garlic tightly into two 2-cup (480 ml) Mason jars.
2. Allow the brine to cool to room temperature then pour over the vegetables in the jars, ensuring they're fully immersed. Close the lids and allow to come to room temperature before storing in the refrigerator.
3. Refrigerate for a minimum 24 hours before serving. The flavours will continue to intensify for 5 or 6 days. Store in the refrigerator for up to 6 weeks.

Quick-Pickled Fiddleheads

Used in Chartier (page 134)
Makes 4 cups (960 ml)

1 lb (450 g) fiddleheads (see note)
1 cup (240 ml) water
1 cup (240 ml) rice vinegar
½ cup (120 ml) lemon juice
3 Tbsp packed brown sugar
3 Tbsp granulated sugar
1 Tbsp kosher salt
1 jalapeño, stemmed and sliced into rounds (with seeds)

1. Bring a medium pot of water to a rolling boil over high heat. Meanwhile, wash your fiddleheads and remove any brown sheathing you see. Add the fiddleheads to the water, boil for 4 minutes, then strain and run under cold water to stop the cooking process. Drain and pack the blanched fiddleheads in two 2-cup (480 ml) Mason jars.
2. Meanwhile, in a second medium pot, combine the water, vinegar, lemon juice, both sugars, salt, and jalapeño. Bring to a boil over high heat and continue to boil for 1 minute until the sugars dissolve. If you would like less spice, remove the jalapeño slices at this point.
3. Carefully pour the boiling hot pickling brine over the blanched fiddleheads, ensuring they are fully immersed. Close the lids and allow to come to room temperature before storing in the refrigerator.
4. Refrigerate for a minimum of 24 hours of pickling before serving. The flavours will continue to intensify for 5 or 6 days. These keep well refrigerated for up to 6 weeks.

Note: If fiddleheads are not in season, substitute sliced Kirby or pickling cucumbers.

Quick-Pickled Growshow Vegetables

Used in Growshow (page 86)

Makes 2 cups (480 ml)

8 oz (225 g) garden vegetables (such as carrot, pickling cucumber, radish, asparagus)

½ cup (120 ml) water

½ cup (120 ml) white vinegar

2 Tbsp granulated sugar

2 Tbsp kosher salt

1. Slice the vegetables about ½ inch (1 cm) thick and pack tightly into a 2-cup (480 ml) Mason jar.
2. Add the water, vinegar, sugar, and salt to a medium pot over high heat. Bring to a rolling boil and boil until the sugar and salt are dissolved. Remove from the heat.
3. Once the brine has cooled to warm, pour it into the jar, ensuring the vegetables are fully submerged. Seal and refrigerate for a minimum of 24 hours of pickling before serving. The flavours will continue to intensify for 5 or 6 days. These keep well refrigerated for up to 6 weeks.

Quick-Pickled Mixed Vegetables

Used in Windowsill (page 80)

Makes 4 cups (960 ml)

1¼ cups (300 ml) water

1¼ cups (300 ml) rice vinegar

3 Tbsp granulated sugar

2 Tbsp kosher salt

1 tsp fennel seed

1 tsp black peppercorns

1 tsp coriander seed

2 garlic cloves, smashed

1 lb (450 g) mixed vegetables, sliced into bite-size pieces (such as carrot, pickling cucumber, radish, cauliflower)

1. To prepare the brine, add the water, vinegar, sugar, salt, fennel seed, peppercorns, and coriander seed to a medium saucepan over high heat. Bring to a boil and boil until the sugar and salt are dissolved, 1 minute. Meanwhile pack your garlic and mixed vegetables tightly into two 2-cup (480 ml) Mason jars.
2. Carefully pour the boiling-hot pickling brine over the vegetables in the jars, ensuring they are fully immersed. Close the lids and allow to come to room temperature before storing in the refrigerator.
3. Refrigerate for a minimum of 24 hours before serving. The flavours will continue to intensify for 5 or 6 days. Store in the refrigerator for up to 6 weeks.

Quick-Pickled Pearl Onions

Used in Untitled (The Amaro One) (page 186)

Makes 2 cups (480 ml)

8 oz (225 g) pearl onions, peeled

3 to 4 sprigs fresh thyme

½ cup (120 ml) water

½ cup (120 ml) red wine vinegar

¼ cup (60 ml) granulated sugar

1 Tbsp kosher salt

1 tsp red peppercorns

1 tsp white peppercorns

1. Bring a medium pot of water to a rolling boil over high heat. Add the onions to the water, boil for 3 to 4 minutes (the onions should still be tender-crisp and not soft), then strain and run under cold water to stop the cooking process. Drain and pack the onions and fresh thyme in a 2-cup (480 ml) Mason jar.
2. Meanwhile, add ½ cup (120 ml) water, vinegar, sugar, salt, and peppercorns to a medium saucepan and bring to a boil over high heat. Boil until the sugar and salt are dissolved, 1 minute.
3. Carefully pour the boiling-hot pickling brine over the vegetables in the jar, ensuring they are fully immersed. Close the lid and allow to come to room temperature before storing in the refrigerator.

4. Refrigerate for a minimum of 24 hours before serving. The flavours will continue to intensify for 5 or 6 days. Store in the refrigerator for up to 6 weeks.

Roasted Duck Sausage

Used in Bingo (page 184) and
Duck Fat Washed Gin (page 301)
Make 4 sausages

4 duck sausages (see note)

1. Preheat your oven to 325°F (160°C). Roast the sausages in a casserole dish until they reach an internal temperature of 165°F (75°C).
2. Once cooked, remove the sausages from the dish, reserving the rendered fat. (Carefully pour the rendered fat into a bowl, for making Duck Fat Washed Gin, page 301.) Let the sausage cool and then refrigerate in an airtight container for up to 4 days.

    Note: We recommend the duck and smoked wild mushroom sausages from Renegade Harvest but any duck sausage will do.

Roasted Dulse

Used in The Diplomat (page 180) and
Ketchup Chip Rim (page 289)
Makes ½ oz (14 g)

½ oz (14 g) dulse

1. Preheat your oven to 350°F (175°C) and line a baking sheet with parchment paper.
2. Place the dulse on the prepared baking sheet and roast until crispy but not coloured, 15 minutes. Let cool, then store in an airtight container in your pantry for up to 1 week.

Roasted Marrow Bone

Used in It's a Thing, Man (page 128)
Makes 4 split marrow bones

2 centre-cut beef or veal marrow bones (each 4 inches/10 cm long), split lengthwise (see note)
1 tsp sel gris
1 tsp cracked black pepper
4 thick slices sourdough bread
Olive oil

1. Preheat your oven to 450°F (230°C).
2. Place the beef bones marrow-side up in a roasting pan. If they seem to be falling over on their sides, prop them up with aluminum foil on either side to keep them level and prevent the marrow from slipping out.
3. Season with the sel gris and pepper and then roast until the bones are browned and the marrow is soft but not melted, 10 to 15 minutes. The timing depends on the thickness of the bones. The marrow can easily liquefy and leak from the bones if overcooked, so check in on them at the 10-minute point.
4. Brush one side of the bread with oil. In the last 2 minutes of the marrow cooking time, place the bread oil-side up in the oven until well toasted.
5. Finish with a pinch of sel gris, alongside the toasted sourdough and a small spoon for scooping and spreading the melt-in-your-mouth marrow.

    Note: You can source marrow bones from your local butcher or grocery store. Ask them to split them for you.

Serrano Ham & Blue Cheese Croquetas

Makes 16 to 20 croquetas

3 Tbsp butter
1 medium onion, finely diced
4 oz (120 g) serrano ham, cut into thin ½-inch (1 cm) long strips

1 cup (240 ml) all-purpose flour, divided

1½ cups (360 ml) whole milk

2 oz (55 g) creamy blue cheese, crumbled

Cayenne pepper

Kosher salt and cracked black pepper

2 large eggs, well beaten

1 cup (240 ml) dried bread crumbs

Canola oil

1. Line a baking sheet with parchment or wax paper.

2. Melt the butter in a medium-size heavy pot over medium heat. Add the onions and cook until soft but not browned, about 4 minutes. Add the ham and cook for about 1 more minute. Stir in ½ cup (120 ml) of the flour and cook, stirring constantly, until well incorporated, about 4 minutes. In the meantime, heat the milk in a small saucepan over medium heat until hot but not boiling.

3. Gradually add the hot milk to the flour, stirring constantly until thickened and the mixture starts pulling away from the sides of the pot.

4. Take the pot off the heat and stir in the cheese until completely melted. Season this sauce with cayenne pepper, salt, and pepper to taste.

5. Pour the thickened sauce onto the prepared baking sheet using a rubber spatula to spread evenly. Let cool to room temperature, then cover with plastic wrap and refrigerate until set, at least 1 hour.

6. Prepare a dredging station by placing the remaining ½ cup (120 ml) flour, the beaten eggs, and bread crumbs in three separate mixing bowls. Dust your hands with flour. Spoon the mixture into walnut-size pieces and then roll each piece into a ball. Roll each ball in the flour, then drop into the egg mixture with a fork, and finally transfer to the bread crumbs. They must be completely coated in bread crumbs or they'll leak when they're cooking (see note).

7. Pour about 3 inches (7.5 cm) of oil in a large, deep-sided, heavy skillet and warm over medium-high heat to 360°F (180°C) (use a candy thermometer to check the temperature). Working in batches so as not to crowd the pan, carefully add the croquetas to the hot oil. Gently turn until golden brown on all sides, about 3 minutes. Remove with a slotted spoon and drain on paper towels, season lightly with salt. Reheat the oil to 360°F (180°C) between batches. Serve immediately.

Note: Once croquetas have been formed and breaded, they can be frozen on a baking sheet. Once frozen store in a freezer bag for up to 1 month. Do not defrost before frying.

Smoky Pickled Egg

Used in Scotch Creek (page 96)

Makes 12 eggs

12 large eggs, hard-boiled and peeled

3 cups (720 ml) water

1 cup (240 ml) white wine vinegar

2 Tbsp tamari

1 Tbsp liquid hickory smoke

1½ Tbsp sea salt

1. Divide the eggs evenly between two 4-cup (960 ml) Mason jars.

2. Pour the water, vinegar, tamari, and liquid smoke in a medium pot over high heat. Stir in the salt, bring to a boil, turn down the heat, and simmer for 1 minute. Remove from the heat to cool slightly.

3. Pour the brine over the eggs, ensuring they're fully submerged. Place the lids on the jars and let cool to room temperature before refrigerating. Allow the eggs to pickle for 3 days before serving. The eggs will keep well in the refrigerator for up to 1 month.

Taro Chips

Used in Vegeta (page 170)
Makes 24 to 36 chips

1 medium taro root, peeled
Canola oil
Fleur de sel
Aonori (see note)

1. Using a mandolin or sharp knife, thinly slice the taro root into ⅛-inch (3 mm) rounds.
2. Heat 2 to 3 inches (5 to 7.5 cm) of oil to 350°F (175°C) in a heavy, wide, deep-sided saucepan (use a candy thermometer to check the temperature). Deep-fry the taro rounds until golden and crispy, 2 to 3 minutes. Fry them in batches to avoid overcrowding the pan. Let oil come back to temperature between batches.
3. Drain the taro chips on paper towel–lined trays and, working quickly, season to taste with the fleur de sel and aonori while they're still hot.
4. Let cool to room temperature before eating and/or using as a garnish. Before storing any extra chips, let them dry at room temperature, uncovered, for 6 to 12 hours. Once they're completely dry, the chips can be stored in an airtight container at room temperature for up to 2 weeks.

Note: Aonori (also known as green laver) is a traditional Japanese green seaweed that is typically sold dried or powdered. Ideally, you will want powdered for this recipe. Aonori can be found at Asian grocery stores or online. If you can't find it, you can substitute with finely crushed dried nori or nori flakes.

Tteokbokki

Used in K-Pop (page 172)
Makes 2 to 3 pieces

1 tsp sesame oil
1 Korean rice cake (4- to 6-inch/10 to 15 cm), sliced into 2-inch (5 cm) pieces
K-Pop Rim (page 289)
Black sesame seeds

1. Preheat a pan or grill to medium. Once it's hot, add the sesame oil and rice cake pieces. Sauté the rice cake pieces, turning occasionally, until crispy and light brown on all sides (more colour = more flavour), 2 to 3 minutes.
2. Once they're crispy, season with a pinch of rim spice and a pinch of sesame seeds. Remove the pan from the heat. Place the rice cakes on a skewer. Return to the pan and cover to keep warm while you make your drink.

Note: Tteokbokki is a classic Korean dish made of stir-fried rice cakes and is often served as a bar snack or by street vendors.

Rims

Bingo Rim

Used in Bingo (page 184)

Makes ¾ cup (180 ml)

2 Tbsp granulated sugar

2 Tbsp flaked sea salt

1 Tbsp cracked black pepper

1 Tbsp ground white pepper

1 Tbsp ground mustard seed

1 Tbsp ground coriander

1 Tbsp garlic powder

1 Tbsp onion powder

1 Tbsp dried dill

1 Tbsp red pepper flakes

1. Mix all the ingredients together in a bowl.
2. Transfer to an airtight container and store in your pantry indefinitely.

Caribou Jerky Rim

Used in Nunavut Country Food Arctic Caesar (page 254)

Makes about ¾ cup (180 ml)

½ cup (120 ml) caribou, elk, or beef jerky, dry and loosely packed (page 276 or store-bought)

¼ cup (60 ml) roasted unsalted pecans

1½ tsp Montreal steak spice

½ tsp sweet paprika

¼ tsp ground coriander

¼ tsp dried oregano

¼ tsp crushed red pepper flakes

1. Place the jerky in a food processor and chop it to a fine shred.
2. Add the pecans, steak spice, paprika, coriander, oregano, and a pinch of red pepper flakes and pulse to combine.
3. Transfer to an airtight container and store in your pantry for up to 6 weeks.

Celeriac Rim

Used in Garde Manger (page 166)

Makes about 1½ cups (360 ml)

1 small celeriac (celery root), trimmed, peeled, and grated finely (roughly 2 cups/480 ml, loosely packed)

2 Tbsp dried onion flakes

1 Tbsp cracked black pepper

1 Tbsp dried garlic flakes

1 Tbsp dill seed, slightly crushed

1 Tbsp coriander seed, slightly crushed

1 Tbsp kosher salt

1 tsp sweet paprika

1. Preheat your oven to 200°F (95°C) and line a baking sheet with parchment paper.
2. Mix all the ingredients in a large bowl until the celeriac is well incorporated with the dried spices.
3. Spread the rim spice mixture evenly across the prepared baking sheet. Dry out in the oven until the mixture is completely dry and brittle, 5 to 6 hours. (This is done to dry out the wet celery root and infuse the other spice flavours. The end result is delicious and worth the effort.)
4. Let cool and crush to the consistency of coarse sand with a mortar and pestle.
5. Transfer to an airtight container and store in your pantry for up to 6 months.

Celery Salt

Used in Smoked Herb (page 82), Growshow (page 86), and others

Makes about ½ cup (120 ml)

2 cups (480 ml) celery leaves, loosely packed

3 Tbsp celery seed, whole

3 Tbsp kosher salt (ideally Diamond Crystal)

1. Preheat your oven to 200°F (95°C). Line a baking tray with parchment paper.
2. Place the celery leaves (no stems) on the prepared baking tray. Dry in the oven until the leaves are brittle and crushable with no moisture remaining, 20 to 25 minutes. Let cool completely and then crush gently in a small mortar and pestle, leaving some flakes and texture. You're not looking for celery leaf dust. Transfer to a small bowl.
3. Using the mortar and pestle again, grind the celery seed to a fine powder. Add to the celery leaf flakes along with the salt. Mix to incorporate.
4. Transfer to an airtight container and store in your pantry for up to 6 months.

Everything Bagel Spice

Used in Double Double (page 102) and Bagel Cracker (page 272)

Makes about 1 cup (240 ml)

½ cup (120 ml) sesame seeds

¼ cup (60 ml) poppy seeds

1 tsp whole fennel seed

½ tsp whole caraway seed

¼ tsp red pepper flakes

¼ tsp citric acid

2 Tbsp nutritional yeast

½ tsp garlic powder

½ tsp onion powder

½ tsp Celery Salt (page 288 or store-bought)

1. In a small saucepan on medium-low heat, lightly toast the sesame and poppy seeds until the sesame seeds are golden, 3 to 5 minutes. Add the fennel and caraway seeds, and toast for 2 to 3 minutes more until fragrant. Remove from the heat.
2. Using a mortar and pestle or spice grinder, crush the toasted seeds, red pepper flakes, and citric acid into a coarse grind (like beach sand). Pour into a small bowl and add the nutritional yeast, garlic powder, onion powder, and celery salt and mix well.
3. Store in an airtight container in the freezer for up to 1 year.

Fashion Rim

Used in The Fashion Caesar (page 262)

Makes about ½ cup (120 ml)

⅓ cup (80 ml) Walter Rim Spice

1 Tbsp cane sugar

1 tsp ground cloves

1 tsp ground nutmeg

1. Mix all the ingredients together in a bowl.
2. Transfer to an airtight container and store in your pantry indefinitely.

Fed Rim

Used in The Fed (page 188)

Makes about ¾ cup (180 ml)

5 Tbsp (75 ml) kosher salt

2½ Tbsp Tajín

2 Tbsp granulated sugar

1 Tbsp Old Bay seasoning

1 Tbsp smoked paprika

1. Mix all the ingredients in a bowl.
2. Transfer to an airtight container and store in your pantry indefinitely.

Garlic Scape Salt

Used in Scotch Creek (page 96)
Makes about ½ cup (120 ml)

½ cup (120 ml) sea salt
¼ cup (60 ml) roughly chopped garlic scapes (see note)

1. Preheat oven to 200°F (95°C). Line a baking tray with parchment paper.
2. Pulse the salt and garlic scapes in a spice grinder or food processor, or grind with a mortar and pestle, until it makes an even paste. Place the mixture on the prepared baking tray. Dry in the oven for 1 hour shaking halfway through until uniformly dried.
3. Transfer to an airtight container and store in your pantry up to 6 months.

Note: If garlic scapes are not readily available, you may substitute green onions.

Ketchup Chip Rim

Used in The Diplomat (page 180)
Makes about 2 cups (480 ml)

1 bag (165 g) ketchup chips
¼ oz (7 g) Roasted Dulse (page 284)
1½ Tbsp pink peppercorns
2 tsp sweet paprika
2 tsp granulated sugar
1½ tsp dried dill
½ tsp Celery Salt (page 288 or store-bought)

1. Reserve a few nice big chips for the garnish, then crush the rest of the chips in the bag until they're about bread crumb–size.
2. Grind the dulse and peppercorns in a spice grinder or crush with a mortar and pestle.
3. Mix together the ketchup chip crumbs, ground dulse and pink peppercorn mixture, paprika, sugar, dill, and celery salt in a medium bowl.
4. Transfer to an airtight container and store in your pantry until the chips go stale (about 1 week).

K-Pop Rim

Used in K-Pop (page 172)
Makes about ½ cup (120 ml)

¼ cup (60 ml) kosher salt
2 Tbsp cane sugar (organic, if possible)
2 Tbsp black sesame seeds
1 tsp gochugaru (see note)

1. Mix all the ingredients in a bowl.
2. Transfer to an airtight container and store in your pantry up to 6 months.

Note: Gochugaru (sometimes labelled as Korean-style red pepper) is medium-spice crushed chili pepper widely found in Korean cooking, including kimchi.

Lemon Dust Rim

Used in Quahog (page 162)
Makes about ⅓ cup (80 ml)

½ cup (120 ml) lemon zest (6 to 8 lemons)
¼ cup (60 ml) Celery Salt (page 288 or store-bought)

1. Preheat your oven to 200°F (95°C) and line a baking sheet with parchment paper.

2. Spread the lemon zest on the prepared baking sheet and cook until completely dry but not browned, 12 to 15 minutes. Once it's dry, crush the zest into a fine dust with a mortar and pestle.
3. Mix together the lemon dust and celery salt in a bowl.
4. Transfer to an airtight container and store in your pantry for up to 6 months.

Lemon Pepper Sea Salt

Used in Garden (page 176)
Makes about ⅓ cup (80 ml)

2 Tbsp sel gris (or sea salt)
2 Tbsp cracked black pepper
2 Tbsp grated lemon zest

1. Mix together all the ingredients in a bowl.
2. Transfer to an airtight container and store in your pantry for up to 1 month.

Nordic Rim

Used in Nordic (page 256)
Makes about ⅓ cup (80 ml)

1 Tbsp flaked sea salt
1 Tbsp cracked black pepper
1 Tbsp caraway seed, crushed
1 Tbsp dill seed, crushed
1 Tbsp grated lemon zest
1 tsp dried dill
1 tsp granulated sugar

1. Mix together all the ingredients in a bowl.
2. Transfer to an airtight container and store in your pantry for up to 1 month.

NWT Rim

Used in Bug Repellent (page 258)
Makes about ¼ cup (60 ml)

2 Tbsp sea salt
1 Tbsp granulated sugar
1 tsp mustard seeds, ground
1 tsp coriander seeds, ground
1 tsp dill seeds, ground
½ tsp red pepper flakes
½ tsp allspice

1. Mix together all the ingredients in a bowl.
2. Transfer to an airtight container and store in your pantry indefinitely.

Primal Rim

Used in Chanterelle (page 126)
Makes about ½ cup (120 ml)

¼ cup (60 ml) kosher salt
2 Tbsp cracked black pepper
1 Tbsp freshly grated horseradish
1 Tbsp dried thyme

1. Mix together all the ingredients in a bowl.
2. Transfer to an airtight container and store in your pantry for up to 5 days.

Roasted Rice Rim

Used in Vegeta (page 170)
Makes about ¾ cup (180 ml)

1 Tbsp dry Japanese short-grain rice
¼ cup (60 ml) togarashi spice
¼ cup (60 ml) Celery Salt (page 288 or store-bought)
1½ Tbsp white pepper

1½ Tbsp black sesame seeds

1 Tbsp Tajín, classic

1 Tbsp dashi powder

1. Preheat your oven to 350°F (175°C). Roast the dry rice on a baking tray until golden brown, 15 to 20 minutes, tossing every 5 minutes for even browning. Let cool.
2. Mix the roasted rice with all the other ingredients in a bowl.
3. Transfer to an airtight container and store in your pantry for up to 6 months.

Salted Coffee Rim

Used in César Cubano (page 236)

Makes ½ cup (120 ml)

¼ cup (60 ml) kosher salt

2 Tbsp granulated sugar

2 Tbsp Café Bustelo espresso ground coffee (see note)

1. Mix all the ingredients together in a bowl.
2. Transfer to an airtight container and store in your pantry indefinitely.

Note: The iconic yellow and red Café Bustelo coffee cans can be found everywhere in Miami. Their strong espresso-style coffee holds a special place in the hearts of many Cuban Americans. If you can't find it online you can use any ground espresso.

Smoked Meat Spice Rim

Used in Chartier (page 134)

Makes about ½ cup (120 ml)

3 Tbsp ground black pepper

2 Tbsp kosher salt

1½ Tbsp ground coriander

½ tsp ground mustard seed

½ tsp ground celery seed

½ tsp garlic powder

½ tsp onion powder

½ tsp red pepper flakes

1. Mix together all the ingredients in a bowl.
2. Transfer to an airtight container and store in your pantry indefinitely.

Spicy Chartreuse Candy

Used in Deep River (page 130)

Makes about ½ cup (120 ml)

1 cup (240 ml) Yellow Chartreuse

¼ cup (60 ml) Tajín, habanero

1. Place the Chartreuse in a small pot and cook on medium-high heat until it reaches the hard crack stage (see note), or 300°F to 310°F (150°C to 155°C) on a candy thermometer. The sweet liqueur can burn quickly, so keep a close eye out when it starts to become thick and sticky.
2. Once it's ready, remove the pot from the heat and pour the liquid onto a parchment-lined baking sheet. Let cool completely until brittle, about 10 minutes.
3. Break into small pieces with the back of a spoon and pour into a medium mortar. Crush to a coarse sugar consistency with a pestle. Mix together the Tajín and crushed Chartreuse candy until combined.
4. Transfer to an airtight container and store in your pantry for up to 4 weeks.

Note: To test for the hard crack stage without a candy thermometer, fill a glass with cold water and a little bit of ice. Take a teaspoon and drop a little bit of the boiling Chartreuse into the ice water. Let the Chartreuse cool completely and then remove it. It should be hard and brittle and snap in half when bent. If it's still pliable and won't crack when bent, it's not hot enough yet.

Wild Yarrow Rim

Used in Miner's Daughter (page 252)

Makes about ⅓ cup (80 ml)

2 Tbsp kosher salt

2 Tbsp sweet paprika

1 Tbsp slightly crushed wild yarrow flowers (see note)

½ Tbsp white pepper

1 tsp dried thyme

1 tsp dried basil

1 tsp dried oregano

¼ tsp cayenne pepper

1. Mix together all the ingredients in a bowl.
2. Transfer to an airtight container and store in your pantry indefinitely.

   Note: Yarrow is a wildflower that grows widely in Northern Canada. It is commonly made into herbal teas and has an astringent anise-like flavour. It can be purchased dried at specialty food stores or online.

Sauces, Syrups, Shrubs, Vinegars & More

Agave Syrup

Used in Friend of the Devil (page 234)

Makes 1½ cups (360 ml)

1 cup (240 ml) agave nectar (100% blue agave, if possible)

½ cup (120 ml) hot water

1. In a heatproof bowl, stir together the agave and hot water until evenly blended. Depending on how thick your agave is, you might need to add a little more water. The goal is to make a syrup that is easy to pour (and easier to measure) and will dissolve more quickly in your drink. Let cool.
2. Transfer to a jar or squeeze bottle and store in the refrigerator for up to 4 weeks.

Bagel Shrub

Used in Double Double (page 102)

Makes about 12 oz (360 ml)

¼ bagel (everything or sesame seed), chopped into 1½-inch (4 cm) cubes

2 tsp olive oil, divided

½ tsp sea salt

½ tsp cracked black pepper

1 tsp sesame seeds

1 tsp poppy seeds

2 cloves garlic, minced

1 small onion or shallot, thinly sliced

1 cup (240 ml) red wine vinegar

½ cup (120 ml) water

¼ cup (60 ml) lemon juice

2 bay leaves

1. Preheat your oven to 250°F (120°C). Toss the bagel cubes in 1 tsp of the oil, the salt, and pepper. Place on a baking sheet and bake in the oven until golden brown, about 10 minutes, turning once or twice during baking.

2. Meanwhile, in a small saucepan over medium-low heat, lightly toast the sesame seeds and poppy seeds, stirring occasionally, until the sesame seeds are golden, 3 to 5 minutes. Transfer the toasted seeds to a small bowl.

3. Add the remaining 1 tsp of oil to the same saucepan and cook the garlic and onions on medium heat, stirring occasionally, until golden but not brown, about 5 minutes. Add the vinegar, water, lemon juice, bay leaves, toasted sesame and poppy seeds, and toasted bagel cubes and bring to a simmer. Simmer, stirring occasionally, for 5 minutes, then remove from the heat. Let the mixture stand for 30 minutes.

4. Strain the mixture through a fine-mesh strainer or cheesecloth to extract as much shrub liquid as possible while keeping any bread crumbs or seeds out of the liquid.

5. Transfer to an airtight container and store in the refrigerator for up to 7 days.

Black Pepper Jam

Used in Chartier (page 134)

Makes about 1½ cups (360 ml)

2 Tbsp canola oil

6 green onions, roughly chopped

1 small yellow onion, diced

¼ cup (60 ml) minced fresh ginger

3 Tbsp minced garlic

1 Tbsp cracked black pepper

⅓ cup (80 ml) granulated sugar

¾ cup (180 ml) kecap manis (see note)

¼ cup (60 ml) low-sodium soy sauce

¼ cup (60 ml) lime juice

1 tsp sea salt

1. Add the oil to a large, heavy-bottomed pot over medium heat. Sauté the green and yellow onions, ginger, and garlic until golden and soft, about 15 minutes.

2. Mix in the pepper, then add the sugar, kecap manis, soy sauce, lime juice, and finally the salt. Continue to cook over medium heat, stirring frequently, until the mixture coats the back of a spoon, 20 to 30 minutes.

3. Place the mixture in a blender, or use an immersion blender, and blend until smooth.

4. Transfer to an airtight container and store in the refrigerator for up to 3 months.

Note: Kecap manis is a sweet, viscous soy sauce that originates from Indonesia. It can be found at Asian grocers or in the specialty aisles of your local grocery store.

Celery Juice

Used in Dear Friend (page 232)

Makes 2 to 4 oz (60 to 120 ml)

2 celery ribs

1. The easiest way to make celery juice is with a juice extractor. You probably don't own a juice extractor, but fear not. You can easily extract an ounce or more of celery juice from a couple of celery stalks by blending (or super finely dicing) the celery and then squeezing it through a cheesecloth or a fine-mesh strainer. Store in an airtight container in the refrigerator for up to 2 days.

Chanterelle Purée

Used in Chanterelle (page 126)

Makes about ½ cup (120 ml)

¼ cup (60 ml) Quick-Pickled Chanterelles (page 281)

¼ cup (60 ml) brine from Quick-Pickled Chanterelles

1. Place the pickled chanterelles and brine in a blender, or use an immersion blender, and blend until smooth.
2. Transfer to an airtight container and store in the refrigerator for up to 6 weeks. Extra purée can be added to a creamy pasta sauce or used as a condiment on burgers.

Citrus Brown Butter

Used in Citrus Brown Butter Washed Vodka (page 301) and Lobster Tail (page 278)

Makes about ½ cup (120 ml)

½ cup (120 ml) cold salted butter, cut into ½-inch (1 cm) cubes

1 Tbsp lemon juice

Sea salt

Cracked black pepper

1. Place the butter in a small saucepan over medium heat. Allow it to melt and then foam, watching it closely—be careful not to heat it too quickly or it will burn and become bitter. You'll see brown particles form within the foam. These are milk proteins toasting and a pleasant nutty aroma should arise. This will take 5 to 8 minutes once the butter is melted.
2. Remove from the heat and swirl in your lemon juice and a pinch each of salt and pepper.
3. Transfer to an airtight container and store in the refrigerator for up to 2 weeks.

Cloudberry Syrup

Used in Nunavut Country Food Arctic Caesar (page 254)

Makes about 1¼ cups (300 ml)

1 cup (240 ml) granulated sugar

1 cup (240 ml) water

1 cloudberry tea bag

1. Combine the sugar and water in a small saucepan over medium heat and bring to a boil to dissolve the sugar, stirring occasionally.
2. Remove from the heat and add the tea bag. Let it steep for 5 to 10 minutes to release its flavours.
3. Discard the tea bag. Transfer the syrup to an airtight container and store in the refrigerator for up to 6 months.

Concord Grape Vincotto

Used in Chanterelle (page 126)

Makes about ¼ cup (60 ml)

1 lb (450 g) Concord grapes

Granulated sugar

1. Juice the grapes with a juicer, run them through a food mill, or chop them up and squeeze them through a fine-mesh strainer or cheesecloth to remove the seeds and release their juices. The yield should be approximately 1 cup (240 ml) of juice.
2. Bring the juice to a boil over medium-high heat in a wide saucepan. Reduce, stirring frequently, until thick enough to coat a spoon (you want it to be around 20% of its original volume). Keep in mind that the reduction will continue to thicken while cooling, so err on the side of less thick. Remove from the heat.
3. Once the vincotto is cool enough to taste, taste it and see if any additional sweetness is needed. It should be almost as sweet as honey or molasses. If additional sweetness is desired, while the vincotto is still warm, add the sugar ½ tsp at a time, stirring constantly until

the sugar is dissolved. (If the grapes are in season, you may not need any sugar.)

4. Transfer to an airtight container and store in the refrigerator for up to 2 months. Extra vincotto can be used in any recipe that calls for honey or molasses.

Herb-Infused White Wine Vinegar

Used in Garden (page 176)
Makes about 1 cup (240 ml)

1 small handful each of fresh dill, flat-leaf parsley, cilantro, and basil
1 cup (240 ml) white wine vinegar

1. Roughly chop the herbs and place them in a 1-cup (240 ml) jar. Add the vinegar. Cover and let infuse for 3 to 4 hours, then strain out the herbs through a fine-mesh sieve or cheesecloth.
2. Transfer to an airtight jar and store in the refrigerator for up to 6 months. Use this infused vinegar in salad dressings or drizzled over anything grilled.

Honey Syrup

Used in Rebuttal (page 168) and Miner's Daughter (page 252)
Makes about 1½ cups (360 ml)

1 cup (240 ml) honey
½ cup (120 ml) hot water

1. In a heatproof bowl, stir together the honey and hot water until evenly blended. Depending on how thick your honey is, you might need to add a little more water. The goal is to make a syrup that is easy to pour (and easier to measure) and will dissolve more quickly in your drink. Let cool.
2. Transfer to a jar or squeeze bottle and keep in the refrigerator for up to 4 weeks.

Horseradish Mignonette

Used in Dear Friend (page 232)
Makes about 1 cup (240 ml)

1 cup (240 ml) champagne vinegar
1 Tbsp freshly grated horseradish
1 tsp kosher salt
1 tsp granulated sugar
1 tsp cracked black pepper
¼ tsp grated clove

1. Mix all the ingredients in a jar.
2. Transfer to an airtight container and store in the refrigerator for up to 1 week.

Josh's Fermented Hot Sauce

Makes about 2 cups (480 ml)

Ferment

1 medium red bell pepper, cored and sliced into ½-inch (1 cm) strips
1 medium carrot, chopped into ½-inch (1 cm) pieces
½ medium white onion, sliced into ¼-inch (6 mm) rounds
6 cloves garlic, peeled
4 oz (120 g or one head's worth) celery hearts and leaves
4 oz (55 g) horseradish root, peeled and cut to ¼-inch (6 mm) pieces
4 oz (55 g) red chilies, stemmed, halved, and seeded (about 16 to 20 chilies)
½ lemon, cut into ¼-inch (6 mm) rounds
5 tsp fine sea salt
3 cups (720 ml) lukewarm filtered water

Post Ferment

2 to 5 Tbsp maple syrup or honey
2 to 5 Tbsp apple cider vinegar

1. Wash all the vegetables and utensils thoroughly. Clean a 32 oz (946 ml) Mason jar and allow to air-dry.

2. Place the red peppers, carrots, onions, garlic, celery hearts and leaves, horseradish, chilies, and lemon in the Mason jar.

3. In a medium bowl, mix the salt into the water until dissolved and pour the salt water into the jar until full. If vegetables are not fully immersed, top up the jar with more salt water.

4. Fill a clean medium-size freezer bag half full with water and remove as much air as possible before sealing. Place it inside the jar on top of the vegetables to weigh them down and keep the vegetables fully submerged under the brine surface.

5. Place a clean kitchen towel on top of the jar opening and secure it with an elastic band around the mouth of the jar to prevent foreign materials from entering. (Alternatively, you can use a fermentation air-lock lid and weight instead of the freezer storage bag and towel.) Store in a cool dark location for a minimum of 5 days. After a couple of days you'll start to see the brine get cloudy, which means it's working! The longer you ferment the more "funk" you'll add to the sauce, but Josh recommends 5 to 10 days as the ideal range.

6. When it's nice and fermented, drain the vegetables through a colander or strainer over a large bowl, reserving 1 cup (240 ml) of funky brine.

7. Place all the fermented vegetables in a blender with ½ cup (120 ml) of your reserved brine. Blend until very smooth.

8. Add 2 Tbsp of maple syrup and 2 Tbsp of vinegar, and blend to incorporate. Taste and adjust to your perfect flavour and viscosity. (Want some more salt? Add a bit of brine. Want some sweet? Add some honey. Want some tang? Add some vinegar.) This allows you to customize the blend to your specific tastes.

9. Place the sauce in an open glass jar and cover with a clean kitchen towel or paper towel secured with an elastic band. Sealing it completely will build up fermenting gases and the jar may pressurize and pop when you open it (or maybe even explode!).

Fermented hot sauce will keep for up to 1 year in the refrigerator, but note that it will continue to ferment and the flavour will deepen over time.

Pomegranate Syrup

Used in Sangrita (page 98)
Makes about 1¼ cups (300 ml)

1 cup (240 ml) granulated sugar
1 cup (240 ml) pomegranate juice (fresh or from concentrate)

1. Combine the sugar and pomegranate juice in a small saucepan over medium-high heat. Stir to dissolve the sugar while slowly bringing the mixture to a low boil. Once it's boiling, turn down the heat, partially cover the pan, and simmer until the mixture has become slightly syrupy and coats the back of a spoon, 15 minutes. Remove from heat and let cool completely.

2. Transfer to an airtight container and store in the refrigerator for up to 10 days.

Note: Pomegranate syrup can also be used as a substitute for commercial grenadine in various drink recipes. Or use it make your teetotaler guests and your kids a Shirley Temple: Stir together 6 oz (180 ml) soda water, 1 oz (30 ml) pomegranate syrup, and 1 oz (30 ml) lemon or lime juice. Serve over ice and garnish with a maraschino cherry.

Roasted Garlic

Used in The Tree House (page 136)

Makes 1 bulb roasted garlic

1 garlic bulb
1 tsp olive oil

1. Preheat your oven to 400°F (200°C). Cut ½ inch (1 cm) off the top of the garlic bulb to expose the cloves. (You only need 1 clove per Caesar, but who doesn't want extra roasted garlic kicking around?)
2. Place the bulb cut-side up on a piece of aluminum foil large enough to wrap it loosely. Drizzle the oil over the exposed cloves and close up the foil. Roast until caramelized, beautifully brown, and quite fragrant, 30 to 40 minutes. Once it's cool enough to touch, remove the cloves by gently squeezing the bulb.
3. Transfer to an airtight container and store in the refrigerator for up to 1 week. Extra can be combined with butter and spread on a baguette to make garlic bread.

Rodney's Back from Hell Hot Sauce

Used in Quahog (page 162)

Makes about 2 cups (480 ml)

8 oz (225 g) scotch bonnet peppers, stemmed (20 to 25 peppers)
8 cloves garlic
2 red bell peppers, stemmed, halved, and seeded
1 large onion
3½ cups (840 ml) white vinegar
1 Tbsp salt
2 tsp dry mustard

1. Pulse the scotch bonnet peppers, garlic, red bell peppers, and onions in a food processor until finely minced. (You can remove the seeds from the scotch bonnet peppers if you want a little less kick.)
2. Place the minced vegetables in a large pot and add

the vinegar, salt, and dry mustard. Bring to a boil over medium-high heat, cover, turn down the heat to low, and simmer for 2 hours, stirring occasionally to prevent sticking. Let cool.
3. Transfer to two 8 oz (240 ml) lidded clean jars and store in the refrigerator for up to 4 months.

Simmered Beet

Used in Nordic (page 256)

Makes about 1 cup (240 mL)

6 oz (170 g) red beet, root and stem trimmed (about 1 billiard ball–size beet)
1 Tbsp sea salt
1 Tbsp white pepper

1. Fill a medium saucepan with water and add the beet, salt, and pepper. Bring to a rolling boil over high heat. Reduce the heat to low and simmer until fork-tender, approximately 20 to 30 minutes.
2. Remove the beet from the water and let cool. Discard the simmering liquid. Gently peel away the beet skin and dice into ½-inch (1 cm) pieces. Store in an airtight in the refrigerator for up to 5 days.

Simple Syrup

Used in Waltermelon (page 226)

Makes about 1¼ cups (300 ml)

1 cup (240 ml) cane sugar (organic, if possible)
1 cup (240 ml) water

1. Combine the sugar and water in a small saucepan over low heat. Cook, stirring constantly, until the sugar has dissolved, about 5 minutes. Let cool.
2. Transfer to a jar or squeeze bottle and store in the refrigerator for up to 4 weeks.

Spruce Tip & Saskatoon Berry Shrub

Used in Deep River (page 130)

Makes about 1½ cups (360 ml)

5 finger lengths (about ⅓ oz/10 g) spruce tips (see note)
10 to 12 Saskatoon berries
1 cup (240 ml) water
¼ cup (60 ml) granulated sugar
¼ cup (60 ml) apple cider vinegar

1. Place the spruce tips, Saskatoon berries, and water in small saucepan over medium-high heat. Bring to a boil, flipping the spruce tips constantly and gently mashing the berries to extract their juice. Once a full boil is reached, remove from the heat and mix in the sugar until dissolved. Steep for 30 minutes.
2. Stir in the vinegar. Strain into a 2-cup (480 ml) Mason jar and store, sealed, in the refrigerator for up to 3 months.

Note: Spruce tips have a citrusy and resinous flavour. But you don't have to go foraging to find them. Check out your local farmers' market for local foraging companies, or you can purchase them online and at many speciality grocers.

Stout Reduction

Used in It's a Thing, Man (page 128)

Makes about ⅓ cup (80 ml)

¾ cup (180 ml) stout or porter beer
1 tsp cane sugar

1. Pour the beer and sugar into a small saucepan and bring to a simmer, stirring regularly, over medium heat. Continue simmering until the liquid has reduced by half, 10 to 15 minutes. Remove from the heat and let cool.
2. Transfer to an airtight container and store in the refrigerator for up to 2 weeks.

Sugar Pie Syrup

Used in Cabane à Sucre (page 160)

Makes about 1 cup (240 ml)

½ cup (120 ml) maple syrup
½ cup (120 ml) packed brown sugar
½ cup (120 ml) water

1. Mix together the maple syrup, sugar, and water in a saucepan over low heat. Cook, stirring constantly, until the sugar has dissolved. Let cool.
2. Transfer to a jar or squeeze bottle and store in the refrigerator for up to 4 weeks.

Tare

Used in Vegeta (page 170)

Makes about 1 oz (30 ml)

1 packet (9 g) dashi powder (see note)
2 tsp mirin rice wine
2 tsp sake
2 tsp soy sauce

1. Dissolve the packet of dashi powder in 2 cups (480 ml) of water in a small saucepan over medium heat. Bring to a boil, then simmer for 3 to 5 minutes. (Note: check the instructions on the dashi powder as they can vary from brand to brand.) You'll only need ⅓ oz (10 ml) of dashi broth for this recipe so sip on the extra broth while you make the rest of the recipe.
2. Combine 2 tsp of the dashi broth, mirin, sake, and soy sauce in a small saucepan over medium heat. Cook until the top starts to show a white foam, which should happen a little before it boils. Do not let the sauce boil. Remove from the heat and let cool.
3. Transfer to an airtight container and store in the refrigerator for up to 2 weeks.

Notes: 1) Dashi powder is readily available at Asian and specialty grocers or online and is usually sold in individual packets. 2) Tare is a traditional Japanese marinade. Try it in a stir-fry or to marinate chicken or beef before grilling.

Tomato Water

Used in Tomato Water Last Word (page 164)
Makes about 34 oz (1 L)

2.2 lb (1 kg) tomatoes (ideally Roma, about 12), roughly chopped
8 oz (225 g) celery (about 3 stalks), roughly chopped
8 oz (225 g) mini cucumbers (skin on, about 4), roughly chopped
1 oz (25 g) fresh basil (about ½ cup/120 ml tightly packed)
½ tsp sea salt

1. Place the tomatoes, celery, cucumbers, basil, and salt in a blender and lightly blend a few times. The mixture doesn't have to be super smooth. You just want to break all the ingredients up evenly so you can extract as much liquid as possible.
2. Pour the mixture into a cheesecloth-lined strainer. Position the strainer over a bowl and refrigerate overnight.
3. In the morning, you'll have a bowl full of clear tomato water. If you want, you can slowly squeeze the solids through the cheesecloth into a separate bowl to extract some additional liquid. Stop when you start to see any colour in the liquid being squeezed out (you want the tomato water to be a nice clear liquid).
4. Once you're done squeezing, pour the liquid from both bowls into a glass bottle or jar and store in the refrigerator for up to 4 days.

Umami Paste

Used in The Umami One (page 104)
Makes about 2 cups (480 ml)

⅓ cup (80 ml) dried shiitake mushrooms, rinsed
1½ cups (360 ml) hot water
½ cup (120 ml) pitted black olives, roughly chopped
½ cup (120 ml) sundried tomatoes, roughly chopped
2 Tbsp soy sauce
2 Tbsp red miso paste
2 Tbsp balsamic vinegar
2 tsp fish sauce
2 tsp anchovy paste

1. Place the dried mushrooms in a bowl with the hot water, cover, and let the mushrooms soak to rehydrate, 20 to 30 minutes. Strain the mushrooms and reserve the mushroom soaking water.
2. In a small saucepan, bring the mushroom water to a boil over medium heat. Reduce the heat to a simmer and let cook until reduced by half (you want about ⅔ cup/160 ml). Transfer to a glass container and place in the refrigerator to cool.
3. Meanwhile, place the olives, sundried tomatoes, soy sauce, miso paste, balsamic, fish sauce, and anchovy paste in a blender and blend until combined. With the blender running, slowly add the cold mushroom water to the blender until the umami paste starts to get super smooth and the paste starts to flow easily in the blender.
4. Transfer to an airtight container and store in the refrigerator for up to 1 week. You can add this paste to soups or pasta sauces for a flavour boost. Or spread it on a baguette like tapenade.

Watermelon Juice

Used in Waltermelon (page 226)

Makes about 1 cup (240 ml)

2 cups (480 ml) chopped seedless watermelon

1. Place the watermelon in a blender and blend until really smooth. Strain through a fine-mesh strainer set over a large bowl—it helps to push it through with a spatula.
2. Transfer to an airtight container and store in the refrigerator for up to 2 days.

Wild Juniper & Spruce Tip Vinegar

Used in Scotch Creek (page 96)

Makes about ½ cup (120 ml)

1½ Tbsp spruce tips, roughly chopped (see note, page 298)

¼ tsp juniper berries, crushed

½ cup (120 ml) apple cider vinegar

1 Tbsp honey

1. In a 1-cup (240 ml) Mason jar, mix together the spruce tips, juniper berries, vinegar, and honey. Stir to dissolve the honey.
2. Transfer to a jar, seal, and refrigerate for 2 weeks before using. It will keep for up to 6 months in the refrigerator. This vinegar is great for dressing salads and especially tomatoes or cucumbers with salt.

Infusions & Fat Washes

Black Pepper-Infused Vodka

Used in The Chucks (page 124)

Makes about 8 oz (240 ml)

8 oz (240 ml) vodka

2 Tbsp peppercorns (black or mixed)

1. Combine the vodka and peppercorns in a 1-cup (240 ml) lidded jar and shake well to initiate infusion. Store in the lidded jar for 4 to 5 days, shaking once or twice a day if you remember (if not, it's fine). Taste once a day after the first 48 hours to see if the flavours are at your preferred levels.
2. Strain through cheesecloth or a fine-mesh strainer into a bowl and transfer to a clean jar. This vodka will keep for up to 12 months at room temperature.

Chili Pepper-Infused Vodka

Used in Friend of the Devil (page 234)

Makes about 8 oz (240 ml)

1 habanero pepper

3 bird's eye chilies

1 scotch bonnet pepper

1 serrano pepper

8 oz (240 ml) vodka

1. Wearing gloves, chop all the peppers (see note). Keep all the seeds and stems for more heat, omit for less. Combine the chopped peppers and vodka in a 2-cup (480 ml) lidded jar, and shake well to initiate infusion. This is going to get spicy fast. Taste every 15 minutes and once you've reached your preferred heat level, strain through cheesecloth or a fine-mesh strainer into a bowl and transfer to a clean jar.

2. This vodka will keep for up to 12 months at room temperature. If it's too spicy, dilute with more vodka.

Note: You can use any peppers you want in this recipe. Also: don't touch your eyes.

Citrus Brown Butter Washed Vodka

Used in Consider the Lobster (page 220)
Makes about 6 oz (180 ml)

2 oz (60 ml) Citrus Brown Butter (page 301)
6¾ oz (200 ml) vodka

1. Combine the butter and vodka in a 2-cup (480 ml) wide-mouth container and seal with its lid. Shake vigorously two or three times over 1 hour to increase the surface area between the vodka and butter. After 1 hour, put the sealed container into the freezer for at least 4 hours or overnight.
2. The butter should create a solid layer on the top of the alcohol. Poke a hole in the butter and pour the alcohol through a fine-mesh strainer over a bowl. Strain the alcohol again through cheesecloth or a coffee filter. Re-strain, if necessary, to remove any remaining fat.
3. Store in a sealed glass container in the refrigerator for up to 3 months.

Dill-Infused Aquavit

Used in Nordic (page 256)
Makes about 8 oz (240 ml)

8 oz (240 ml) aquavit
3 to 5 fronds fresh dill

1. Combine the aquavit and dill in a 1-cup (240 ml) lidded jar and shake well to initiate infusion. Store in the lidded jar for 4 to 5 days, shaking once or twice a day. Taste once a day after the first 48 hours to test the flavour.
2. Strain through cheesecloth or a fine-mesh strainer into a bowl and transfer to a clean jar. This aquavit will keep for up to 12 months at room temperature.

Duck Fat Washed Gin

Used in Bingo (page 184)
Makes about 7 oz (210 ml)

8 oz (240 ml) gin (ideally Spring Mill Distillery Gin)
2 oz (60 ml) rendered duck fat, from Roasted Duck Sausage (page 284, step 2)

1. Combine the gin and duck fat in a 2-cup (480 ml) wide-mouth container and seal with its lid. Shake vigorously 2 or 3 times over 1 hour to increase the surface area between the gin and fat. After 1 hour put the sealed container into the freezer for at least 4 hours or overnight.
2. The fat should create a solid layer on the top of the alcohol. Poke a hole in the fat and pour the alcohol through a fine-mesh strainer over a bowl. Strain the alcohol again through cheesecloth or a coffee filter. Re-strain, if necessary, to remove any remaining fat.
3. Store in a glass container in the refrigerator for up to 3 months.

Garlic-Infused Vodka

Used in Chartier (page 134)

Makes about 6 oz (180 ml)

6 oz (180 ml) vodka

1 clove garlic, minced

1. Combine the vodka and garlic in a 1-cup (240 ml) lidded jar, and shake well to initiate infusion. Store in the lidded jar for 4 to 5 days, shaking once or twice a day. Taste once a day after the first 48 hours to check the flavour. If you want a super-fast infusion, double the garlic and shake hourly for 8 hours.
2. Strain through cheesecloth or a fine-mesh strainer over a bowl and transfer to a clean jar. This vodka will keep at room temperature for up to 12 months.

Sesame Fat Washed Vodka

Used in Hot & Sour (page 84)

Makes about 6 oz (180 ml)

6¾ oz (200 ml) vodka

1 oz (30 ml) sesame oil

1. Combine the vodka and oil in a 2-cup (480 ml) wide-mouth sealable container. Shake well and emulsify to expand the amount of surface area of the vodka in contact with the sesame oil. Shake it every 5 or 10 minutes for about 30 minutes, then let it settle for about 30 minutes so the fat generally rises to the top.
2. Place in the freezer for at least 4 hours or overnight. Don't let it sit too long with the oil or the flavours will become too strong.
3. The sesame oil should create a solid layer on top of the alcohol. Poke a hole in the sesame oil and pour the vodka through a fine-mesh strainer over a large bowl. Strain the alcohol again through cheesecloth or a coffee filter to remove any remaining fat solids. Transfer to a clean jar and store in the refrigerator for up to 3 months.

References

Arnold, Dave. *Liquid Intelligence: The Art and Science of the Perfect Cocktail.* W.W. Norton, 2014

Bartels, Brian. *The Bloody Mary: The Lore and Legend of a Cocktail Classic, with Recipes for Brunch and Beyond.* Ten Speed Press, 2017

Bishop-Stall, Shaughnessy. *Hungover: The Morning After and One Man's Quest for the Cure.* Harper, 2018

DeGroff, Dale. *The Craft Cocktail: Everything You Need to Know to Be a Master Bartender, with 500 Recipes.* Clarkson Potter, 2002

Dillon, Geoff, and Whitney Rorison. *Craft Cocktails: Seasonally Inspired Drinks & Snacks from Our Sipping Room.* Penguin Canada, 2019

Embury, David A. *The Fine Art of Mixing Drinks*. Cocktail Kingdom, 2013

Hemberger, Allen, Sarah Hemberger, Micah Melton, Nick Kokonas, and Grant Achatz. *The Aviary Cocktail Book.* The Alinea Group, 2018

Kaplan, David, Nick Fauchald, and Alex Day. *Death & Co: Modern Classic Cocktails.* Ten Speed Press, 2014

Kaplan, David, Nick Fauchald, and Alex Day. *Cocktail Codex: Fundamentals, Formulas, Evolutions.* Ten Speed Press, 2018

Klemm, Eben. *The Cocktail Primer: All You Need to Know to Make the Perfect Drink.* Andrews McMeel Publishing, LLC, 2009

Meehan, Jim. *Meehan's Bartender Manual*. Ten Speed Press, 2017

Meehan, Jim, and Chris Gall. *The PDT Cocktail Book: The Complete Bartender's Guide from the Celebrated Speakeasy.* Sterling Epicure, 2011

Morgenthaler, Jeffrey, and Martha Holmberg. *The Bar Book: Elements of Cocktail Technique.* Chronicle Books, 2014

Newman, Lenore. *Speaking in Cod Tongues: A Canadian Culinary Journey.* University of Regina Press, 2017

Page, Karen, and Andrew Dornenburg. *The Flavor Bible: The Essential Guide to Culinary Creativity, Based on the Wisdom of America's Most Imaginative Chefs.* Little, Brown and Company, 2008

Regan, Gary. *The Joy of Mixology: The Consummate Guide to the Bartender's Craft,* rev. and updated ed., Clarkson Potter, 2018

Robitschek, Leo. *The Nomad Cocktail Book*. Ten Speed Press, 2019

A Brief History of The Caesar (pages 4–6) draws on the following sources:

Dictionary of Canadianisms on Historical Principles, 2nd ed., s.v. "Caesar." http://dchp.ca/dchp2/, accessed August 2020

Caplan, Nina. "The Bloody Mary Is Dead: All Hail the Bloody Caesar." *New Statesman,* October 10, 2015

Cummings, Christopher. "The Bloody Caesar: Who Put the Clam in the Cocktail Hour?" *Canadian Hotel and Restaurant,* June 1984

Hercz, Robert. "Drink Staples: The Caesar." *Food and Drink,* Summer 2006

Kadane, Lisa. "The Caesar: The History of Canada's Beloved Cocktail." *WestJet Magazine,* May 14, 2020

McDowell, Adam. "Canada's Favourite Hangover Cure Has a Secret." *National Post,* August 7, 2010

Mettrick, Alan. "Bartender Prefers Scotch." *Calgary Herald,* February 4, 1972

Naccarato, Michael. "Bloody Caesar Canada's Cocktail." *Toronto Star,* May 11, 1994

Pruden, Jana G. "Hail Caesar!" *Globe and Mail,* March 3, 2017

Remington, Robert. "All Hail Caesar!" *Calgary Herald,* May 13, 2009

Turnbull, Barbara. "Inventor of Bloody Caesar Dies." *Toronto Star,* April 2, 1997

"Walter Chell Is a Familiar Face . . ." *Calgary Herald,* October 15, 1971

Wondrich, David. "Behind the Drink: The Bloody Caesar." https://www.liquor.com/articles/behind-the-drink-the-bloody-caesar/, accessed August 2020

Wondrich, David. *Imbibe!* TarcherPerigee, 2015

Unpublished Sources:
Interviews and emails with Joan Chell, 2019–2020

Family photographs, Chell-related press clippings, and advertising materials from Joan Chell personal archives

Acknowledgements

To start, a perpetual thanks to all of the incredible professionals that contributed recipes to this book: Ned Bell, Michelle Bernstein, Sloane Botting, Matthew Boyle, Trevor Burnett, Julio Cabrera, Jason Chan, Adrian Chappell, Joan Chell, Sylvie Cheverie, Jonathan Chovancek, Bronwen Clark, Anthony Cobb, Derek Dammann, Megan DeHaas, Donna Dooher, Rich Francis, Chuck Hughes, Nathan Hynes, Nicole Hynes, Katy Ingraham, Trevor Kallies, Lora Kirk, Charlotte Langley, Stephen La Salle, Mel Leonard, Reuben Major, Paul Mason, David McMillan, Jess Midlash, Adele Moriarty, Lauren Mote, John Pan, Sarah Parniak, Ranjit "Ray" Pieres, Parker Reid, Ryan Reynolds, Joe Ruhland, Zach Slootsky, Jessica Smith, Michael Smith, Kaitlyn Stewart, Elsa Taylor, Jeffrey Van Horne, JenniLee Vaneltsi, Jesse Vergen, Julien Vézina, Robin Wasicuna, Jordan Watson, Tyrone Welchinski, Chris Whittaker, and Craig Wong. We annoyed you in the midst of a pandemic with requests and plenty of dumb questions when you all had much more important things to do. Yet you still generously found time for us. Thank you for sharing with us and our readers.

In researching this book, many people took time to speak with us about Caesars, Canada, clams, fact-checking, and more, including: Ned Bell, Shaughnessy Bishop-Stall, Anthony Cobb, Shaun Edmonstone, Meredith Erickson, Nicole Gomes, John Hale, Chuck Hughes, Chris Johns, Trevor Kallies, Stephen La Salle, Reuben Major, Josh McFaddin, David McMillan, Sarah Parniak, Agatha Podgorski, Whitney Rorison, Christine Sismondo, Sarah Sowden, Kaitlyn Stewart, and JenniLee Vaneltsi. Elbow bumps to Nick Paton (#blessed) and Nick Nemeth for nerding out with us. Hugs and kisses (post-COVID) to Erika Bolliger, Claire Dawson, and the Ocean Wise Seafood team. Niki Tsourounakis, your test kitchen was a life saver. We are forever indebted to Joan Chell for taking time with us, sharing family photos and news clippings, and telling us stories about her father. We hope Walter would be proud of this book.

Tanya Pilgrim, your photos are stunning and make this book what it is. Working with you so closely on this project has been exceptional, as is your work. You are a trooper doing all of this during a pandemic.

Without question, this book could not, and would not exist if not for the tireless work and support of the following three people. Joshua Linde, you are the ever-calm presence in our world of chaos. As always, credit for keeping your head while we were losing ours. And thanks again for Zack's job in the dish pit at Lansdowne Earls. Jessica Smith, master tester, taster, proofer, creator, and keeper of the detailed notes. We love you. We can only hope you still love us. Mark Braude, you are the best of us. You showed us that it's possible a couple dudes from Richmond can write a book. Without you all the words in this book would be less gooder.

To Rachel (and Leo!) Brown, Lindsay Paterson, Robert McCullough, and the team at Appetite, your guidance and expertise has been invaluable. Should we discuss cover design or paper stock again? Marian Staresinic, thank you for kicking this whole thing off. Our gratitude to Tiffany Ayalik for her words which so beautifully captured the North. Michael Bonacini, Lynn Crawford, Meredith Erickson, Chuck Hughes, and Christine Sismondo, thanks for your time and the kind words. Jason Prendergast and Ryan Reynolds, thank you for your generosity. Glad that our shared love of gin, Caesars, martinis, and Vancouver could come together here.

Alex Rein, Helena Tubis, Nick Paton, and the Kelvin Slush team, as always, you are amazing. Let's not write a Frosé book next.

To our extended Walter Caesar family, including Lorrie Jane Boucher, Stephan Cohen, James Dayson, Leon & Joan Denenfield, David & Lindsay Skabar, Chris Frankowski, Alexander Friel, Scott & Lee Gibson, Michael Hofbauer, Will Jee, Jeremy & Laura Kalenuik, Stuart Langfield, Jennifer Mackie, Yvan Guy Larocque, Simon Mills, Scott Paddington, Dylan & Meryl Rekert, Kyle Russell, Christie Collins, Mark Santarossa, Brandon James Scott, Steven Shafir, Ian Weinstein, and Jane Yuan, thank you for believing in us.

A very deep and humbled thank you to the thousands of grocers, retailers, restaurateurs, chefs, and bartenders who have taken a chance on us and stocked Walter over the years. It still amazes us how supportive the food and beverage community has been of what we do. Cheers to the countless suppliers, vendors, and partners of both past and present. And, of course, thank you to the scores of Canadians who have purchased Walter since we started way back when.

To the Walter team, thank you from the bottom of our hearts for all you do. Stephanie Binnersley, like it or not, we're now family. Howard Harowitz, you too.

Finally, we couldn't do anything without the ceaseless support of our families: Helen, Quinn, and Avery, Amanda, Sienna, Stella, and Nolan. And to our parents and siblings: Howard, Trudy, Josh, Sara, Dave, Marsha, Arne, Deborah, David, Ben, Art, and Lucy. We love you.

This book was written in Toronto and Vancouver. We acknowledge that the City of Toronto sits on the traditional territory of many nations including the Mississaugas of the Credit, the Anishinaabeg, the Chippewa, the Haudenosaunee, and the Wendat peoples. We acknowledge that the City of Vancouver is on the unceded traditional territory of the Musqueam, Squamish, and Tsleil-Waututh First Nations. We recognize the enduring presence of all First Nations, Métis, and the Inuit peoples.

Index